DATE DUE

NO 26 97			

DEMCO 38-296

ISLAM AND THE MYTH OF CONFRONTATION

Published in 1996 by I.B.Tauris & Co. Ltd
45 Bloomsbury Square, London WC1A 2HY
175 Fifth Avenue, New York, NY 10010

In the United States of America and Canada distributed by
St Martin's Press, 175 Fifth Avenue, New York, NY 10010

A full CIP record for this book is available
from the British Library

Library of Congress catalog card number 95–61524
A full CIP record for this book is available
from the Library of Congress

ISBN 1 85043 959 1 paperback
ISBN 1 86064 004 4 hardback

Set in Monotype Baskerville by Lucy Morton, London SE12
Printed and bound in Great Britain by WBC Ltd,
Bridgend, Mid Glamorgan

ISLAM AND THE MYTH OF CONFRONTATION

Religion and Politics in the Middle East

FRED HALLIDAY

I.B.TAURIS PUBLISHERS
LONDON · NEW YORK

In memory of

Manouchehr Kalantari
Shokrallah Paknejad
Abdul-Rahman Qassemlu
Said Sultanpur

Iranian friends and democrats,
opponents of religiously sanctioned dictatorship

Contents

Acknowledgements

The chapters that follow reflect the help of many, from the Middle East and elsewhere, who have given me their time and understanding over more than three decades. I would like to thank, in particular, Nikki Keddie, Kanan Makiya, Afsaneh Najmabadi, Roger Owen, Jim Paul, Joe Stork and Sami Zubaida for their insights into the contemporary Middle East, and above all Maxine Molyneux, my wife, who has shared many of the events and debates addressed in these pages. Emma Sinclair-Webb at I.B. Tauris was all that an editor should be – encouraging, exigent, patient – and without her this book would never have seen the light of day. I am also grateful to those who responded so generously to my need for guidance on their areas of expertise and with particular research assistance – Katarina Dalacoura, Bernard Johnson, Richard Saull, Achin Vanaik. There are many in the Middle East itself whom I would like also to thank, but circumstances currently prevailing in their countries, which have little to do with religion and a lot to do with tyranny, make this, for the time being, impossible.

The author and publisher would like to thank the following for permission to use materials already published in other forms and appearing here in revised versions: Macmillans Publishers; the University of Malta Press; the *Review of International Studies*; the Center for German and European Studies, University of California; the *Times Literary Supplement*; *Political Studies*; *The British Journal of Middle Eastern Studies*.

An earlier version of chapter 1 was published in Ray Bush (ed.), *The World Order* (Cambridge: Polity, 1987).

The main body of chapter 2 was first published in the *Journal of International Affairs* (Columbia, NY), winter 1982/3, vol. 36 no. 2, and reprinted in Fred Halliday and Hamza Alavi (ed.), *State and Ideology in the Middle East and Pakistan* (London: Macmillan, 1988). Additional material is included from 'The Politics of Islamic Fundamentalism: Iran, Tunisia and the challenge to the secular state', in Stanley Fiorini and Victor Mallia-Milanes (ed.), *Malta: a Case Study in International Cross-Currents* (Valetta: Malta University Publications, 1991), and reprinted in Akbar Ahmed and Hastings Donan (ed.), *Islam, Globalization and Postmodernity* (London: Routledge, 1994).

An earlier version of chapter 3 was published in the *Review of International Studies*, vol. 20, no. 2, April 1994.

Chapter 4 combines material originally published in Beverly Crawford and Peter Schulze (ed.), *European Dilemmas after Maastricht* (Berkeley: Center for German and European Studies, 1993), and *The Times Literary Supplement*, 14–20 April 1989.

A version of chapter 5 appeared in *Political Studies*, July 1994.

Chapter 7 is based on the text of the annual British Society for Middle East Studies lecture delivered at the School of Oriental and African Studies, London, on 2 March 1993. An earlier version was published in *British Journal of Middle Eastern Studies*, vol. 20, no. 2, 1993.

Introduction

The chapters that follow are part of the long process of reflection on the contemporary Middle East and on the various ways of thinking about and analysing that region. Some of the themes addressed have underpinned writing on the Middle East for many years and have already been the subject of considerable debate. Others, not least the rise of Islamist movements and the responses of the region to the end of the Cold War, are more recent, but are now interlocked with the older, more enduring, discussions.

In a number of earlier studies I myself have tried to provide analysis of specific Middle East countries, or periods in modern Middle East history, and some of the chapters in this work are in the same vein.[1] However, I have tried here to broach some broader questions of interpretation and analysis, and in so doing not only to cast light on the contemporary Middle East, but also to relate the study of the region to broader trends within the social sciences. If there is one theme that lies behind these essays, it is the denial of the common assumption that the Middle East is a unique case, quite different from the rest of the world and incomprehensible to outsiders. They are an attempt, necessarily incomplete and provisional, to comprehend this region by viewing it within a broader structure of international processes, and through recourse to an intellectual system of general application.

Several of the essays focus on the issue of Islam both as a religion and as a political phenomenon, espoused by some, excoriated by others. Here it is essential to distinguish between the two meanings of the term, and to consider the distinct questions each definition raises. I therefore want to draw a clear distinction between Islam and 'Islam'. In the first sense, Islam as a religion, espousing certain clear doctrines, exists as a system of belief about the supernatural and related questions of morality, destiny and meaning. This is a matter for believers and theologians and is not the subject of what follows: indeed I am not competent to discuss Islam in this theological sense, and do not claim to do so. As far as the second meaning of the term is concerned – 'Islam' as a social and political system – it should quickly become evident that I do not believe there is much to be gained by regarding the many socio-political realities that the term applies to as part of a single phenomenon. As an object of social and political analysis, or as a force in international affairs, there is little that can be explained, praised or denounced by reference to a unitary 'Islam'. What is needed is a full consideration of particular societies and political systems and of the uses, variant across time and place, to which Islamic symbols and doctrines are put. 'Islam' as an object of study must first be dissolved in order to be made concrete in the study of particular events, times and places.

Beyond these themes originating in if not specific to the Middle East, there are broader themes in social analysis which are currently vital in academic and public policy circles and which inform the discussion in this book. One such theme is the question of whether or not contemporary international relations centres upon what Samuel Huntington has termed a 'clash of civilizations' in which conflict between states will increasingly take the form of civilizational disputes, and a division of the world into competing blocs.[2] There is, inevitably, much that appeals in such arguments. Many of those who challenge Western domination, or seek to defend it, do so by invoking 'civilization' as a term of guidance and legitimation. For many of the same people history appears to make sense in terms of a set of such bipolar rivalries – what Arnold Toynbee long ago termed 'challenge and response'. With the Cold War gone, it seems, other rivalries, one of which is that between Islam and the West, will replace it. The rise of the 'Islamic threat' would seem to be just one such case, just as there is an increasing body of literature that links the growing economic and strategic strength of the Far East to 'Confucian' values.

Yet, enticing as it may be, such an approach has its limits. In the first place, it is not at all evident that civilizational difference has been the basis for international conflict, in the 1990s or at any other time. The trade conflicts between Japan and the US, or the rivalries for influence between Russia and Western states, have only a remote relation to civilization. Equally, conflicts involving Middle Eastern states on, for example, oil prices, nuclear weapons or territory, involve straightforward secular concerns. More significantly, the very term 'civilization' needs questioning. It was used originally, in the early modern period, in contrast with barbarism or savagery.[3] Subsequent usage, denoting blocs of culture and/or religion, assumes that such entities exist as coherent, historical givens, and that international forces can be mobilized around them. The following chapters aim to show that what may appear to those outside a society, or be instrumentally presented by those within that society, as timeless essential truths are in fact confections of recent political and social origin, created and used for contemporary purposes. 'Civilizations' are like nations, traditions, communities – terms that claim a reality and authority which is itself open to question, and appeal to a tradition that turns out, on closer inspection, to be a contemporary creation.

A second issue much debated in contemporary social thought is that of universality and relativity: of whether it is possible, or desirable, to analyse and evaluate different societies on the basis of similar criteria, or whether we should accept that each community, and nation, has its own meanings and values, which preclude such universalist 'narratives'. The critique of universalism, long present in philosophic thought, has been reinforced in recent years from three sources: from those who challenge the authority of the West from what one can broadly term an 'anti-imperialist' or multiculturalist stance; from those who, like post-modernists, deny the primacy of all 'grand narratives' or unitary sets of concepts; and from moral philosophers who challenge the primacy of reason, especially in its Enlightenment variety. Broadly, these sources advocate the avoidance of universalist discourses and the acceptance of a diversity of voices in the contemporary world. We must realize, they argue, that beneath all universalist discourse lie structures of domination and power that impose the system of one group of states on the others and inflict a spurious rationality on human experience.

It will soon become clear in what follows that I am sympathetic to one part of this argument, and distinctly unattracted by the other. A diversity of voices is a reality, and a desirable one, both within societies and between them, and there are many contexts in which such diversity should be welcomed. Power, and a hegemonic concept of reason, have done much to distort our understanding of the contemporary world, and of the ethical issues embodied in it. To state this, however, does not necessitate the contention that all arguments are of equal validity, analytic or moral, or that there are not issues on which the recourse to a concept of universalism is appropriate. Statements may be more or less true, and values more or less desirable, and the mere acceptance of diversity does not preclude such judgements. Thus it remains possible to seek agreement on explanations of why a particular event occurred – a war, a revolution, a social trend – whilst being aware of different starting-points and perspectives. Equally, there are ethical issues, notably those pertaining to the conduct of war or to human rights, on which universal standards can be asserted and defended.

Closely related to this is the much debated issue of the need to listen to the voices of those formerly excluded from consideration, not least the voices of Third World peoples. A sustained and thorough rethinking of prevailing interpretations of history and political thought to take account of the hierarchies of power in the contemporary world is both desirable and possible and has, in some areas, already begun. Too often monopolies of power have created monopolies of knowledge. This is manifest in the role of imperialism in creating the international system, and in gender bias in managing to present as natural what are contingent human creations. In both cases, as in many others, a critique of existing power structures and monopolies of knowledge is long overdue. It would, however, be mistaken to go from an acceptance of established orthodoxies to the assertion that *all* alternatives are to be welcomed, or have equal validity. In the first place, to argue that power and the desire to maintain or justify it can serve to distort our knowledge and language does not automatically entail accepting that powerlessness, and the desire and efforts to remedy it, are guarantors of validity, whether explanatory or ethical. If reverence for authority is displaced by uncritical acceptance of every voice 'from below', then little advance will be made.

The very condition of being oppressed, in a collectivity as much as in an individual, is likely to produce its own distorted forms of perception: mythical history, hatred and chauvinism towards others, conspiracy theories of all stripes, unreal phantasms of emancipation. It is, at the same time, important to be initially sceptical about the agendas and interests of those who claim to speak for the silenced: one of the sharpest lessons of the twentieth century is that projects of emancipation, or the discourses associated with them, may in the hands of self-appointed leaders lead to alternative forms of oppression and denial. New forms of distortion may be presented in the guise of authenticity from below. Secular variants – authoritarian ideologies of the left, nationalism – and religious ones – sundry fundamentalisms and communalisms – have illustrated this often enough. Those forces that are often deployed against the oppressive and global – the local, the indigenous, the communal – may therefore conceal as much confusion, and as much instrumentalism and coercion, as the structures they claim to challenge.

The need to be discriminating in this regard is all the more important since the very terms in which arguments are often posed – 'the West' versus 'the East', or indeed 'the West' versus 'the rest' – are themselves misleading. As the discussion of 'civilization' has already suggested, we are not dealing with a world of contrasting political traditions: the very terms in which European power and values have been challenged are ones taken from the European tradition – the state, the nation, rights, independence, sovereignty, democracy. Just as international economic competition concerns disputes over trade, investment, profits within a global system created by the European powers, so political argument about the 'West' versus 'the rest' turns out, on closer examination, to be a conflict between two different interpretations and variants of the Western political tradition itself. At the same time, the treatment of the 'West', and of Europe in particular, as an undifferentiated whole is historically simplistic. The history of Europe, and of the political systems it generated, is itself a contradictory one, in the sense that it produced ideas of both oppression and emancipation. European history was itself the product of conflict between political and social forces. The Europe that imposed its political and economic order on the world also developed its own internal emancipation – at enormous cost both externally and, through the world wars of the twentieth century and attendant ideological conflicts, internally too. To pose choices about political values, or historical narratives associated with them, in terms of a 'European' versus a non-European approach, where the former is cast as somehow 'ethnocentric' and the latter as freed of such particularistic associations, is to deny the diversity and the conflict present within each history. It is to deny the combination of domination and resistance that is present throughout all societies, whether European or other. The arguments that follow have, therefore, a double purpose. If they can in some measure serve to challenge the more simplifying and misleading analyses of Islamist movements and the contemporary Middle East, they may also serve to illustrate, by reference to this region, the limits of some general theories of supposedly global relevance.

The 'myth of confrontation' to which the title of this book refers is, therefore, a myth that is sustained from two, apparently contradictory, sides – from the camp of those, mainly but not exclusively in the West, who seek to turn the Muslim world into another enemy, and from the camp of those within the Islamic countries who advocate confrontation with the non-Muslim, and particularly Western, world. It involves an argument that, while critical of the ideologies of those who have long sought to dominate the Muslim world, is critical too of much of what passes for 'alternative', 'indigenous', 'authentic' contestation from within these countries themselves. This book should, in this sense, be equally unwelcome to both groups of people.

Yet such a critique, and the resistance which such arguments normally provoke, will not in itself do much to dispel the confusions surrounding the issue of 'Islam' in the contemporary world. There are two main reasons for this. First, as this book makes clear in a number of ways, the study of myths may reveal the illusory or false character of discourse, but it also unveils the agenda behind their propagation. Myths of 'Islamic threat', like myths of legitimacy or of nationalism, are part of the rhetorical baggage of political struggle, employed by both those who wish to remain in power and those who aspire to attain power. As long as such interests exist, myths will continue to be generated – to legitimize, to mislead, to silence, to mobilize. In addition, despite the fact that such myths can be revealed as false, once generated and expressed they can acquire a considerable life of their own. Myths of racist hatred, for example, may begin as lies invented by idle xenophobes, but once conveyed into the political realm and diffused in tense inter-ethnic contexts, they acquire a force and a reality they previously lacked. A similar process is occurring with the 'myth of confrontation' pertaining to Islam; propagated against Muslims, such myths are also taken up by Islamists to provide justification for their own causes. All of this should lead to caution about how effective the critique of myth can be, though having said that, it is important that those who propagate myth, from whatever camp, should not go unchallenged. Such, in essence, is the purpose of the chapters that follow.

PART ONE

Interpreting the Middle East

I

The Middle East and International Politics

Introduction: illusions of particularism

In the postwar period the Middle East has consistently *appeared* to be the most unstable and strategically alarming region in the whole Third World. After all, it was there, in the crisis over northern Iran in 1946, that the first Cold War began. It was in the Suez crisis of 1956 that European–US contradictions reached their highest point, and that the Soviet Union, for the only recorded occasion, threatened a direct missile assault upon Western European states. In 1967 and 1973 Arab–Israeli wars occasioned crises between the USA and the USSR more dangerous than any that arose over Indo-China or Europe, less dangerous only than that which erupted in 1962 over Cuba. The years after 1970 provided event after event that placed the Middle East at the forefront of international concern: the OPEC price rises of 1971–73, the Iranian revolution, the protracted agonies of the Lebanese civil war and the Israeli invasion of that country, the Iran–Iraq war of 1980–88, the Gulf war of 1990–91. Events in what President Carter's security adviser Brzezinski termed the 'Arc of Crisis', encompassing Afghanistan, Iran, South Yemen and Ethiopia, played an important part in the onset of the second Cold War in 1978 and 1979. The war between Iran and Iraq was the second longest interstate war of the twentieth century, shorter by only two months than the Sino-Japanese conflict of 1937–45. The events following the Iraqi invasion of Kuwait, from August 1990 to March 1991, comprised one of the major international crises of the postwar epoch, both for the Middle East and for the United Nations.

Whether their intensity is assessed in terms of the impact upon East–West relations, the challenge to the workings of the international market, or the apparent threat to regimes in place in the region, the events of the Cold War decades were clearly of major and sustained importance, both for the Middle East itself, and for the outside world. Little wonder that the Middle East seemed to many to be the most critical and explosive area of the post-1945 epoch.

Yet such an impression needs some qualification, not least in terms of historical perspective. The Middle East was, arguably, the scene of a greater degree of interstate war than any other region of the world in the post-1945 period: the Arab–Israeli wars and Iraq's invasions of its two neighbours saw to that. But on other indices other areas of the Third World were the most contested: it was the Far East which saw the most costly conflicts of the second half of the twentieth century, in Korea and Vietnam, followed in southern Africa by the conflicts of Angola and Mozambique.[1] It was the Far East too which, in conjunction with these wars, saw the greatest levels of political upheaval (most of all in China) and which, from the 1950s onwards, became the site of the greatest economic transformations, in part as a result of the Cold War itself. On none of these three indices therefore – the human costs of war, the degree of political mobilization, the record of economic transformation – was the Middle East the most prominent region of the developing world. While recognizing the importance of the region for the international system as a whole, there is a need to guard against what may be termed a 'regional narcissism', a tendency to see the course of events there as uniquely dramatic by comparison with other areas of the world.

Coverage of this region, both academic and journalistic, reveals another distortion, a tendency towards suspending analytic rigour in the face of what appear to be impenetrable, or at least *sui generis*, political and social developments. Somehow, it is implied, the Middle East is simply *not like* other parts of the Third World: its dynamics, conflicts and patterns of behaviour are different. One version of this particularist approach, examined at greater length in chapter 7, is what has come to be termed 'orientalism' – the assertion of a special, Islam-dominated, area, where canons of rationality and comparative judgement are not applicable.[2] It is asserted that the only way to understand the behaviour of Middle Eastern societies is through analysis of 'Islam': that class politics, or revolutions, or even social consciousness do not arise there, or that democracy, in either its liberal or socialist sense, is not possible in such countries. But the temptations of particularism are not confined to 'orientalists': for, in suitably altered form, they constitute much of the self-image of Middle Eastern peoples themselves. No one could be more 'orientalist' than the Arab nationalist vaunting the uniqueness and specificity of the 'Arabs', and arguing that forms of oppression found elsewhere – based on class, gender or ethnicity – do not operate in the Arab world. Equally, the vision of Islamic radicals of the 1970s and 1980s, epitomized in but not confined to Khomeini, stresses the different social and moral character of Middle Eastern peoples. The Islamist vision denies, explicitly, the relevance to the Muslim world of what are seen as alien, secular, criteria of assessment. Since the early 1970s, as part of the wide disillusion with earlier forms of socialist and secular thought, large numbers of Arab intellectuals have also focused their work upon a search for Arab identity, and the unearthing of what are presented as *al-turath*, the 'roots' of Arab culture and history. Even ex-Marxists and Arabs of Christian origin can be found extolling the virtues of the Arabs' Islamic culture. Essentialism and relativism of many stripes therefore pervade a broad sphere of discussion of the Middle East, both within the region and outside.

In reaction against this there has arisen, predictably, a contrary current, persistent if still subordinate. This dispenses with the apparent exceptionalism of the Middle East and instead seeks to assimilate, without major qualification, developments in the Middle East with those of Europe and/or other regions of the Third World. Thus in the nineteenth and early twentieth centuries, much liberal writing – Arab, Turkish, Persian and European – saw the region as progressing along an increasingly enlightened and optimistic path towards more acceptable democratic norms. In the 1940s, 1950s and 1960s a body of Marxist writing, part of it orthodox pro-Soviet, part of it independent or Maoist, and aspiring to be historical materialist in approach, portrayed the region in class terms, with almost no reference to factors of tribe, nationality, religion or faction. It seemed that here finally the complexes of orientalism and colonial essentialism had been well and truly overcome. In these class analyses the 'petty bourgeoisie', the 'proletariat' and the 'semi-feudal forces', among others, were moved firmly to the centre. As the OPEC-led boom of the 1970s took shape, and led to the spectacular increase in producer-state incomes, it seemed also to many more orthodox economic and social analysts as if the pattern of Middle Eastern economic growth could be tidily assimilated to that of other states and models. This was the view taken by some about Egypt's economic liberalization, and nowhere was this optimism more common than in writing on Iran, where virtually all the literature of the 1970s colluded in some degree with unilinear and apologetic illusions of the Shah's modernization programme. Yet each of these universalist approaches has faced an apparent rebuff by history: the end of the twentieth century has not seen the universal triumph of liberal progress, or rigorous class politics, or orthodox capitalist modernization.

The particularist and the universalist approaches have profound problems associated with them: both have to some extent foundered on the rocks of empirical reality, both rest on questionable theoretical assumptions and both have evidently served ideological functions. But study of their competing ideological approaches is of more than discursive interest, for these ideologies have been espoused by groups, within and beyond the Middle East, who have been striving to gain power over societies and economies. The particularism of the colonialist, like the universalism of the capitalist modernizer, reflects a material interest in the region. Furthermore, the relativism of Arab nationalists or Islamic revolutionaries serves a comparable ideological function (i.e. to obtain or secure political power). The ideologies of Middle Eastern society, exceptionalist and universalist, are therefore themselves inseparable from the overall pattern of conflict and tension in Middle Eastern societies: whether generated from without or within, they are part of a competition for power and resources.

A preliminary solution to this problem can, however, be suggested, and informs the following analysis. The particularist approach to the Middle East, and its universalist antinomy, contain two distinct arguments as to the character of Middle Eastern societies. One is what can be termed an *analytic particularism*, according to which the very categories used to describe these societies must themselves be specific to this region (the nationalist who rejects Weberian sociology or Marxism in the name of 'authentic' national or Islamic concepts, or some revised version of the thought of Ibn Khaldun, could be said to exemplify this analytic relativism). The other can be termed a *historical particularism*, according to which the specificities of the contemporary Middle East can only be comprehended in the light of the historical formation of the societies and politics of the region. In terms of this second particularism the Middle East is peculiar, not because the categories of analysis applicable elsewhere do not apply, but because of the specific processes of historical formation through which Middle Eastern states have passed. The particularity of the Middle East is therefore to be seen in the *manner* in which its contemporary social formations have emerged: these particularities are, however, to be grasped in terms of analytic categories that are universal, and that may be all the more revealing precisely because they *are* of general and comparative application. This approach, matching an analytic universalism with a historical particularism, can provide a means of avoiding both the rampant relativism that has dominated discussion of the Middle East in recent years, and that bland universalism that applies to the Middle East general schemata for the Third World, without taking its special character into account.

The problem of analytic relativism is matched by that of its ethical counterpart, of those outside who argue that it is wrong to criticize Middle Eastern societies in terms of what are termed 'our values' – be these on human rights, women, freedom of speech or even torture. The argument raised earlier can be restated here: that the criteria for such judgements must be universally applied, even if it is possible to comprehend the specific historical forces that led to a particular Middle Eastern abomination. Some of the grotesque positions of Western 'understanding' or of 'solidarity' groups in recent years, of critics of Western imperialism defending the firing squads of Khomeini's *pasdaran* or the clitoridectomy of some Arab Muslim societies, show where such relativism can lead. For many years, no one was a greater beneficiary of such confusion than the Iraqi dictator Saddam Hussein. Those who criticized the brutalities of his regime were all too often accused of collusion with Western imperialism, a charge all the more spurious when it was directed against Arabs, and above all Iraqis, who voiced such criticisms.[3]

Analytic relativism has equally affected questions of national rights – a good example of this being the metropolitan left's attitude to the Arab–Israeli dispute. If in the period after the mid-1960s the majority of the Western left sided with the Palestinians, the majority before that, and a significant minority since, sided with Israel. There have been all too few who have taken up clear, critical and independent positions on this issue. Two who did, and who were repeatedly denounced for so doing, were Isaac Deutscher and Maxime Rodinson.[4] Both criticized the chauvinism and repression of the Israeli state, and declared their support for Palestinian statehood. But both also named and opposed the chauvinism of many Arab politicians, a chauvinism meekly reproduced in much metropolitan 'anti-imperialism' which simply called for the abolition of an Israeli state. Where such direct expressions of this view were judged unwelcome, coded formulations, such as that equating Zionism with racism, were espoused. The clear democratic position adopted by both Deutscher and Rodinson argued that *each* nation should have its own state in a partitioned Palestine. Such a position required both a detailed study of the issues involved and a political willingness on the part of both to distance themselves from two political camps that have managed virtually to monopolize the terms of discussion. The great tragedy of so much external concern with the Middle East is that for too long it took the form of support for one or other chauvinism in the Arab–Israeli dispute and, indeed, in other conflicts.

Determinations: external and internal

To look for a common pattern or cause in the conflicts that ravaged the Middle East in recent decades is futile.[5] The societies themselves are too different, their distinct political characters and state formations already too diverse, to permit of any unified *endogenous* explanation. To invoke one common *external* factor would also be misleading. For many years, Cold War writers tried to blame all the problems of the Middle East on Islam or Soviet influence. Equally simplistically, others ascribed these events solely to the workings of imperialism. Imperialism, conceived of as a system of external domination, formal or informal, certainly played a part – whether it be understood as the historic legacy of colonial rule and capitalist penetration, with all its disruptive impact, or as the subsequent exercise of Western (and particularly US) power in the region, both directly and through local allies. The external factors must be incorporated into the picture; but regional conflicts arose equally from forces located *within* these diverse societies themselves. This can be seen by examining three of these conflicts: the war in Lebanon of 1975–90, the Iran–Iraq war of 1980–88, and the Gulf war of 1990–91. Beyond their intrinsic importance, these conflicts may serve as examples of how internal and external factors combined to produce, and sustain, specific Middle Eastern antagonisms.

The war in Lebanon that exploded in 1975 arose from the long and unresolved crisis within that country that had been developing ever since independence from France in 1943.[6] The initial political arrangement reached at independence, the National Pact, had established a form of power-sharing between representatives of the Christian and Muslim bourgeoisies: positions in the state, from the president down, were to be allocated by religious affiliation; the two confessional elites and their allies were to run the state's policies together. Lebanon was to occupy a correspondingly cautious place within the Arab world: part of that world, but to a considerable degree insulated from its politics.

The main problem with this 1943 system was that it took inadequate account of change, internal or external. Internally, the demographic balance shifted in favour of the Muslims, while within each community new social forces emerged that did not accept the dominance of their respective elites. The most striking case of the latter process was the rise of a Shi'ite Muslim community that rejected the Sunni Muslim leadership, and which constituted much of the poorer population of Beirut. An initial attempt in the 1950s to challenge the balance of forces in Lebanon that had begun to favour the rise of Arab nationalism in the country ended abruptly in 1958 with the intervention of US marines, at the request of the Christian leader and President Camille Chamoun. The US intervention was, in the short run, successful. Internal change at the political level, and the appeals of Arab nationalism to the Muslim population, were contained.

But social change did not stop and the class and confessional conflicts within Lebanese society only festered the more as they failed to find political expression. Hence by the mid-1970s Lebanon faced an explosive domestic situation, born of the inability of the political system to adjust to changes within the society.

External factors then compounded the internal and played a significant role in generating the explosion. Lebanon's Christians did not feel themselves to be part of the Arab nationalism that swept the region in the 1950s and Lebanon stayed out of the Arab–Israeli wars. But it was not possible to insulate Lebanon completely from the turmoil of the Arab world. Its economy was a satellite of the oil-producing states, in that moneys from the oil producers were invested and spent on services in Lebanon. It was thus sensitive to developments in the Gulf. The Muslim community was increasingly drawn to Arab nationalism, and Syria never accepted that Lebanon was entirely a separate state (even after 1943 Damascus continued to regard Lebanon as within its sphere of influence). Most important, however, was the presence within Lebanon of a Palestinian exile community which from the early 1970s became politically and militarily mobilized against the Israeli state to the south. This Palestinian community established a loose alliance with the political representatives of the Muslim community; it increasingly became an autonomous and unassimilable factor within Lebanese politics.

So the civil war that broke out in 1975 had several dimensions. It was a war between confessional groups – Christians and Muslims – and between social forces within each group. The Palestinians sought to ally with the Muslims, but found no stable alliance either with the Sunni leaders or with the representatives of the Shi'ites. At the same time, Syria became increasingly involved, first on one side, then on the other, trying to re-establish some coalition of confessional groups that could govern the country under its direction. In 1978 and, more importantly, in 1982, Israel intervened directly, hoping to assist the Christians to re-establish domination, and to crush the Palestinian forces in Lebanon. It failed, and was forced in the end to withdraw from Lebanon. A decade of civil war, and of intervention by Syria and Israel, had not produced a new coalition to replace that which had been swept away by the explosion of 1975. If a

complete disintegration of Lebanon was improbable, the fragmentation, destruction and bitterness occasioned by the war certainly
made any new stable political system the harder to achieve.
Confessional hatred, social tension and the dynamics of war-
lordism in each camp made restabilization all the harder to
attain. Only in 1990, with the establishment of a Government of
National Reconciliation on 24 December, did a combination of
internal exhaustion and external realignment make possible a
slow, often interrupted, return to peace and to the reconsolidation
of a single state.

A different combination of confessional, social, national and
international factors contributed to the other major war of the
early 1980s, that between Iran and Iraq that began in September
1980.[7] The immediate cause of this war was the Iranian revolution of the previous year. Like virtually all revolutionaries,
Khomeini in a rhetorical way sought to spread his revolution: he
advocated a set of universal revolutionary ideals and believed that
the security of his new regime could best be ensured by the
establishment of similar regimes elsewhere. Although he did not
envisage all-out war with Iraq, his call for a generalized Islamic
revolution led his new regime within months into conflict with
neighbouring Iraq, and into support for dissident Islamic groups
within that country. Ethnic factors also played a part: antagonism
between Arabs and Persians was fanned by both sides, and each
sought to encourage ethnic dissidents within the other's state –
the Iraqis backing Kurds and Arabs in Iran, the Iranians assisting
Kurdish rebels in Iraq.

The resort to history alone cannot explain such wars. One has
always to ask the question of why the past comes to influence the
present. However, deeper causes of the conflict lay in the rivalry
between Iran and Iraq within the Persian Gulf region. Evident for
more than a decade, this rivalry had led Iran, then under the
Shah, to wage a long, destabilizing covert war against Iraq in the
early 1970s. Temporarily halted by an agreement between the two
states in 1975, this regional rivalry was reopened by the Iranian
revolution of 1979. The Iraqis, facing what appeared to be a
determined new challenge from Iran, decided to hit first and to
press their cause in the regional contest. When they attacked in
September 1980 they expected a rapid victory. Instead they

became embroiled in a massive land and air war they could scarcely sustain. Both sides had played their part in the outbreak of the war, and both suffered terribly in the killing and destruction that followed.

After eight years of war, neither side was able to achieve its combat goals. Iraq had failed to defeat Iran in its initial attack: by the summer of 1982 Iraq had withdrawn its forces from enemy territory and was calling for peace on the basis of a return to the status quo. Iran, while unable on its part to defeat Iraq, was occupying some Iraqi territory and proclaimed itself determined to continue the war until its goals were met. These included the removal and 'punishment', presumably execution, of Iraqi President Saddam Hussein, the payment of war damages of $150 billion or more by Iraq, and the condemnation of Iraq as the aggressor by an international tribunal. On some occasions, Iranian leaders implied that they would continue the war until an Islamic Republic like their own had been established in Iraq. For six further years, Iran persisted in these demands despite its inability to prosecute the war successfully. Only in 1988 did Khomeini, with bitter reluctance, agree to a compromise peace.

Claims about external control of both states involved in this war were not hard to find: the Iranians accused Saddam of being a tool of the Americans, and having attacked on Washington's instructions; the Iraqis accused Khomeini of being, among other things, an Israeli agent and of sending envoys to Tel Aviv to receive instructions. Demagogy aside, neither party to this war was wholly or mainly motivated by exogenous factors, though neither side could have fought the war that they did without external support. Both needed money, and this they obtained from selling their oil and, in the case of Iraq, from sympathetic Arab states. Both also needed arms, since they had only limited domestic arms-production capacity. Iraq experienced no difficulty in obtaining arms, since most Arab states, the Soviet Union, France and the USA supported its cause. Iran did face much greater difficulties and no states, apart from Libya and Syria, were willing openly to support it. But Iran was able to obtain substantial supplies of arms for cash payment on the world market, from Western sources and from North Korea, and thus acquired at least part of the outside help it needed.

Yet despite these external inputs, neither state could be said to be acting at the behest of or under the control of other states. None of the many suggestions to this effect managed to demonstrate that any outside power was actively encouraging or prolonging the war for its own interest. The outbreak of the Iran–Iraq war, and its long duration, underlined the considerable autonomy of the states involved and of the tensions within them that led to war.

The Gulf war of 1990–91 lends itself, as do these earlier two examples, to analysis of an almost wholly exogenous or endogenous kind. Thus there were many who saw Iraq's attack on Kuwait as the result of external factors, be these the crisis of the Middle East state system at the end of the Cold War, the cold war between Arab states themselves, going back to Egypt's peace with Israel in 1977, or (for those favouring a more conspiratorial approach) direct US enticement of Iraq into the war, with the hope of then crushing an Arab state that threatened Western hegemony in the region. On the other hand, there was no shortage of analysis that stressed factors within the states themselves: the crisis of the Iraqi state, frustrated and empty-handed after its eight-year war with Iran, the very ideological dementia of the Ba'thist regime and of its leader, for whom war was an attractive way forward, and, on the other side, the political crisis in Kuwait which led the leaders of that country to risk confrontation with Iraq in the hope of silencing domestic critics within. There will be a more detailed analysis of the Gulf war, and of explanations of its origin, in chapter 3. Suffice it to say here that no simple explanation, focusing wholly on the external or the internal, is possible. Rather, a combination of international and regional, domestic and personal factors combined to lead Iraq's leader to provoke a war.

The examples offered by these three conflicts – the Lebanese civil war, the Iran–Iraq war and the Gulf war – underline two of the most salient features of the contemporary Middle East, and of its place in the overall pattern of world conflict. One is the apparent explosiveness of the region and of the political systems within it: this is why the Middle East has been consistently a source of international concern since the end of World War Two. The second salient characteristic is the considerable independence of these conflicts from the broader skein of international politics.

The contemporary Middle East cannot be understood apart from the historical experience it underwent in the colonial era, the character of its economic links to the developed countries, and the impact upon it of prolonged Soviet–American rivalry. But while these international factors provide a context and often a catalyst, it is equally important to locate the conflicts of the region in their specific, local origins and to develop judgements and political assessments also based on these particular factors. It is, indeed, in the tension between these two approaches that the specific difficulty of analysing the Middle East lies. Of inescapable importance for international conflict as a whole, and for an informed, critical evaluation of the contemporary world, the Middle East remains the site of violent local conflicts that are largely independent of broader international patterns.[8]

Historical formation

The Middle East, a region in 1995 of 20 independent states with a combined population of around 300 million, is the only area of the Third World geographically contiguous with Europe. Conflict between it and Europe, taking military, economic and religious-ideological forms, has been in train for centuries, reaching far back beyond the era of contemporary imperialism into the epoch of feudalism, the Crusader wars and the rise of Islam. The modern period of interaction between Europe and the Middle East began in the late eighteenth century, first with the Russian assaults upon the Ottoman empire in the war of 1768–74, and then with Napoleon's invasion of Egypt in 1798.

European interest in the region was, until this century, mainly strategic. Throughout the nineteenth century, external rivalry took the form of the 'Eastern question', the competition between rival powers, especially Russia and its competitor Britain, for influence in the region and control over communications at the expense of the Ottoman empire. Until 1914 the Ottoman empire survived, in part through a system of flexible alliances with Western powers, but in the preceding decades various imperial powers had succeeded in establishing themselves on its periphery – France in Algeria (1830), Tunisia (1881) and Morocco (1912), Italy in Libya

(1911), Britain in Egypt (1882), in Sudan (1898), in South Arabia (1839) and in the string of coastal Persian Gulf states (late nineteenth century to 1914).

With the end of World War One the Eastern question was dramatically transformed. On the one hand, the Ottoman empire was dismembered, its heartland becoming the nation state of Turkey and its former Arab dominions divided into seven separate states or colonial entities. Two of these new entities (Lebanon and Syria) were now ruled by France, three (Iraq, Jordan and Palestine) by Britain, and two (Saudi Arabia and North Yemen) became independent Arab monarchies. While the territory of the Ottoman empire was thus divided, the strategic rivalry in the region was simultaneously redefined by the new developments: by the discovery, just prior to World War One, of substantial quantities of oil in and near the Persian Gulf, by the entry of a rival imperial power, the USA, into the Middle Eastern arena for the first time, and most important of all by the political transformation of Russia, one of the powers central to the Eastern question, through the 1917 revolution. Thus, if World War One meant the end of the old order and its Eastern question, new problems simultaneously emerged to elicit a renewed interest in the region. Hitherto of *geostrategic* importance, with the discovery of oil the Middle East now became of *intrinsic economic* significance. The pre-existing inter-European imperial rivalry between France, Britain, Italy, Germany and Tsarist Russia was now complicated by the entrance of the American challenger – albeit, at this early stage, mainly in the form of oil companies. Superimposed upon these economic and inter-capitalist concerns, there emerged a new global conflict, between the Bolshevik revolution and the Western capitalist powers as a whole. This impinged directly on the Middle East. One of the first acts of the Bolshevik revolutionaries was to publish the secret agreements on the Middle East between Britain, France and the Tsarist government, and thereby stimulate Arab nationalist hostility to Western intrigues.[9]

In addition to these changes, the decline of the Ottoman empire and the events accompanying and succeeding World War One had produced two other major changes *within* the Middle East itself: one was the entry into the political arena for the first time of popular movements, the other the consolidation of Zionist settlers in Palestine. A combination of factors stimulated the former development – the increased economic impact of the industrialized world, foreign occupation, the spread of new ideas of religious and national radicalism, peasant resistance to agricultural change, urban resistance by the traditional merchant class to foreign imports. Together these produced considerable resistance and revolt across the region in the decades after 1880. In Egypt it was nationalist military forces under Urabi Pasha that resisted the Anglo-French invasion of 1882, while in 1919, as Britain was preparing to deny Egyptian nationalists their right to attend the Versailles Conference and demand independence, a major revolt broke out in the villages of the Nile delta and in the cities. To the south, in the Sudan, a mass revolt led by the Mahdi wiped out the expeditionary force of General Gordon in 1885 and prevented Britain from establishing control there for more than a decade. In the Arab areas of the Ottoman Empire World War One was preceded by substantial political organization against Turkish rule, and in the war itself Arab nationalists and officers rose up to join the British in driving the Ottomans northwards.[10] The imposition of colonial rule in the territories freed from Ottoman rule was itself followed by a series of uprisings – in Iraq in 1920, in Syria in 1926 and in Palestine in 1936–9. In Iran there had been a nationwide project against foreign economic influence in 1891, a major urban uprising against the Shah in the Constitutional Revolution of 1906–08, while in the aftermath of World War One communists and nationalists established a distinct revolutionary regime in the northern Gilan province.[11] The complex new strategic situation in the Middle East was therefore tied to the onset of widespread popular dissent and resistance to foreign domination, both of which were to prove formative influences in the twentieth century.

This mobilization of elements in the indigenous populations of the Arab countries and Iran was matched by the simultaneous movement to colonize Palestine by Zionist settlers. This movement had begun with the first emigration or *aliya* in the 1870s, and by World War One there existed a substantial, but still minoritarian, Jewish community in Palestine.[12] The world war dramatically altered the conditions under which this settlement took place: it provided in Britain an administrative power whose more favourable attitude towards such settlement was enunciated as policy in the 1917 Balfour Declaration, which promised Jews a 'national home' in Palestine; and it laid the basis in Europe of the political and social conditions that were to drive many of those Jews able to survive Nazism towards the comparatively safer haven of the Middle East. Substantial Jewish migration to Palestine continued between the wars, and by the end of World War Two the Jewish community there was strong enough to demand, and establish, an independent state.[13] Britain purported to be even-handed as between the two nationalities, Palestinian and Jewish. But it had itself opened the door to the new settlers in Palestine (while closing the door to them in Britain itself) and by the end of World War Two it was so vulnerable to American pressure, by then firmly pro-Zionist, that it in effect abdicated in the face of mounting pressure for an Israeli state. The result was that in 1948 a third non-Arab state emerged in the Middle East: it was one that the Arab states long refused to accept and which was to provide the focus for nationalist and religious resentment for decades to come. It is common to talk of 'the Middle East problem' as if it consists solely of the Arab–Israeli dispute. This is a simplification. However, if the modern history of the Middle East cannot be *reduced* to the conflict between Israelis and Arabs, it was nonetheless affected, enflamed and warped by it to a remarkable extent.[14]

It was the World War One settlement, for all its contradictions, that established the state system of the Middle East as it has emerged today.[15] Immediately after the war, there were only four fully independent states in the region. Saudi Arabia and North Yemen were conservative monarchies: these arose in those parts of the Arabian Peninsula that the Ottomans abandoned but where no colonial power sought to exercise its domination and where new tribal coalitions seized power. The two others were non-Arab states that had escaped colonial rule after World War One, partly because of their size and partly because of the need felt by all outside powers to create buffers on the south of the USSR: these were Turkey and Iran. Both had been the sites of major resistance to the victors of World War One – in Turkey this took the form of Kemal Pasha's military revolt of 1920–2, in Iran it led to a popular mobilization that forced Britain to abandon its 1919 plan to turn Iran into a protectorate.

The remaining Arab states all now fell under colonial rule, and divided up into three main groups. The states of the Maghreb, or North Africa, all already subjugated before World War One, comprised three French colonies (Morocco, Algeria and Tunisia), one Italian (Libya) and two British colonies (Egypt and Sudan). In the Arabian Peninsula, Britain maintained control over six distinct administrative entities around the coast (Kuwait, Bahrain, Qatar, the Trucial Oman States, Oman and Aden or, as it later became known, South Arabia). It was in the third Arab region, the east, or Mashrik, that the territories taken from the Turks were parcelled out as five distinct entities between Britain and France.

Imperial control of the Middle East was to prove relatively transient, and the decolonization process began in the interwar years. By the end of World War Two, Egypt, Syria, Lebanon and Iraq were all formally independent: but the process of decolonization then became a much more bloody and conflictual affair. In Palestine, the process led to open conflict between Jewish settlers and Palestinians; when in 1948 the predominantly Jewish state was established, half the Palestinian population became refugees.[16] British troops only finally left Egypt's Suez Canal zone in 1954, in the face of nationalist opposition: they then tried to return in the Suez invasion of 1956. France hung on in the Maghreb: it took the deaths of over one million Algerians, out of 14 million, for the nationalists to prevail in the war of independence that lasted from 1954 to 1962.[17] In South Yemen, Britain's plans to establish a strategic pivot for its east of Suez policy at Aden were only thwarted by the nationalist, and increasingly radical, guerrilla-led revolution of 1963–67.[18] British rule elsewhere in Arabia lasted until 1971, when the last of the Persian Gulf colonies acceded to independence. The transition in the Gulf involved substantial repression, of a workers' movement in Bahrain and of the guerrilla resistance in the Dhofar province of Oman.[19] Short as it had been, imperial rule in the Middle East was only established and terminated amidst substantial resistance and conflict. These conflicts over decolonization did not usher in a new more quiescent period. The outbreak of the first Cold War over Iran in 1946 set the scene.[20] The tensions of the Middle East since decolonization were consequently of far more than local interest.

The 'conformity' of the Middle East: six Third World characteristics

Recognition of the international importance of developments in the Middle East tends to coexist with a markedly uncertain, and persistently mystified, approach to the internal character of these societies. One central aspect of the countries of the Middle East is their great diversity, a factor often ignored in generic statements about them. The modern history of the Middle East, and the decisions of the World War One victors, have produced a region of great variety and instability. Of the 20 independent states in the region, 17 are Arab, and three – Israel, Iran and Turkey – non-Arab. This ethnic diversity is matched by that of demography. The total population of around 300 million is divided up most unevenly between these states, three of them – Egypt, Turkey and Iran – having near 60 million each, and some – Bahrain, Qatar and Oman – having populations of under one million. The salience of certain shared characteristics – strategic position, Islamic culture, arid geography and, for most, the Arabic language – is offset by great differences and conflicts between them. As much as any other area of the Third World, the Middle East is united by some common features and relations to the outside world, but riven by contradictions and distinguished by variations within.

Before analysing what is specific about the Middle East, it is useful to recognize a number of characteristics of Middle Eastern societies that, in general terms, are shared with other regions of the Third World.

The Middle East has for a century or more been subjected to domination by the developed capitalist world, through direct colonialism in some areas and through indirect control in others. This experience of domination provides the fundamental context in which Middle Eastern politics and society have been formed and has given rise to certain features that are also visible in other societies of the Third World. These include movements of nationalist resistance, frequently unstable post-colonial states, extremes of economic distribution, manipulation by metropolitan states and penetration by metropolitan economies. For all its apparent eccentricity, the Middle East has *not* escaped the colonial and post-colonial experiences characteristic of the rest of the Third World.

In common with parts of Sub-Saharan Africa and the whole of the Americas and the Antipodes, the Middle East also endured, for a period, *direct* colonial settlement. In general, colonial settlement in Asia and Africa took three broad forms: settlement followed by long-term accommodation to the local population (Kenya and Morocco); settlement followed by forced departure (Angola and Vietnam); settlement and elimination of the local population (the bulk of the Americas). But there was a fourth intermediate model where neither accommodation nor elimination was possible, an unstable situation of prolonged post-colonial conflict – South Africa. In the majority of Middle Eastern cases, the first options prevailed and settlers were either assimilated or later expelled (Algeria, Libya and Egypt). But in one case, that of Palestine, there occurred precisely that intermediate and unresolved situation found also in South Africa.

In common with all others of the post-colonial world, the state structures and interstate boundaries of the Middle East reflect not long-established divisions, but the decisions of colonial administrators that cut across pre-existing regional linkages. This is as true for North Africa as it is for the Arab states of the Mashrik (Iraq, Syria, Lebanon and Jordan) and for the states of the Arabian Peninsula. Yet, arbitrary as they were in origin, Middle Eastern state boundaries have survived beyond the departure of the colonial powers. States have neither disintegrated nor, with the possible exception of Yemen, have they successfully or lastingly merged. Rather they have endured, under the control of ruling groups with roots in the colonial period. These groups have seen their interests as being best served by the preservation of a state system inherited from colonialism.

In their conflictual relationship with the metropolitan states, the countries of the Middle East have followed the pattern of other Third World states and developed forms of nationalism that exalt their specificity and distinct historical origins, while at the same time maintaining and developing economic relations with the metropolitan countries. The image of Arab oil ministers negotiating over OPEC prices from beneath their headdresses epitomizes the two sides of this attitude. The exaltation of the Islamic past, or of the supposed greatness of the Arabs and their component individual nations, is part of a much wider Third

World pattern of simultaneous rejection and acceptance of the international system dominated by Western states. The rejection focuses on the symbolic, the acceptance on the material.

Again in common with the Third World as a whole, a violent relationship with the metropolitan countries, and the tensions generated within Middle Eastern societies by this contact, have led to recurrent waves of popular unrest and mobilization against the forces of external domination and against those who have cooperated with them. The history of the modern Middle East has been punctuated time and again by uprisings, riots, demonstrations, revolts and protests, in cities, villages and oases, against the influence, real and imagined, of foreign powers. The uprisings in Egypt (1919 and 1952), the Iranian revolutions (1906 and 1979), the Yemeni revolutions of North (1962) and South (1963), the Algerian revolution (1954–62), the repeated popular upheavals of the Sudan (notably, 1964 and 1985), and a host of other resistance movements testify to this recurrent pattern of uprising and mobilization. The energies of the Middle Eastern peoples may have too often been misdirected, but they have been frequently rebellious and intransigent.

The Middle East shares with other Third World regions the character of its local state structures and ruling classes. The post-1945 period has seen the seizure of control by rulers of the state structures inherited from colonialism, and their exploitation of the economic opportunities resulting from integration into the world economy. In this way they have succeeded in consolidating power domestically against their subjects and regional rivals. For all the rhetoric of Islamic or national communality uniting rulers and subjects, the tenures of these rulers and their administrations have been marked by a persistent, often ruthless, use of the instruments of political and social control – repression, massacre, demagogy, censorship, bribery. Moreover, while maintaining political power over subjugated classes has been the predominant and most general concern of these ruling groups, they have demonstrated equally their concern to preserve other forms of power – over subject ethnic groups, such as the Kurds in Turkey, Iran and Iraq, over subject confessional groups, such as the Shi'ites in Lebanon, and over women, whose subordinate position throughout the Middle East has been perpetuated through a ferocious combination of violence, law and ideology. When it comes to maintaining the mechanisms of domination, on class, ethnic and gender bases, Middle Eastern rulers have resorted to all too characteristic practices in order to sustain their position.[21]

Regional anomalies? Islam, Palestine, Arab unity, oil, terrorism

The dimensions of Third World societies described above show how little the Middle East has escaped the experience of other regions of the Third World in the era of imperial domination and then of post-colonial independence. They also serve to place the apparent particularities of the Middle East in another, less anomalous context. Indeed events or trends that are often taken as distinguishing the Middle East from other parts of the Third World can, in this comparative light, appear far less particular. This can be illustrated by reference to what are most commonly held to be five key examples of Middle Eastern particularity: the hold of Islam, the Palestine question, the devotion to Arab unity, the rise of the oil states, and the incidence of terrorism. Far from relativizing the region, these five prominent features of the modern Middle East can in fact illustrate the analytic universality of its politics and society.

The Islamic religion, which originated in the Arabian Peninsula in the seventh century, is, first of all, no preserve of the Middle East. Most of the world's one billion or so Muslims are not only not Arabs, but do not live in the Middle East: the largest Islamic countries lie elsewhere and are Indonesia, Bangladesh, Pakistan and Nigeria. At the same time, significant numbers of Arabs – in Lebanon, Palestine, Egypt and Iraq – are Christians. By definition, therefore, an *Islamic* political or social character can hardly define what is *specific* to the Middle East; generalizations about 'politics' or 'society' deployed to explain the Middle East would have to apply to these other non-Middle Eastern societies as well and would have to exclude the behaviour of the region's Christians. Examination of what Muslims *do* also reveals the fact that Islam cannot dictate a politics: Islam itself is politically and socially contingent. While the Islamic religion does have certain specific implications in theory for social and even political practice, and legislates for areas some other religions exclude, these doctrinal specifications are meagre and partial; they tell us very little about how Muslims will or do act in any society or political situation. The very variety of behaviour in Muslim societies bears this out.

To explain the *particular* social forms and political beliefs of people in Muslim societies, other factors, external and additional to Islam, have to be examined. These include the patterns of state domination and class rule, the relation to external forces and the historical formation of the country and its economy.[22] Certainly, as we shall see in chapter 2, the Iranian revolution of 1979 took the form it did in part because of the belief systems of the Iranian people and the presence of a clergy committed to a course of political action. But the particular version of political Islam espoused by Khomeini, the willingness of the population to follow him, the inability of the state to defeat its unarmed opponents, and the failure of the Shah's allies to help him – none of these can be explained by reference to the Quran.[23] In a comparative perspective, the Iranian revolution, which took place in the major cities of Iran after a decade of rapid socio-economic change, has much in common with urban-based populist movements in other Third World countries, from Peronism in Argentina and Getulism in Brazil to the mass movements of the Hindu right in India.[24] It had an Islamic ideological character, yet it cannot be explained by Islam any more than an abstracted Christianity can explain the peasant movements of Germany in the early sixteenth century, or the *Solidarnosc* movement of the 1970s in Poland.

Many in the Middle East, and outside, consider the region to be unique because of the Arab–Israeli question – the refusal of the Arabs for many years to accept the state of Israel, the protracted struggle of the Palestinians and Israel's resistance to any compromise with the Palestinians. In some ways, this dispute is unique; but it is not *so* anomalous. For as has already been suggested, the Palestine question is in origin the product of a colonial situation which in the nineteenth century saw the outward expansion of European settlement. Trans-Mediterranean colonialism was by no means specific to Palestine: it encompassed every country on the southern Mediterranean shore from Morocco to Palestine. What *was* specific to the case of Palestine was, first, the

particular ideological and religious character of that settlement
movement embodied in Zionism; second, the fact that the Zionist
settlers evolved into a separate Israeli nation while neither of the
two conventional resolutions of colonialism occurred (the local
inhabitants were not eliminated or definitely crushed, nor were
they able to resist the establishment of a settler state); and third,
the very intense and ultimately decisive support which this settler
community obtained from the metropolitan countries, and in
particular from the USA. The specific character of this colonial
experience, one in its origins and essence nonetheless similar to
dozens of other colonial settler processes, produced the conflict
now seen as the Arab–Israeli dispute. That the immigrants, initially
a multi-ethnic community drawn from many lands, should themselves have become a distinct nation is by no means unique: many
of the current nations of the Americas were so formed.[25]

Of equal importance in the panorama of Middle East politics,
and ideologically linked to that of the Palestine issue, is a third
special feature: the drive for Arab unity.[26] The Middle East
contains 17 independent states, plus Palestine, which consider
themselves to be Arab; they are formally committed both to Arab
unity and to 'solidarity' on the Palestine issue. They are members
of a regional body, the Arab League, founded in 1945. In the post-
1945 period there have been several attempts by Arab states to
merge, most notably that by Egypt and Syria in the period 1958–
61. The failure of such attempts at unity has not apparently
lessened the formal commitment of Arab states to this goal. On
closer examination, however, this anomaly is not quite as peculiar
as it may appear. Commitments to unity are not specific to the
Middle East. In some cases they have succeeded (the German and
Italian unifications of the nineteenth century), in others they have
faded after initial enthusiasm (notably, the aspiration for unity
among Latin American revolutionaries in the 1820s, briefly revived
by Che Guevara, and among African states in the early 1960s, as
advocated by Nkrumah). The European states have, in the past
decade or two, also proclaimed an interest in greater unity and,
short of that, coordination. Arab unity is one of those unificatory
movements.

If the *reality* of Arab unity is examined more closely then it
appears even less surprising. First, there is the reality of unity at

the economic and cultural levels. The growth of economic ties within the Arab world, as a result of the oil boom, is substantial; this can be measured in terms of migration and financial flows. But these linkages are not in any way unique, being comparable to other flows of labour and capital in the contemporary world economy. They have, moreover, created a new hierarchy between Arab societies rather than greater fraternity or equality. The sense of *cultural* unity which Arabs have, based on language but extending to music, poetry, film and humour, is certainly stronger than that within most parts of Asia and Africa. But that of Spanish-speaking Latin America is certainly comparable, and that of the English-speaking world is becoming so.[27] On the other hand, when we come to the political, the reality is one of Arab *disunity*. Abstracting from the rhetoric, the post-colonial states of the Middle East have remained as separate and as jealous of their state and rulers' interests as any other. After decades of demagogy about unity, the post-colonial divisions have endured in the Arab world, just as they have in Africa and Latin America. Nor did the Palestine question in reality provide a transcendent, unificatory cause; it led to little common action or sacrifice, except where states actually had common frontiers with Israel, and in those cases the conflict invariably took the form of a border war, a phenomenon by no means unique to the Middle East.

Solidarity with the *Palestinians* themselves was largely rhetorical. In practice Arab states used the issue of Palestine for domestic legitimacy, while avoiding direct confrontation with Israel and trying for self-serving purposes to manipulate the Palestinian resistance movement itself. The zenith of Palestinian activity, from 1967 until the mid-1970s, generally concealed this. However, from 1948 until 1967 the Palestinians were permitted no independent political presence in the Arab world, and were afforded scant attention. Developments after the mid-1970s – Sadat's independent initiative towards Israel in 1977, the division of the Arab world into several camps, and then, in 1983, Syria and Libya's direct attack upon the Arafat leadership of the PLO – helped to strip away the mythology about a unificatory and pan-Arab commitment to the Palestinians. These events revealed the separate, self-regarding interests of Arab states that lay behind their supposedly common position on Palestine.

Oil is a fourth issue that has, for many, come in recent years to symbolize the uniqueness of Middle Eastern societies. Yet, as with Islam, so with this black gold. In the first place, the majority of OPEC producers have not been Arabs, and many are outside the Middle East – Venezuela, Ecuador, Nigeria and Indonesia amongst them. Secondly, the impact of oil upon producer states varies greatly depending upon the character of the society in question. Only a few Arab producers – Saudi Arabia, Kuwait, Qatar and the Emirates – have enjoyed substantial oil surpluses in the post-1973 period. The rest remain capital-hungry and, with large populations, they are beset by many of the problems of other developing countries. Most importantly, the reality of 'oil power' has been far more restricted than was thought in the 1970s. In political terms, the Arab states have not been able to any significant extent to alter metropolitan policies on Palestine: the 'oil weapon' has proved a chimera. Economically, the producers were able for some years to raise the price and their real incomes by combining to enforce a near-monopoly position in a favourable market. But it is the law of supply and demand rather than any Middle Eastern specificity that explains this success. About all the Arabs did achieve politically were some increased arms sales by the USA to Saudi Arabia and a few anodyne utterances by the then EEC: after 1973, only one OECD country – Japan – recognized the PLO. Moreover, even in economic terms OPEC's power proved to be temporary: in the early 1980s OPEC's share of the world market declined.

The uniqueness of oil resides quite elsewhere, in the peculiar form of payment resulting from it, a rent to producer states that does not entail the forward and backward linkages within the local economy that are characteristic of other primary production in the Third World.[28] The collection of this 'rent' enables the producer state, and those controlling it, to amass enormous sums of money without engaging in any form of production; it is this which has generated such major social tensions within the producer states. These tensions – growing income inequality, rampant corruption in the state, grandiose development projects, neglect of productive activity and skills, especially in agriculture – have been seen as much in Lagos and Jakarta as in Tehran and Riyadh. Islam, the Palestine question, Arab unity and oil do not, there-

fore, define a *sui generis* Middle East. Neither the determination of
the geological substructure nor those of the religious-ideological
superstructure can establish a Middle East exempt from analytic
universality.

Finally, there is the issue of terrorism, a question widely
associated in the Western public mind with the Middle East and,
in particular, with a special brand of Islamist bent on acts of
hijacking, kidnapping and bombing of civilians. Actions of such
kinds have indeed been carried out by militants of a variety of
ideologies in the Middle East. Yet there is much confusion in the
discussion of terrorism.[29] A measure of historical proportion is
essential. In the first place, taking 'terrorism' as any act of terror
by a civilian political group directed against non-combatant
civilians, the phenomenon is by no means specific to the Middle
East. Acts of terror of this kind have been present throughout
much of recorded history, and have been a pervasive part of
political life in many countries and cultures during the twentieth
century. The first terrorists of modern politics did not come from
the Middle East but were Russian anarchists, Irish republicans,
Armenian and (Hindu) Bengali nationalists, later to be followed
by Zionist Jews, Greek Cypriots and others in the post-1945 period.
Modern political terrorism did not originate in the Middle East,
or among Muslims, nor has it been predominantly carried out by
such people.

Discussion of terrorism suffers not just from a selective application of the term, but also from problems of definition. The term
itself was originally used in the context of the French revolution
to refer not to acts of unofficial terror, but to the use of terror, for
political purposes, by the state. In that sense, of course, it has
been a widespread instrument of Middle Eastern states in the
modern period, but by no means exclusively so. Terrorist acts
against one's own subjects, or against populations deemed to
represent a threat in neighbouring states, have been committed by
many Arab states, and by Israel, Turkey and Iran. They have also,
it need hardly be underlined, been committed by states in much
of Europe and elsewhere during the twentieth century.

Perhaps the greatest confusion in the 'terrorism' debate has
been the idea that the practice is usually directed outside the region
itself – at Europeans, or at visitors to the region, at journalists,

tourists or diplomats. Criminal attacks on such people have occurred, but by the far the highest incidence of terror, be it by states or unofficial groups, has been carried out within the region *against peoples of the region themselves*. And the greatest number of victims of terror by a state are invariably the subjects of that state. Equally, the killings in inter-communal conflict (Lebanon providing the most obvious example) have exceeded anything seen in the foreign operations of militant groups.

Discussion of 'terrorism' is as often as not an instrument, a tool in a polemical exchange rather than a means of clarification. What much usage of the term serves to obscure is the issue of why a given group is fighting in the first place: the implication which those who use the term hope to convey is that, by dint of the very methods they use, the militants concerned have no legitimate cause. But this is, on a moment's reflection, untenable. Some groups, or individuals, may commit acts of terror for the sake of it, for revenge or because of psychological disturbance. But this has been true of very few terrorist groups. In the main, such actions have been carried out by groups which, while employing reprehensible means, have been motivated by political goals that at least merit discussion. These goals are usually related to some form of national independence. To brand such people as 'terror- ist' is a means of using a (probably legitimate) condemnation of their means as a way of excluding discussion of their goals. But whether it is Palestinians or Zionists, Algerian FLN or Egyptian fundamentalists, there are issues beyond terror which such actions draw attention to. In any moral calculation of such situations, as in major wars, criminal behaviour must detract from considera- tion of the legitimacy of its goals; but it is rare indeed for the former wholly to invalidate the latter. Here, as much as in any of its other analytic dimensions, the question of terrorism in the Middle East is part of, rather than distinct from, the broader political issues and debates of modern times.

The discriminations of history

Such are the historical origins of the contemporary Middle East and those formative characteristics which it shares with the colonial and post-colonial world as a whole. This discussion should make it apparent that those features of Middle East politics that are often thought to define its distinctiveness do no such thing. It now becomes possible to identify with greater accuracy the real particularities which are born not of the workings of a socially abstracted religion, or of a timeless 'Arabism', but out of the specific history of the Middle Eastern region, and of its component societies.

The Middle East in the post-colonial period continues to be markedly influenced by the individual character of its pre-colonial societies.[30] Modern forms of communication and ideas of nationalism obviously did not exist prior to the impact of imperialism: but in the context of the great Muslim empires, the far-flung regions of the Middle East were to a considerable degree bound by ties of trade, administration, religion and migration in a way that gave a certain cultural and social unity. The current ideology of its unity as a region, or of the Arabs as one people, despite its imaginary quality, does reflect the fact that some elements of a certain *pre-colonial* cohesion have endured. Of equal import are many of the specific features of pre-colonial social structures: the prevalence of tribal forms of organization, not only amongst nomads but amongst settled agricultural populations in the Peninsula and in some other countries such as Libya; the adherence of much of the population to Islamic values which, for all their political contingency, provided a common demotic culture in the face of external, imperial and post-imperial, domination; and the presence in the cities of trading and financial sectors opposed to central government and able (as in Syria and Iran) to express political opposition to them under propitious circumstances. These, among other features of the pre-colonial Middle East, have substantially affected the politics and society of the more recent decades.

The influence of these pre-colonial factors has been all the greater given the comparatively superficial impact of colonial rule itself and the limited transformation of society by European imperialism in the region. In North Africa imperial rule did take the form of colonial settlement and agricultural transformation: the former was particularly strong in Algeria, the latter in Egypt. But in the rest of the region – in Turkey, Iran, the Arabian Peninsula and, with the exception of Palestine, the Mashrik – no comparable transformations of the pre-colonial society were effected. Four of the states escaped colonial domination altogether; in the remaining Mashrik and peninsular states, colonial rule was effected through local social and political forces, either inherited from the pre-imperial period, as in Kuwait and Oman, or in the form of monarchies and local administrations installed by Britain and France in the wake of the Ottoman retreat. This relative absten-tion happened partly as a consequence of colonial parsimony, and partly because apart from oil – whose production as described above requires little social or economic linkage – there was little in these arid lands to attract metropolitan economic transformation. The result of that uncharacteristic forbearance was that in contrast to most of Africa, to Latin America and to the rest of Asia, the Middle East states of the Peninsula and the Mashrik acquired independence with many archaic social and political structures intact. Many retained their pre-colonial ruling classes. Even in the Maghreb the degree of continuity was striking, as the survival of the kings of Morocco and, up to 1969, Libya demonstrated.[31]

Another distinctive feature of Middle Eastern societies has been the virulence of ethnic and confessional differences. As elsewhere in the Third World, the current force of these divisions derives from a combination of pre-colonial historical legacies with later colonial and contemporary social and political divisions. Histori-cal evidence shows that relations between different religions and ethnic groups in the pre-colonial period were *certainly not* wholly harmonious or egalitarian: the idea that they were, and that current divisions are *solely* the work of an external factor, imperi-alism, is part of contemporary nationalist mythology. But colonial rule often did much to worsen divisions, by playing off one group against another, by provoking forms of nationalism that exalted one group's past and so antagonized another's, and by stimulating the divisive search for 'genuine' national values. The pattern of confessional conflict in Lebanon and Egypt has in this way much in common with that of Cyprus and India, Sri Lanka and Indonesia. In Palestine it had additional elements, combining settler–native conflicts, nationalistic but in some measure theo-logically sanctioned Jewish–Muslim enmities, and a comprehensive interstate rivalry between Israel and the Arab states.

In the modern Middle East there has been no shortage of

popular movements, social in origin, that have been warped and diverted by sectarian and confessional forces. Time and again social, inter-class contradictions have developed in Middle Eastern societies but have then taken a confessional, religious or even chauvinist form. As we have seen, the Lebanese civil war that began in 1975 was a result of the long maturing of social contradictions within the country, as the power bloc established in the 1940s came under increasing pressure from underprivileged groups. Similarly, the Islamic fervour of the Iranian revolution reflected the sharp social tensions within Iranian society created by the oil boom and the Shah's autocracy. The sense of outrage and solidarity among Arabs at the plight of the Palestinians has often cascaded into an anti-Jewish demagogy and chauvinism as retrograde as it is ineffective. At the same time, large sections of the Israeli population, including the more deprived social groups, have swung behind the semi-religious bigotry of the Likud and its overtly religious satellites.

The Middle East is characterized by what *is* peculiar to oil, the anomalous economic and social consequences of its production. Less than half of the Middle Eastern states are oil producers, and the majority of those have small populations. The majority of states with large populations do not have oil. This asymmetry of population and oil resources has provoked substantial migration from oil-less to oil-producing states, while at the same time enabling the oil producers to use their wealth for individual political purposes in the region. That ability to focus their power has been compounded, however, by the peculiar economies of oil production itself, which has a minimal linkage with the society in which it is taking place. In this context the main, indeed sole, significant effect of oil is that the producer state obtains a substantial rent from overseas sales. Inputs of labour, capital or agricultural goods are very small: hence oil production has an enclave character. Taken together, these two features of oil production – its asymmetrical distribution, its provision of rent rather than generation of national income – mean that some of the states most marked by pre-colonial continuities have been the very ones endowed with substantial quantities of surplus capital. This they have deployed to promote not only their particular political values but also their social values as well: a form of conservative 'Islam', whether in its Saudi or Qaddafi-ite varieties.

If the degree of international conflict has in comparison with other regions been exaggerated, the politics of the Middle East have been characterized by a combination of popular mobilization and political regression unique in the Third World. This had, however, only an indirect relationship to the dominant world contest of the post-1945 period, the Cold War. For all the West's anxiety up to 1991 about Soviet influence, the fact that the Middle East bordered the Soviet Union and that the USSR played a role there in support of states allied to it, had in the end rather little impact on the domestic character of politics within that region. Egypt's ability to manipulate Soviet aid and, under Sadat, to expel Soviet advisers was a case in point. So too was the denunciation heaped upon Moscow by the leaders of the Islamic Republic of Iran. The USSR's role in the Middle East was a strategic and military rather than a political one. The forces of the left that emerged were in some cases substantial: communist parties were, at certain times, powerful in Iran, Sudan and Iraq. But these parties were subjected to severe repression and faced increasing competition from rival Islamic radicalisms. In other cases where groups of an 'anti-imperialist' and allegedly socialist character emerged, these took the form of military dictatorships of a most repressive and chauvinist kind, as in the Ba'thisms of Syria and Iraq. Those left-wing regimes that survived and avoided the degenerations of the Ba'th, as in Algeria and South Yemen, were comparatively isolated from the mainstream of Middle Eastern politics, and in time succumbed to the authoritarian temptations of their own.

The end of the Cold War has, in several respects, revealed to what extent the region shares many of the broader features of Third World development, even as its politics retain a particular character. With the waning of the Soviet–American conflict from the mid-1980s onwards, it became possible for a range of regional conflicts to be approached in a more diplomatic way. The Iran–Iraq war ended in 1988, and at the end of the same year Palestinian recognition of the need for a two-state solution paved the way for subsequent Arab, and particularly Palestinian, negotiations with Israel. At the same time, the collapse of the Soviet system led to a dual realignment of regional powers by permitting both new relations with Moscow and Washington, and the emergence of new centres of regional influence such as Turkey in the context of a wider Middle East that included some of the former Soviet republics. Perhaps the most conspicuous issue to surface in the changed international environment was the generally alarming condition of Middle Eastern economies, an underlying crisis often obscured in the past by military confrontation and by oil money. The triple challenge of demographic explosion, declining water supplies and stagnant agricultural production confronted most Middle Eastern states, irrespective of political structure or ideological orientation.[32] It is these problems, eminently comparable to the challenges facing the rest of the Third World, that confront the Middle East.

2

The Iranian Revolution in Comparative Perspective

The preceding chapter has argued, in a broad overview of modern Middle Eastern history, that the development of the region's politics cannot be explained by reference to a set of religious doctrines, or to some fixed social and political entity called 'Islam'. The purpose of this chapter is to test that argument against the key event in modern Middle Eastern history which appears more than any other to show the importance of Islam. The Iranian revolution of 1978–79 was made in the name of religion and its call for a resurgent Islam resonated through the Middle East and beyond. Nowhere in the modern period has the challenge of explanation, of showing how an apparently religious event was the result of other, more mundane, processes, been so sharply posed.

The Iranian revolution was indeed one of the epic events of postwar history, involving a remarkable level of political mobilization, crisis on an international scale and political brutality. Contrary to the expectations of many, the apparently stable regime of the Shah was overthrown in 1978–79 and a new post-revolutionary system successfully established and maintained. Yet beyond its importance for the history of modern Iran and of the world as a whole, the revolution has posed complex analytic questions both for those who seek to relate it to the overall course of modern Iranian history, and for those who want to compare it to other modern revolutions. It can also serve as an important case-study of how far Islam as a religion can explain the course of political events in a late twentieth-century context. If the Iranian upheaval deserves the name 'revolution' – defined in terms of a high level of mass mobilization, destruction of an existing political and social order and the establishment of a distinctly new order – then it would seem to be a quite unusual variant, a development as atypical as it was unexpected.

It is, however, worth remembering that all revolutions exhibit characteristics that are unexpected, that they can upset the schemata of social analysis as much as they overthrow established systems of power. The French revolution challenged many of the rationalist assumptions of the Enlightenment. Antonio Gramsci, himself a communist leader in Italy, called the Russian revolution 'the revolt against *Das Kapital*' because of the way it appeared to defy the economic determinism that underlay earlier Marxist thinking. The Iranian revolution was certainly an original event, but it is advisable to be more than a little cautious about specifying just where this originality lies.

A tentative discussion of this revolution's originality can therefore serve three functions: to prevent facile locking of the Iranian case into preconceived patterns of Iranian history or the sociology of revolutions; to counter claims that the Iranian revolution represents a wholly original process, a *sui generis* event to which available concepts of historical analysis and rational explanation cannot be applied; and to match general conceptions of how 'Islam' affects politics and society against a particular case, and one in which an Islamic regime has been established and maintained. A proper emphasis upon the novelty of the Iranian revolution and of its Islamic character can be balanced by some comparative caution, by suggesting that not all that has occurred in Iran is either unique, or as resistant to external comprehension as many would suggest.

The novelty of the Iranian revolution can be said to reside, in the first instance, in the role played within it by religion and in particular by what is loosely termed 'religious fundamentalism'. For the first time in modern history (that is, since 1789), a revolution took place in which the dominant ideology, forms of organization, leading personnel and proclaimed goal were all religious in appearance and inspiration. This in itself distinguishes the Iranian from other revolutions of the modern era. Given the manner in which Islam seeks to legislate for many areas of social activity, this religious imprint has involved an attempt to transform law, culture, polity and social practices in Iran in line with a model supposedly elaborated in the seventh century AD.

A consideration of various other features of the ideology of the Iranian revolution, often overlooked in the too generalized emphasis on religion, serves to show that paradoxically they too have a religious derivation and also distinguish the Iranian case. The first of these ideological features is the rejection of ideas of historical progress: Ayatollah Khomeini explicitly proposed a return to an earlier model of social and political practice and a rejection of many aspects of modernity. Such historical and ideological throwbacks have been seen in other revolutions and nationalist movements: the past can always be used to provide convenient legitimation. But the Iranian case went much further, because such a regression was the basis of the whole revolutionary programme. In the proper sense of the word, what happened in Iran was a comprehensively *reactionary* revolution, restoring to the term its original, astronomical, meaning of *return* to a previous order. A second consequence follows from this. While economic and material factors and aspirations played a part in the Iranian revolution, the leadership was reluctant to recognize the fact and tended rather to reject the idea of material improvement. Khomeini attempted to lower the material aspirations of the population by inculcating his ideal of generalized austerity, in which Western consumer goods were rejected and the faithful could live in a state most conducive to religious devotion.[1] Khomeini on one occasion declared that the goal of revolution was not to provide the people with cheap melons. On another, he told President Bani-Sadr that the American embargo during the hostage crisis would not be detrimental to the population for 'In the time of the Prophet, they ate only one date a day.'[2] Thirdly, while nationalist themes of assertion and rejection were articulated, the Iranian revolution was undertaken in the name of universalistic religion, and comparatively little stress was placed on Iran as a national entity. Its universalism was more pronounced than that of the French or Russian revolutions. This was evident both in the cultural shift that accompanied the revolution, which saw the rejection of many features of indigenous Iranian culture as well as values that were regarded as Western, and in the projection of Iran's revolution as the first episode by an insurgent Muslim world in the overthrow of its oppressors.[3]

A fourth ideological peculiarity, the rejection of history, followed from this. Far from vaunting the heroes and strugglers of earlier generations, as other revolutionary and nationalist movements have tended to do,[4] Khomeini appeared to regard almost all the earlier leaders of Iranian opposition movements, both secular and religious, as obstacles to his legitimacy, which he derived from the Islamic leaders of the seventh century, the Prophet Muhammad, and the founders of Shi'ite Islam. Khomeini's symbolic recourse to doctrine to secure legitimacy accounts for the fifth ideological quirk of the Iranian revolution, namely the fact that while it was a mass uprising, it cannot even theoretically be considered a democratic revolution.[5] Khomeini's writings and the constitution of the Islamic Republic made clear that ultimate power rests with the divinely inspired religious authority, the *faqih*, who can override all elected bodies and can dictate his views to the faithful. Khomeini tended to suggest that this presented no problem since there could be no contradiction between the faithful and the *faqih*; but were such an unexpected event to occur then he was in no doubt that the will of the *faqih* held sway. The reality of the Iranian revolution therefore contrasted markedly with the conception of revolution that had prevailed since the late eighteenth century: it rejected historical progress, material improvement, national assertion, historical legitimation, and democratic sovereignty – five themes which, however violated in practice, were at least invoked formally by modern revolutions from 1789 onward.

Yet this wholesale religious character is not, even in its appearance, as all-encompassing as might be assumed. Khomeini's ideas were fundamentalist in their claim to derive everything from sacred texts, but they were not fundamentalist or traditional in the sense that these terms imply inheritance from the past. Both the ideas themselves, and even more the political and social effect they had, were novel, dependent upon modern social conditions and modern political debates on which they drew quite freely, though without attribution.[6] Furthermore, it is possible to pose the same questions of Khomeini's ideas as one would of any set of radical ideas that find a mass following and make an impact on history. Which social groups supported these ideas, and why? What were the determining factors in the history of the country concerned which enabled such a movement to gather force at the time it did? Why was it possible for this opposition to defeat the established state? What kinds of social and political change have accompanied its triumph? The Islamic revolutionaries have their own answers to these questions which usually involve divine agency. Others may be hesitant about accepting these answers, even while viewing them with interest for what they tell us about the intentions and ideology of those who directed the revolution itself. Different responses may, therefore, be suggested.

If we depart for a moment from its religious character, the Iranian revolution appears more familiar. It was made by a wide-ranging alliance of social groups, drawing its support from dissident sections of the civil service and trading communities, and from much of the poor urban population. These forces were mobilized against a dictatorial political regime by a charismatic leader and by an ideology of revolutionary legitimacy.[7] In other words, the Iranian revolution developed in the context in which populist movements have arisen in many other Third World societies. Even the religious character of the revolution is, in historical perspective, not so unique. History is replete with instances of rebel movements challenging temporal rulers in the name of God, and of clerical leaders organizing such movements. The aspiration to create a sanctified order on earth runs through much of the history of medieval Europe and the Middle East and through that of nineteenth-century China. Newly urbanized populations in other countries have been known to turn to religion as a means of responding to the tensions of their new environment. In Iran itself, the mullahs were at the forefront of other protests in modern times, specifically the 1891 Tobacco Protest and the Constitutional Revolution of 1906.[8] What is unique about the role of religion in the Iranian revolution is that it became prominent in the latter half of the 1970s and, in particular, that it succeeded in overthrowing the established regime.

However, the originality of the Iranian revolution does not lie only in its religious character. If Iran's upheaval was unique in the prominence occupied by this 'traditional' theme, it was unique too for its very 'modern' features. The first contemporary revolution to be religious in orientation, the Iranian revolution was also the first ever 'modern' revolution.[9] This 'modernity' is evident in four respects. First of all, the revolution took place in a society far more socio-economically developed, in major respects, than was Russia in 1917 or China in 1949. Half of the population lived in urban areas, per capita income was over $2,000 and, however unevenly this was distributed, it meant that most Iranians living in the cities were materially better off than a decade before. It was not the *sans-culottes* who made the revolution, but people who had benefited materially from a process of rapid capitalist modernization.[10] Second, in contrast to all other Third World revolutions, the Iranian revolution happened in the cities. Many of those who took part in it may have been peasants (that is, of rural origin), but it was an urban event, produced by the conditions of the major cities in the 1970s. The contrast with China, Vietnam and Cuba is evident. Third, and again in contrast with other Third World revolutions, the Iranian upheaval was carried out through political confrontation rather than armed conflict. Thousands of people died in the last months of the Shah's regime, but they were mainly unarmed demonstrators, not guerrillas. Only in the last days of the Shah's regime did armed confrontation become the dominant form of resistance: the preceding months had been dominated by the street demonstration and the political general strike, forms of opposition associated with the schemata of revolution in the most advanced Western countries.[11] Finally, the fall of the *ancien régime* happened without it having been weakened through confrontation with any external force, as is normally believed necessary for the removal of an authoritarian regime. Neither defeat in war nor serious international economic pressure assisted the advance of the Islamic revolutionaries, and they themselves received no significant help from abroad.

From the perspective of twentieth-century revolutions, these 'modern' features are as original as the Islamic character of the Iranian case. It can therefore be said that the originality of the Iranian revolution resided neither in its 'traditional', nor in its 'modern' character but in the interaction of the two.[12] It is this combination which accounts for both the success and the peculiarity of the revolution in its initial stages, but it was also the increasing disassociation of the two which complicated the establishment of a post-revolutionary order.

The course of the revolution

The events that led directly to the fall of the Shah spanned a period of little more than one year. Mohammad Reza Pahlavi had been on the throne since 1941 and had been an autocratic ruler since 1953 when, with the assistance of the United States and Britain, a military coup had overthrown the nationalist government of Mohammad Mosaddeq. Since that time there had been only sporadic open opposition to the regime; the period 1960–63, when nationalist politicians and a section of the clergy led by Ayatollah Khomeini had protested against the Shah's control of political life and against the reforms he was instituting, was the notable exception. After over a decade of apparent calm, marked only by minor urban guerrilla activities, the opposition became more active in 1977, circulating critical statements and holding protest meetings. In January 1978 street protests began, organized by religious students in the city of Qom protesting at a newspaper article which insulted the exiled Khomeini. For the next few months there were successive protests and strikes in the main urban centres of Iran, in which the local clergy usually played an important organizing role and in which the bazaars, the historical centres of trade and finance, gave support by going on strike.

The regime did not appear to be in mortal danger, however, until September 1978 when, at the end of the fasting month of Ramadan, the traditional religious processions rallied over one million people in Tehran for what became political protests. The imposition of martial law on 8 September, followed by the shooting of demonstrators, only temporarily stemmed the protest movement, and in October a wave of strikes began. Although at first organized to make economic demands or as protests at press censorship, these strikes set in motion a process which led to a nationwide political general strike in late November and December. The first victims were the oilfields, whose standstill effectively blocked off Iran's export earnings and deprived the armed forces of diesel fuel. On 5 November, under pressure from a restive military leadership, the Shah appointed a military government. Lacking political cohesion, the new government was in any case unable to end the strikes and in early December found itself forced to permit a new round of street demonstrations to mark the traditional Shi'ite festival of Ashura. This provided the opportunity for the demand to be made more clearly than ever before that the Shah must depart. By this time, Khomeini had become not only a symbol of opposition but also an increasingly active leader; from his base in Paris he insisted on no compromise with the Shah or those in any way associated with him.

On 15 January 1979 the Shah left Iran, leaving behind a demoralized and divided army, and a government headed by former opposition leader Shahpour Bakhtiar. A committed secularist and courageous individual, Bakhtiar overestimated both his own political resources and the loyalty of the army. He also underestimated the degree to which he had discredited himself by being seen to accept his office from the Shah. Khomeini refused to negotiate with the Bakhtiar government and, after returning to Iran on 1 February, he pronounced Mehdi Bazargan head of a rival government. For ten days Iran had two governments; but on 10 and 11 February, following pro-Khomeini mutinies in the garrisons of Tehran, groups of armed civilians seized control of government buildings and military camps. The army command declared itself neutral in the conflict between Khomeini and Bakhtiar; the latter and his associates, together with remnants of the royalist court, either fled or were arrested.

The new Bazargan government then proceeded to institutionalize the post-revolutionary regime. On 30 March a referendum proclaimed Iran an Islamic Republic. In November 1979 a new Islamic constitution was similarly passed by referendum, and Khomeini was officially accepted as the *faqih* or supreme judicial authority with extensive powers. In January 1980 Abol-Hasan Bani-Sadr was elected president and, following its election, the *Majlis* or parliament, dominated by the Islamic Republican Party, selected as prime minister Mohammad Ali Rajai, an opponent of Bani-Sadr. These institutional developments were, however, overshadowed by other processes and crises: the virtually undisputed dominance of Khomeini as leader of the new republic weakened any other political forces and encouraged factionalism among those eager for his support. Meanwhile, the deterioration of the social and economic structures of the country, combined with increasingly antagonistic international relations, impeded attempts to create a new and viable post-revolutionary order.[13]

Beyond those traditional and modern aspects that gave this revolution its unique and paradoxical character there were other remarkable features. One was the suddenness of the event. Despite the underground opposition of the 1960s and 1970s, and despite the socio-economic tensions associated with uneven and rapid economic expansion, the years prior to the revolution were not marked by major political or social unrest. Neither was the upheaval preceded by a significant economic crisis such as a recession affecting substantial parts of the population. Nor did this crisis develop inside Iran as a result of conflict with other states: the frequently observed pattern of revolution following war or comparable international challenges to the power of a state could not be applied to Iran. Few people, whether observers or participants, were conscious even six months before the Shah fell that the regime was in serious trouble, and even the pronouncements of the Ayatollah Khomeini indicate that his growing sense of confidence, reflected in his more and more militant demands, developed in response to the course of events in Iran itself. Yet the revolution was not a chance event: it defeated not a decayed autocracy but a state that had appeared to be one of the stronger and more decisive of Third World regimes, and one, moreover, that had enjoyed considerable support from abroad. Although it is necessary, in the light of subsequent events, to revise the picture of the Shah's regime as one at the zenith of its power, it would be a mistake to underestimate the combined force of the revolutionary pressures which were necessary to overthrow the established Iranian state. In a condensed and schematic form, there are five central areas in which the causes of the revolution may be discerned.

Rapid and uneven economic development

In the two decades prior to the revolution Iran had undergone substantial socio-economic transformation and had made considerable advances towards becoming an industrialized capitalist society.[14] Yet in previous decades Iran had undergone relatively little transformation, and the accelerated changes of the 1960s and 1970s both produced exceptional tensions within the society and sustained certain pre-capitalist or pre-industrial sectors that were to facilitate the upsurge of 1978.

The main reason why the revolution occurred was that conflicts generated in capitalist development intersected with resilient institutions and popular attitudes which resisted the transformation process.

The impetus for economic expansion came from Iran's oil industry, whose revenues rose from $45 million in 1950 to $1.1 billion in 1970 and, following the multiplication of prices by OPEC, to $20.5 billion in 1976. By the late 1970s, per capita income in Iran was over $2,000, industrial output was growing at over 15 per cent a year, and up to half the population was living in the towns. Urban Iran appeared to be enjoying widespread prosperity, and virtually no social groups in the cities suffered a net fall in income. But the very process of transformation, mistermed 'modernization', was itself contradictory.

This oil-fuelled growth generated its own problems. First, the availability of oil revenues subsidized many areas of the economy and so enabled them to remain uncompetitive and unproductive. Oil assisted economic changes, but it also subsidized inefficient sectors, fostered a large service sector and state apparatus, and gave the Iranian government the illusion that it could dispense with the disciplines that developing societies without oil had to respect. Although much of the economic change was real, there was also much that was illusory. Even in its own terms, however, the oil boom could not last, and the period 1977–78 saw a relative slowing down. GNP stagnated in these years; inflation increased, particularly in rents; certain commodities grew scarce; and power cuts occurred, angering urban-dwellers. There was no widespread hardship, but the slowing down had political effects as entrepreneurs lost confidence and as the government enforced price controls on merchants to combat inflation. The decision of the cost-cutting Amuzegar government to suspend state subsidies to the clergy in 1977 must also have had its consequences.

More important for the mass of urban poor, however, were the inequalities and tensions associated with the boom itself: while the gap between rural and urban incomes began growing in the late 1960s, inequalities in the urban areas themselves began to be increasingly pronounced. By the mid-1970s it was calculated that the top 10 per cent of the population accounted for 40 per cent of expenditure; in addition, the urban poor suffered from the housing shortage, with the result that some had to spend up to 70 per cent of their income on rents. The population of some cities doubled in a decade, and while the migrants may have benefited from higher incomes there, they suffered the loss of the support systems of village society. To make matters worse, there was wide-spread corruption, involving members of the royal family. Beyond the unevenness of the economic expansion lay the unevenness of the transformation itself: the fact that despite industrialization and partial modernization, the transition was not taking effect. In agriculture the land reforms of the 1960s produced a cash-crop sector tied to the urban economy, but far more of the land was cultivated in family-sized units relatively isolated from the rest of the economy. The towns had a long tradition of commercial and religious institutions grouped around the bazaars which, in the face of the changes from above, adapted but retained their inde-pendence and their hostility to the Shah's state. There was a high degree of industrialization, with two and a half million people employed in manufacturing of some kind – a very high figure by Third World standards, representing about a quarter of the total labour force. Yet the great majority were employed in small artisanal units, retaining the production processes and cultural values of an earlier epoch.

Comparable dichotomies could be observed in the fields of distribution and finance. Despite the emergence of a modern banking system and of modern retail outlets, a good deal of financial and commercial activity remained under the control of the bazaar which had in the past fully controlled these sectors. The bazaar merchants resented their relative demotion by banks and new retail systems, yet their absolute position improved greatly with the expansion of economic activity in the country, so that the two-thirds of retail trade they retained enabled them to lend to those whom the banks regarded as unacceptable. It was also the bazaar that had traditionally financed the religious institutions, the mosques, shrines and religious schools.[15] This was, then, a sector that combined considerable influence in the country with deep antagonism to the new economic structures and to a regime which posed a direct threat to its influence by attempting to restrict the area in which the bazaar merchants could manoeuvre. Those merchants were one component in an explosive triangular partnership that also incorporated the clergy and the urban poor, the latter retaining the values of the pre-industrial society. The transformation of Iranian society therefore preserved and even promoted institutions of economic and social activity that acquired new potential for opposition within the altered context created by this transformation.

The political weakness of the monarchy

The Shah's personality helped weaken not only the army but also the state. The role of the individual in history is not only that of instigator and agent, but also of being a weak link in a system of political power. This factor alone cannot explain the Iranian revolution, any more than the characters of Louis XVI and Nicholas II can explain the fall of the Bourbons and Romanovs. But the Shah's grandiose distance from the realities of Iran helped introduce those development programmes which created the socio-economic context of the revolution; his ignorance of conditions in the country, together with his tendency to withdraw into silent meditation and his paralysis of will, were ill-suited to his coping with the crisis of 1978.[16] He seems to have known from about 1974 that he had cancer, and this may account both for the recklessness of some of his projects and for the fatalism he displayed in his final months of power. If such speculation is permissible, one could argue that no monarch could have saved the regime in the last few months of its existence, but that an autocrat of a different stamp might have been able to prolong its existence or take effective corrective measures early in 1978. Whatever the importance of this personal factor, it certainly seems to have contributed to the unexpectedly rapid disintegration of the regime.

In certain respects, the Pahlavi regime never enjoyed widespread legitimacy. Both the Shah and his father had come to power through military coups, and both ruled through political dictatorship. By the time of his fall, the Shah had had many thousands imprisoned and tortured. Khomeini's designation of the Shah and his father as 'usurpers' therefore struck a chord in Iranian political life, although the precise interpretation of this term may have varied, depending on whether it was alternative secular forces that were seen as having been displaced (in the cases of the 1906 Constitution and the coup that removed Mosaddeq) or rather the legitimate leading role of the clergy. Both Pahlavis were also seen as illegitimate rulers because of their reliance on foreign support. Certainly the attempts by the Shah to generate intermediate institutions of legitimation in the post-1960 period were a failure; the *Majlis* and the parties in it were phantoms, and neither Pahlavism as a national ideology stressing the pre-Islamic past, nor authoritarian concepts of *farmandari* or 'commandism', were widely accepted.

Yet the quality of the Shah's political illegitimacy was not constant: the dictatorship of the 1950s, and the prospects of economic improvement of the 1960s and early 1970s, seem to have produced at least some tacit acceptance. But the ironic consequence of the boom of the mid-1970s was to undermine this tacit acceptance by highlighting the inequalities and corruption inherent in the regime. Nor did this concern only the urban poor and the bazaar merchants: it also exposed one of the fatal weaknesses of the regime, namely the alienation of large sectors of the middle class. Despite the fact that this class benefited from the regime and could have had little expectation of improvement without the Shah, they failed actively to support his government. Their alienation cannot be attributed solely to the fact that the regime was a dictatorship which denied the rich and educated a voice in the affairs of a government which simply reflected the specific factions at court and the skewed distribution of oil wealth. Here Iran differed from Franco's Spain and Pinochet's Chile: while the material improvement offered to the middle classes was far greater in Iran, so too was the separation of those in power from the middle class. The result was that the Shah failed to mobilize an active social constituency in his period of success and was thus left isolated throughout the course of the revolution.

This fissure helps explain another important feature of the revolution, the demoralization of the army. One cause was the form that the confrontations of the revolution took. Huge unarmed crowds assembled, backed by the disconcerting and potentially hegemonic ideology of Islam. This was a threat any army would have had difficulty resisting in the absence of an occasion to take the offensive. The structure of the army, with its corrupt top officer corps and mass of conscripts beneath, also made it more liable to political demoralization. Khomeini himself devoted considerable attention to this issue, making appeals that would be most likely to undermine the army while at the same time seeking to avoid bloody confrontations. Another important factor was the conduct of the Shah himself and his failure to give strong leadership in the final months. When he left the country in January 1979 the army leadership was divided. The crisis of the final days was settled because, in the face of Khomeini's movement, the top army leadership signed a secret agreement with the opposition.[17] Yet beyond all these factors lies the fact that the army was, from the beginning, isolated in Iranian society: it was the instrument of the Shah. It had never fought a successful war and lacked any martial legitimacy. The gap between the majority of the middle class and the regime meant that in Iran, in contrast with other countries where armies have seized power to pre-empt revolutions, the military lacked the political and social support which an active political constituency can provide.

The broad coalition of opposition forces

Theda Skocpol's study of the French, Russian and Chinese revolutions forcefully contests the idea that revolutions are purposive activities in which a group of people consciously organize to overthrow a regime.[18] She points out that revolutions arise in situations of structural crisis for the society in question, and that those who initiate revolutions are not necessarily those who ultimately wield power in the post-revolutionary order. All revolutions produce groups who say the cause has been 'betrayed'. In Iran, the liberals and guerrillas who were openly contesting the regime in 1976 and 1977 were displaced in January 1978 by the clerical and bazaar forces; indeed, even within the Islamic forces the leadership gradually passed from cautious clergy like Shariat-Madari and from reformist Muslim militants like Bazargan and Bani-Sadr to the more hardline clergy of the Khomeini–Beheshti variety. At the same time, the revolution was not carried out by a political party. One of the proudest claims of the Islamic militant was: 'Our greatest strength is our lack of organization.'[19]

The broad and rapidly congealed coalition of forces that over-threw the Shah was strong precisely because of its diverse and spontaneous character; it was also one of the causes of the factionalism and paralysis of the post-revolution period. On the other hand, political organization did play its part in the Iranian revolution. The secular political parties were small and played only a secondary or even marginal role in the events of 1978–79; even when they participated they were forced to join the dominant Islamic trends. Far more important was the organization of the clergy; based in each locality of the city and with centres in the mosques and shrines, they were able to use religious networks to mobilize the population. These networks may have been de-centralized and, initially, not designed for political purposes, but they acquired a leading organizational role in the crisis of 1978 and had, by the latter half of the year, acquired in Khomeini a determined and appealing leader. Behind the clergy there also lay the underground *Fedayin-i Islam* grouping, a militant sect founded in the 1950s. There is reason to doubt whether Khomeini himself was a member, but some of the leading clerical figures were, and they had been determined for over two decades to wrest power from the Shah. The case of the Iranian revolution demonstrates the possibility of purposive action in a revolutionary situation: it was the clergy who directed the struggle throughout.

The social forces that responded to the movement varied. In the first clashes of 1978 the main components were theology students and bazaar merchants, but these groups, far more in touch with the population than the secular parties, were able to call on the urban poor who became the foot-soldiers of the major demonstrations in the latter part of the year. Parallel to these protests, the students and parties continued their actions, and in the final weeks of the regime it appears that significant numbers of middle-class people also joined in the demonstrations. The slogan raised in the final weeks was simple enough: 'Independ-ence, Freedom, Islamic Republic'. The one commanding aim was to oust the Shah: many who doubted the suitability of Khomeini none the less supported the movement in the hope that it could achieve the desired aim. Among the secular and middle-class forces many hoped that once the Shah had gone they could deflect the movement away from its clerical patrons. This enabled such people to support the movement with appropriate optimism, but it represented an underestimation of the strength of the religious forces.

The resulting relationship between social classes and political leadership was an example of the combination of traditional and modern forces in the Iranian revolution, which mobilized large numbers of people representing various social groups. Without such numbers, and the arousing of insurrectionary consciousness in these groups, the revolution would not have succeeded. The strikes that paralysed the country from October 1978 on became a great and unified exertion of social power by different classes in pursuit of a defined political goal. Yet these classes acted in the name of, and under the leadership of, an Islamic force that denied the relevance of class forces and class goals. The post-revolutionary period showed that the workers and merchants, despite the power they had demonstrated in the revolution, were unable to wield their power independently of the religious authorities, let alone in opposition to them. Subsequent accounts would argue either one side of this process or the other – that this was an Islamic revolution brought about by the exertions of an undifferentiated body of believers, or that the revolution was a proletarian upheaval later betrayed and crushed by a usurping and counter-revolutionary clergy. Neither account appears to be sufficient. The strength, as well as much of the tragedy, of the revolution lay in the manner in which both aspects were combined.

The mobilizing role of the Islamic religion

In the Iranian revolution several factors together produced the unique result of a twentieth-century state run by the clergy along lines derived from the Quran and Islamic law, in which the major influence lies in the hands of a personage constitutionally designated as the interpreter of holy texts. One negative factor which played its part in giving prominence to Islam as an ideology of opposition was the systematic destruction by the Shah and his father of the *secular* opposition forces that had mobilized protest movements in earlier decades.[20] Even the guerrilla groups, the

Fedayin and *Mujahidin*, were at a low ebb by the mid-1970s. The result was that, as in other societies where secular forms of protest are blocked off, religion in Iran became a symbol and an organizing centre for a protest that might otherwise have taken a more conventional secular form. Had Mosaddeq not been kept inside Iran and subsequently died, he might have developed some of the allure of the Ayatollah Khomeini.

This 'vacuum' theory is not, however, sufficient. Several other factors have to be taken into account. First, in all its forms Islam claims to be able to legislate for the whole of human activity. In Islam there is no formal distinction between church and state (though in practice the clergy has through history tended *not* to challenge *fundamentally* the legitimacy of a state governed by a monarch or other ruler who is not a cleric). The very concept of the secular is theoretically excluded, and all social ideas must be legitimated by derivation from the holy texts. In terms of political theory this assertion finds its expression in the attempt to define an 'Islamic' concept of government. In social activity, Islam prescribes modes of behaviour for everyday life and human relations. Like Judaism and Hinduism (though not Christianity), it has concepts of clean and unclean and stipulates ritual activities for each day: in the language of anthropologists, it enjoins *orthopraxy* as well as *orthodoxy*. As a result, the call for an Islamic society or Islamic polity is far more deeply rooted in the basic doctrine of Islam and in the historical consciousness of Muslim societies than comparable Christian claims. Islamic countries have in practice often exhibited a wide gap between the religious and secular domains, but this has not altered the theoretical overlap of the two upon which Islamic thinkers can draw.

A second factor is the ideological ductility of Islam in general, and of Shi'ite Islam in particular.[21] While considerable energy is expended by believers and non-believers alike in arguing which political principles can be derived from Islam, both the evidence of interpretation and the fluid formulations of the Quran itself suggest that Islamic theory allows a wide range of derivations. According to the external circumstances of the time and the concerns of individual interpreters, different principles may be derived with equal authority from the holy texts. The doctrine does not enjoin a specific course of action but provides themes that can justify a variety of courses. One possible line of interpretation is what one may term the *demotic* (as opposed to *democratic*). Islam does not have a religious hierarchy and the position of its clergy depends to a considerable extent upon popular assent. At the same time some of the themes of Islam, such as emphasis on the common concerns of the community of believers, opposition to tyrants and support for struggle, can serve the cause of popular mobilization.[22] The very plainness of Islamic prayer meetings, in contrast with the ceremonials of Christianity, confirms this demotic tendency. Because all such policies claim to be derived from the word of God and are interpreted by those with authority, they are not at all democratic, but can still serve the purposes of political mobilization.

In Shi'ite Islam there are further dimensions to this demotic and undemocratic potential. Traditionally, in Sunni Islam the caliph or his equivalent was the head of state. The caliphs were direct descendants of the Prophet, and since they embodied temporal and religious power, in theory at least, there was no problem of ensuring legitimate government. Born of a division in the Islamic movement, Iranian Shi'ism holds that the Twelfth Imam went into hiding, and believes in the occultation or *gheiba* of this Imam, God's representative on earth. Great stress is also laid on the sufferings of Shi'ites at the hands of unjust rulers, and upon the cult of the Shi'ite martyrs, Ali and his sons, Hasan and Husein. Both these factors combine to *permit* the idea that Shi'ism is an ideology which rejects temporal order, a permanent dissidence *vis-à-vis* both orthodox Sunni Islam and established state authorities. (At the time of the revolution some – Western-educated – advisers to Khomeini liked to say: 'We are the Trotskyites of Islam.') Other interpretations are, of course, possible. Conservatism and political quietism are just as reconcilable with Shi'ism because Shi'ism is neither inherently radical nor inherently compliant. For over a century after Iran became an officially Shi'ite state in 1501 the clergy was properly integrated into the state structure. Shi'ism in sixteenth-century Iran served the function of Protestantism in Elizabethan England – as a state religion designed to distinguish the monarch's realm from other states, in Iran's case from Ottoman Turkey. But this arrangement broke down in the eighteenth century, and from then on there has tended to be opposition

between state and at least some *ulema*, a clash that broke out at
the turn of the twentieth century.[23]

Within the many variant and contingent consequences of original Shi'ite theory, two have had particular political pertinence –
one institutional, the other ideological. The institutional consequence concerns the financial bases of the clergy. In Sunni Islam
where the state is legitimate the faithful pay their *zakat* and a
further levy known as the *khoms* (fifth) is paid directly to the clergy.
This means that the clergy are independent of the state in a
manner unique in the Muslim world, and that the populace is
able to make the religious personnel responsive to their demands.
In Iran in the 1960s and 70s there existed a religious establishment of several thousand mosques and shrines, several tens of
thousands of *mullahs*, and a network of *madrases* (religious schools).
Mainly funded by *bazaaris*, these were independent of the Shah's
control.[24] Ideologically, this link with the people meant that the
clergy had little room for improvisation or change. Reflecting the
concerns of a conservative constituency, the Iranian *mullahs* were
far less concerned to face the intellectual challenges of the
modern world than their more autonomous counterparts in the
Arab Sunni countries.[25] One of the central Shi'ite debates concerned the status of authority in the period of the *gheiba*: while
one school accepted temporal authority or advised a process of
patient dissimulation or *taqiye*, others advocated a political role
for the clergy and derived this course of action from certain
Quranic principles. It was this latter option that Khomeini was
to embrace. In popular Shi'ism, there also lay ideological themes
that could be used for political advantage. One was the theme of
martyrdom and sacrifice, celebrated every year in the passion
plays commemorating the death of the Shi'ite leader Husein in
the seventh century. The other was the belief in a future golden
age, a time when the Twelfth Imam would come out of occultation to create a just society upon earth. If the former was conducive to extremes of political militancy in a revolutionary period,
the latter provided a theological goal that enabled many to hope
that an Islamic Revolution would indeed create a new and better
society on earth. By failing to specify the characteristics of such
a society, Khomeini maintained the support of a wide range of
social groups.

Revolutions require organization and ideology, and both were provided in some measure by Shi'ism in its institutionalized Iranian form. But revolutions also require leaders, and in Ayatollah Ruhollah Khomeini the Islamic movement found such a person. Khomeini had a history and a personality appropriate to his role. He had opposed the Shah in the early 1960s and had been exiled in 1964. He was known to be honest and courageous; he spoke in a clear, uncompromising, and often cruel tone. He also exhibited shrewd political judgement: he saw that his greatest asset was to have nothing to do with the Shah's regime, and he kept his intentions for the future regime as vague as possible in order to maximize political support. He also found the proper moment to strike – mobilizing his supporters for the final push in late 1978, skilfully weakening the army, and returning to seize decisive control of the Iranian state. As a revolutionary leader Khomeini had luck, but he also had skill.

Khomeini was in many respects the epitome of a charismatic leader. He came to the fore during a time of rapid social change and tension, and appeared to be exempt from the sinful and compromising world around him. He also appropriated the religious title of Imam, which gave some suggestion that his role was analogous to that of the returning Twelfth Imam. Another reason for his assuming this title was that it circumvented the problem of his not being the senior ayatollah while investing him with a (higher) religious authority. There are certainly many who seem to have believed not that he was the Twelfth Imam, but that he would none the less introduce a just society as promised in the Shi'ite dramas.[26] He himself never claimed to have the specific attributes of the Imam in Shi'ite doctrine – the ability to transmit the word of God as conveyed by angels, the power to effect miracles, and the quality of being *ma'sum* (immune from sin). But the position of *faqih*, or supreme interpreter of the law, where both interpretation and law are invested with religious authority, certainly raised him well above other mortals and members of the Shi'ite clergy. Assuming this religious legitimacy had been established *before* the revolution, the very success of the events of 1978–79 appeared to strengthen Khomeini's authority and the aura of God-given power he sought to cultivate.[27]

It is in this context that the thought of Khomeini became

particularly influential. Khomeini belonged to that minority faction within Iranian Shi'ism who held to the activist interpretation of the Shi'ite dilemma: he criticized monarchy and thought the clergy should play a leading role in government. Yet the logical development of this thesis came only in response to the potential effect it might have. While his early writings of the 1940s were critical of monarchy, they did not go as far as to condemn it outright; and even in the 1960s Khomeini accepted the legitimacy of the 1906 Constitution. However, his lectures on Islamic government published in 1971 reject monarchy and advocate the concept of *velayat-i faqih* (*velayat* means government or legal authority, here combined with *faqih*, the standard Islamic term for someone who interprets the law). The concept of *velayat-i faqih* as elaborated by Khomeini is therefore a forthright attempt to legitimize governance by Shi'ite clergy in the temporal as well as the spiritual realm. In 1978, however, he went further and openly rejected the 1906 Constitution, instead introducing the concept of Islamic Republic, his idea of the society Muslims should try to recreate on earth.

For all its invocation of a return to the past, however, the concept of the Islamic Republic was, like many of Khomeini's other ideas, a skilful fusion of Quranic and modern themes with the Shi'ite aspiration of one day seeing a just society on earth created by the returning Imam. Khomeini divided societies into two categories of people – the *mostazafin* and *mostakbarin* (literally, those made weak and those made big) – two Quranic terms which began to be used in the populist sense of 'oppressed' and 'oppressor'.[28] His attacks on *fesad* or corruption certainly had a Quranic moralism about them: the main charge on which many of the Shah's supporters were executed was of 'spreading corruption upon the earth'.[29] Yet the term corruption would, in the eyes of many poorer Iranians, include more secular derelictions as well. Even Khomeini's relation to nationalism was ambiguous, because in the first period of his rule he virtually never mentioned the word Iran at all, laying stress instead on Islam and on the need to recreate the Islamic 'Universal State'. Yet much of his diatribe against the West and Western values had an unmistakeably nationalist ring, and followed what some secular Iranian intellectuals had been saying for a long time.[30] It picked up on the influence of Frantz Fanon mediated to Iran via the thought of Ali

Shariati, the lay Muslim philosopher whose writings had a great impact upon the younger generation.[31] The war with Iraq that began in September 1980 forced Khomeini to lay greater explicit stress on nationalist themes: just as Stalin was forced by the German invasion of 1941 to evoke the greatness of Mother Russia, so Khomeini turned to mobilizing support in the name of Iranian patriotism. In this sense even the *faqih* and the role of the Imam could epitomize standard populist–nationalist leadership themes.[32]

However, as his attitude towards modernity shows, Khomeini did not accommodate secular forces. In contrast to some earlier Islamic thinkers such as al-Afghani, who did emphasize the need for Islam to come to terms with science and democracy, and who openly acknowledged the ductility of Islamic thinking, Khomeini reasserted the hostility of Islam to modern ideas and the need to re-establish authoritative doctrinal purity in all matters.[33] Yet even this misleading traditionalism was not, as we have seen, simply based on an extrapolation from doctrine, but was rather an accommodation to the popular mood in Iran itself, at least as the clergy perceived it. Indeed, both the political strength of the Islamic movement in Iran and the particular theological interpretations that emerged in the 1970s were made possible only by the new socio-economic conjuncture in which the clergy found themselves. In sum, the transformation of Iran, with the unevenness and transitional features already discussed, provided the context for the fusion of a discontented urban coalition with the opposition current within the clergy. What might otherwise have been a more recognizable populism, a movement of the oppressed against the oppressor and in search of a perfect society, was shaped and was given the necessary organization and ideological confidence with which to prevail by the clerical forces led by Khomeini.

The ambivalent international context

At first glance international factors seem to have played an atypically minor part in the course of the revolution itself. The Iranian state had not been weakened by any foreign military defeat or comparable external challenge to its prestige and capacity to govern.[34] Neither the opposition movement nor the Shah enjoyed active foreign support in the final months of the contest. Indeed the absence of any financial or other material backing for the opposition, and the failure of the United States more actively to intervene on the Shah's behalf, are among the most striking characteristics of the whole process.

The Iranian revolution was nonetheless in a definite sense international. It had deeply unsettling effects on the West Asian region, appearing to challenge the rulers of Iraq and the Arabian Peninsula and to stimulate Shi'ites in Lebanon, and to encourage the Islamic forces fighting the revolutionary Afghan government which had come to power in April 1978. After the revolution, Iran extricated itself from the alliance system that the United States had created in the region and became embroiled in two major international conflicts: the fifteen-month dispute over the American hostages and the war with Iraq that began in September 1980. If the Iran crisis of 1946 was (together with Poland) one of the two issues which started the Cold War, the rejection thirty-five years later of the arrangements of 1946–47 by the populations of the two countries introduced a major element of international uncertainty in the 1980s.

Yet the revolution was international in another overt sense, namely in the manner in which Iranians perceived it. Despite the revolutionary universalism posed by Islam, it was felt to be a nationalist movement against the political, economic and cultural influence of the West, and of the United States in particular. This perception was reinforced by one of the most enduring features of Iranian political culture, the belief that political events are determined by a foreign hand. This is as true of the Shah and his supporters, who blamed the revolution on a Western conspiracy to bring Khomeini to power, as it was of Khomeini and the forces associated with him, who regarded the Shah as *sag-i Carter* ('Carter's dog') and continued after the Shah's departure to uncover foreign conspiracies at every turn of events. There was a considerable degree of foreign influence in Iran prior to the revolution, and in this sense the perspective of the revolutionaries had some justification; but the real extent of external interference was far less than was supposed and pointed to the prevalence of that collective paranoia which is such a strong feature of Iranian political life. It fosters such a debilitating atmosphere of helplessness that, far from enabling Iranians to emancipate themselves from foreign domination, it all too often incapacitates them.

Although such conspiracy theories are common in many societies, it can be argued that their particular virulence in Iran owes much to the pattern of foreign policy domination in earlier decades. Never a formal colony of any European power, Iran did not therefore pass through the clear break with foreign authority that independence involves. Moreover the patterns of semi-colonial control used by Britain, Tsarist Russia and later the US – influencing ministers, fostering dissension in the provinces and suborning the military – were precisely those most likely to engender a conspiracy mentality among Iranians.[35] Once this was coupled with the intense exposure to foreign influences at an everyday level in the 1960s and 1970s, and to the fact that the Shah himself *had* been brought back by American covert assistance in 1953, it was less surprising that a simplified picture of foreign control should persist and should substitute for more accurate and intellectually more demanding analyses.

Essentially, foreign forces shaped the revolution in at least three respects. First, the whole context in which the upheaval occurred was one of socio-economic transformation under which Iran was increasingly integrated into the world market and exposed to the economic, social and cultural influences of the West. The rate of Iran's oil output – over 6 million barrels a day – was dictated not by a rational calculation of what revenues Iran could most effectively absorb but by the demands of other countries for greater supply. The political and military build-up of the Shah's regime came about as a result of strategic decisions made in Washington. The cultural gap between the Westernized middle class and the class of new migrants in the major towns was one of the underlying tensions that helped ignite the revolution. Above all, oil introduced external revenue into the society without any comparable transformation of its socio-economic and productive structures.[36] Unregulated oil revenues progressively dislocated the regime from its social context and thereby rendered Iran more vulnerable to a sudden upsurge from below.[37]

A second international factor was the Shah's reliance on foreign support in 1953 and his visible friendship with the United States, together with his quiet but overt sympathy for Israel. This support certainly facilitated his control of Iran in the 1950s and 1960s, but in the longer run, like the oil revenues, it undermined his internal bases of support and encouraged his belief that a loyal domestic following could be dispensed with. For this reason, the United States was unable to intervene to save him. The pattern of such interventions, from Vietnam to Iran in 1953, shows that in order to succeed, an action of this kind requires that certain internal conditions prevail. These conditions, which would include a sympathetic middle class or a motivated, repressive army, were absent in Iran by the time the full dimensions of the crisis had become clear in the late 1970s.

The third aspect was US policy in the 1977–79 period. Certainly, it would be a mistake wholly to exclude those factors to which the Shah himself, in his memoirs, draws attention: the Carter human rights policy and the confusions of US policy-making in the final weeks.[38] Yet these were not the determinant factors. Those issues upon which US critics focused attention – human rights violations and the high level of arms sales – were not those most prominent in the complaints of Khomeini and his followers; the subsequent vicissitudes of Islamic justice do not suggest that a desire for due process or improved prison conditions was paramount in the minds of those who flocked to the December 1978 Ashura demonstrations. What can be said is that the Carter policy on human rights reinforced the internal process of political decompression in Iran in 1977 that the problems of the 1974–76 boom had created, and through which certain liberal politicians were able to begin some public activity. It was the example of these secular forces that contributed to the feeling among the *bazaaris* and *mullahs* that they too could now be somewhat bolder.

The events of 1978–79 themselves show little signs of having been influenced by Washington. Until early November 1978 the American government did not recognize that Iran was undergoing a revolution, and by that time no course of action, except the dispatch of substantial numbers of troops, would have staved off defeat. The USA was constrained by domestic considerations such as the post-Vietnam reluctance to engage in foreign wars, and also by Iran's strategic position. US intervention, as Brezhnev warned in November 1978, would have run the risk of triggering Soviet intervention in accordance with the Soviet interpretation of their 1921 treaty with Iran. But, beyond such considerations the overriding explanation of why such a course of action was impossible lay in the crumbling of the Shah's own regime and of his own sense of determination. There remains the question of whether, in the final days, the United States could have achieved some compromise between Khomeini and the army commanders which would have stemmed the full tide of insurrection that followed.[39] This too is an unlikely scenario, since there was little incentive for Khomeini to accept it and, once in power, Khomeini failed even to respect the agreement on immunity of top commanders which he had signed in early February. Therefore, despite the fact that the revolution was affected by both the realities and the myths of Iran's international context, the actual course of events did not entail the involvement of foreign states.

Islamism in power: the record of the Khomeini decade

The analysis so far has focused on the period of the revolution itself and on its immediate aftermath. The passage of time enables us, however, to look at this revolution with a measure of hindsight: not least among the issues which it is possible to consider in retrospect is the way in which 'Islam' was shaped by political requirements, and the needs of those in power. The death of Ayatollah Khomeini on 3 June 1989 brought to an end the first decade in the life of the Islamic Republic of Iran and provides one point from which to assess the character and consequences of Iran's revolution. The consolidation of the regime after 1979 and its continuation after Khomeini's death provide much material for analysis of what the practice of Islamism means in terms of political and social control. It also illustrates the greatest failing of Islamist movements in general: namely, their lack of an economic programme.

Khomeini's achievement in his ten years in power was considerable – in making the revolution, in remaining in power and, not least, in ensuring a smooth transition after his death. Two factors aided that transition. One was that his regime had been run by a group of clergy who had been his students years before and who constituted a loose but effective revolutionary cadre around him.

It was these people who maintained sufficient unity after 3 June 1989 to ensure that Ali Akbar Hashemi-Rafsanjani, already the most influential government personality after Khomeini, was able to assume power and be elected to the new chief executive position of president. The other factor, evident in the popular response to Khomeini's death, was the immense authority which the revolution and the Ayatollah in particular retained among the population, despite all the difficulties of the post-revolutionary period. The revolution and eight-year war with Iraq had brought immense privations to Iran, and sections of the population had been alienated by repression. But there can be no doubt that, ten years after Khomeini came to power, the Islamic Republic enjoyed considerable legitimacy within Iran: it was this support that made it more possible for Khomeini's associates to organize a smooth transition.

Khomeini's last years were, however, marked by great difficulties for Iran: these followed, to a considerable extent, from uncertainty within the ideology of the revolution itself. The first uncertainty lay in the precise role of the state in the new post-revolutionary situation, and the relationship between government and Islam itself. In the early period of the Islamic Republic, greatest emphasis was laid on the question of how Islamic thinking could influence state policy. Thus the constitution was rewritten to include the concept of the *velayat-i faqih*, the vice-regency of the jurisconsult; economic policy was altered to preclude the taking or granting of interest-bearing loans; education was transformed to reflect Islamic thinking, as was the law; women were forced to wear the *hijab*. However, this Islamization of the state went together with another debate on how far the precepts of Islam could act as a constraint upon the actions of government. This was a debate opened in the first instance by religious opponents of the Khomeini regime, who argued on Islamic grounds for a limitation of the new republican regime's power; but the argument soon came to be prevalent within the state itself, in discussion of such issues as government control of trade and finance, and intervention in the economy in the name of planning. Those within the government who adopted a more conservative attitude to economic policy, opposing state intervention, used this Islamic argument to block reform measures.

It was in this context that Khomeini, in January 1988, made one of his most important political pronouncements, in the form of a letter to the then president, Ayatollah Khamene'i. Khamene'i had apparently argued that the government could exercise power only within the bounds of divine statutes. But Khomeini disagreed, stating that government was 'a supreme vice-regency bestowed by God upon the Holy Prophet and that it is among the most important of divine laws and has priority over all peripheral divine orders'. He itemized a set of issues on which, if this view was not valid, the government would not be able to take action. These included:

Conscription, compulsory despatch to the fronts, prevention of the entry or exodus of any commodity, the ban on hoarding except in two or three cases, customs duty, taxes, prevention of profiteering, price-fixing, prevention of the distribution of narcotics, ban on addiction of any kind except in the case of alcoholic drinks, the carrying of all kinds of weapons.

Khomeini continued:

I should state that the government which is part of the absolute vice-regency of the Prophet of God is one of the primary injunctions of Islam and has priority over all other secondary injunctions, even prayers, fasting, and *hajj*. The ruler is authorized to demolish a mosque or a house which is in the path of a road and to compensate the owner for his house. The ruler can close down mosques if need be, or can even demolish a mosque which is a source of harm ... The government is empowered to unilaterally revoke any Shari'a (Islamic law) agreements which it has concluded with the people when those agreements are contrary to the interest of the country or to Islam. It can also prevent any devotional or non-devotional affair if it is opposed to the interests of Islam and for as long as it is so.[40]

This explicit statement was not just a legitimation of what already existed in Iran, namely a clerical dictatorship. The concept of the 'absolute vice-regency' (*velayat-i mutlaq*) was a major new formulation of Islamist politics in the context where an Islamic state had already been created. Yet like all such legitimations (for example, the dictatorship of the proletariat) it contained its own internal contradiction: for the legitimation of the state and of the *faqih* lay in their fidelity to Islamic precepts, and yet these two authorities, derived from Islam, were now being used to justify overriding whatever Islam enjoined. The key to this new legitimation was given by the concept, invoked in the quotation above, of *maslahat* or the 'interest' of the Muslim people. It was in the name of this interest, which the *faqih* alone could identify, that the specific injunctions of Islam could be overridden. Conservative opposition had been based in the Council of Guardians, a clerical body designed to see whether parliamentary decisions contradicted Islamic precepts. Khomeini broke this deadlock by creating a new committee, for the 'Discernment of the Interest of the Islamic Order' (*Tashkhis-i maslahat-i nizam-i Islami*), which now had overall power. Never were the underlying political priorities of Islamism clearer: the tactical concern of Khomeini was to use the concept of 'interest' and of the absolute authority of the jurisconsult to override conservative opposition within the regime; the overall goal was to invert Islamic authority so as to free the actions of the state from any Islamic restrictions, particularly in regard to property.

A similar political determination could be seen in the manner in which Khomeini handled another difficult area of state policy, that of the export of revolution. In common with all revolutions, Iran's was presented as a model which could be promoted and reproduced elsewhere. The concept 'export of revolution' (*sudur-i inqilab*) was commonly used by Iranian officials. It included the conventional means of exporting political radicalism – arms, financial support, training, international congresses, propaganda and radio programmes. Islamic tradition also provided specific elements that could be added to this process. Thus, at the ideological level, Khomeini could claim that the Islamic peoples were all one and that in Islam there were no frontiers. In organizational terms, the already established links between different religious communities across the Muslim world provided a network for building revolutionary links. Until the clashes of 1987 when around 400 Iranians were killed, the *hajj*, the annual Pilgrimage to Mecca, acted as a means for propagating Iran's revolutionary ideas.[41]

The most important component of this militant policy was the attempt to export Islamic revolution to Iraq. Iran had called for this before the Iraqi invasion of September 1980, and it became Khomeini's rationale for continuing the war after July 1982 when the Iraqis were driven out of Iranian territory. In the end, of course, it failed: the Iraqi population did not rise up, and the Baghdad regime did not collapse. In August 1988 Iran was forced to accept a ceasefire. In his speech calling for a ceasefire, Khomeini stated that for him this was worse than drinking poison, but that he was forced by political and strategic necessity to do it. This enormous setback in the promotion of revolution abroad did not, however, lead to an acceptance that promotion of Islamic radicalism abroad was impossible. Iran continued to play a role in arming and guiding Shi'ite guerrillas in two countries, Lebanon and Afghanistan, and in the bitter aftermath of the war it maintained a steady criticism of Saudi Arabia, whose 'corrupt' rulers it saw as enemies of Islam.

The proclamation of Iran's continuing role as leader of the oppressed across the world was important not just for external reasons, promoting the image and prestige of Iran, but also internally as a means of sustaining the morale of the population, distracting from domestic economic crisis, and preventing an emergence of 'liberalism', a spirit of compromise or accommodation with the outside world. After the August 1988 ceasefire, Khomeini felt there was a danger that the Iranian revolution would falter and would lose its revolutionary orientation. It was in this context that he reasserted his view that Iran should remain independent of international economic forces, even at the cost of austerity.[42] But he also used an issue that gave him the opportunity to provoke a major crisis with the non-Islamic world and at the same time to present Iran as the leader of the Islamic cause. Khomeini's call for the death of Salman Rushdie, the author of *The Satanic Verses*, was a means of meeting his two main policy goals – mobilization at home, confrontation internationally.[43]

Both of these policies reflected Khomeini's political thinking: the way in which priorities of power and the maintenance of state control determined his use of Islamic concepts and interpretation of 'tradition'. Ultimately, the political assessment of Khomeini's legacy will depend on the extent to which the Islamic Republic endures and whether the regime can resolve the most pressing problem it faces, namely that of revitalizing an economy in collapse. Whether or not it succeeds, however, the measure of Khomeini's achievement should not be understated.

Conclusions

Three general conclusions seem relevant to the overall issue of the relationship between religion and politics, and the extent to which the Iranian revolution exemplifies the course of other upheavals in the contemporary world.

The unique combination of modern and traditional in the Iranian revolution had both institutional and ideological features. The modernity of the revolution was above all accounted for by the transformation of Iranian society in the 1960s and 1970s, the rapid urbanization and industrialization, and the demographic and social tensions this produced. Without this transformation, the Islamic movement could have arisen again, as it had in the 1890s, in the 1900s, and in the early 1960s, but it would have been much less likely to succeed. The destruction of the monarchical regime and the neutralization of its foreign support were made possible by the great force with which the urban movement erupted, a force derived from this process of profound social transformation. Even in ideological terms, the movement reflected the contemporary world environment, both in the themes it invoked and in the manner in which the enemy was viewed. At the same time, the movement drew on traditional forces which had survived and even flourished in the years of transformation. In the cities, the bazaars (and the link of bazaar and mosque) gave the opposition a rallying point and an organizational backbone. The clergy provided an ideology of resistance and the principles for an alternative society. The political culture of the mass of the urban population continued to be characterized by religious beliefs and an acceptance of the role of the clergy in political life.

The Iranian revolution was only to some extent a religious revolution. The values, personnel and goals were all defined in religious terms, the society which has subsequently been created is one which its creators would argue is modelled on the Quran and on Islamic law, and undoubtedly religious beliefs and the specific interests of the clergy made indispensable contributions. Yet the image of an 'Islamic revolution' is too simple. First of all, the concept of religion is itself variable. In Islam it encompasses far more than in Christianity, where the principle of a division between church and state has existed for some centuries.

Doctrinally, Islam does not admit the secular. Though a separation of the secular and the religious has come to prevail over the centuries, it has been far easier for those who wish to reassert the comprehensive claims of Islam over all areas of social and political life to do so than it would be in the case of Christianity. Second, the factors enabling the clergy to challenge and overthrow the Shah were eminently secular ones. Thus the Iranian revolution has more in common with revolutions in other societies than the specifically religious dimension will permit. Material living conditions, opposition to royal dictatorship, and hostility to foreign influence all played important roles in preparing the Shah's downfall. Third, even the very ideology and programme of the revolutionaries contained many themes common to other revolutionary situations: re-establishment of national independence, expropriation of the rich, punishment of the guilty and corrupt, and redistribution of wealth. The decisive manner in which Khomeini's forces took control of the state and consolidated their hold by the creation of a set of new revolutionary institutions was eminently intelligible to anyone aware of what is involved in the establishment of a new state power.

The paradoxical unity of the 'modern' and the 'traditional' in the Iranian revolution accounted for the success of the Shah's opponents, but this unity did not long survive the monarch's fall. The history of post-revolutionary Iran is to a considerable extent that of a growing dislocation of these two components. The attempt to create a clergy-dominated or hierocratic society based on allegedly seventh-century principles in the last quarter of the twentieth century has encountered many problems that permit no easy resolution. The impact of the revolution and its aftermath on the economy has been to lower living standards throughout urban society and to provoke considerable unemployment and inflation. The defiance of all outside powers, together with Iran's call for the spread of Islamic revolution, led the regime into a full-scale war with Iraq, with enormous loss of life and catastrophic consequences for the economy. The imposition of a new form of centralized rule, dominated by the clergy, generated widespread opposition from political forces who supported the overthrow of the Shah but did not support the establishment of an Islamic Republic ruled by the *faqih*. These three dimensions, economic, international and political, therefore presented very real limits to the plan of creating an Islamic Republic.

The Iranian revolution achieved great levels of mobilization and political impact in the struggle against the Shah and in the immediate post-revolutionary aftermath. Once difficulties arose, and the broad united front that had toppled the Shah broke up, Khomeini was able to establish a regime built in his own image and successfully to crush the various opposition forces he faced. The success of the revolution lay not only in the destruction of an old regime, but in the successful establishment of a new one, different in many significant respects from that which it had replaced. If it shared more than it admitted with the Pahlavi regime, it was none the less built on very different systems of power, social support and values. Yet, while this regime survived its first sixteen years, the prospects for its long-term stability remain uncertain.

The hopes raised by the Iranian revolution were extremely high, and it is not the only revolution to have disappointed its original supporters, let alone to have failed to create a perfect society on earth. The post-revolutionary history of Iran has not only highlighted the limitations of the solutions offered by the Islamic clergy, but also soon after his accession to power led Khomeini to stress an archaism inherent in his thought in appealing to blood and sacrifice, the persecution of enemies and former allies, the brutal imposition of discriminatory Islamic codes of behaviour for women, the callous neglect of human life in the war with Iraq, and the incitement to persecute sexual and religious deviants. All these and more are the themes and policies to which the Imam resorted in order to implement his programme.

Through the revolution Iran became the site of a competition between the theological and the material, the clerical and the secular. The first round certainly went to the theological and the clerical. But how far these forces could sustain their advance in the face of material problems and an inability to meet many of the basic needs of the population remained an open question. As time passed, the impact of the material, and of a broad popular aspiration for economic improvement, became more evident.[44] The regime itself began to lay stress on its economic achievements, and to justify the revolution in terms of what it had provided in this domain.[45] Yet, by all accounts, this appeared to be too little, and too late. It was an ironic comment on the fate of the revolution, and of its Islamic aspirations, that by the early 1990s the story was circulating in Tehran that there was now only one authoritative Ayatollah left in the country: his name was 'Ayatollah Dollar'. Itself a product of social and material conditions to an extent that it was reluctant to admit, by the mid-1990s the Islamic Republic of Iran appeared to be in danger of foundering on the very worldly considerations it had sought, sixteen years before, to deny.

3

The Gulf War,
1990–91

Introduction: analysing a contemporary war

The Gulf crisis of 1990–91 was, by any standards, one of the most significant international crises of the post-1945 epoch.[1] It involved the mobilization of around one million armed men, the diplomatic involvement of much of the international community, and a war that, despite its limited character, was a significant case of interstate conflict. What follows avoids dwelling on the actual course of the war or examining in detail specific aspects of the history, not least because the broad outline of what happened is already well known.[2] Instead the conflict will be considered in its broader perspective, and from two vantage points in particular, each pertinent to the study of international relations. This was a war which began as one between two Islamic states, but there is relatively little to say about the role of Islam in this conflict for the simple reason that as a system of belief, and indeed as a legitimating discourse, it had no significant role in the origins, course or outcome of the conflict.

First, with the benefit of hindsight, it is useful to consider the significance of this war, and to ask how our evaluation of it may already have shifted. The other, more extended vantage point from which this chapter will examine the war is for its implications for the study of International Relations as an academic discipline (IR). IR is often faced with two problems, two forms of reserve. On the one hand, many people, practitioners and general readers of the press, doubt the validity of IR as an academic discipline, or assume that it is simply commentary on current affairs with some added historical and moral depth. Those of us who work in the field of IR theory are continually told that there is no need for *concepts* in such a field. To which one might reply with the question: where were the men of 'reality' on the night of 2 August 1990, when Saddam was occupying Kuwait? Asleep in Surrey, or about to go sleep in Arlington, Virginia, or Bethesda, Maryland, is the answer. The justification for IR theory must be not that it enables predictions but that, beyond any insights it can cast on events contemporary or historical, it can bring out underlying issues, analytic and moral, that are posed by international politics.

On the other hand, in part because of this public depreciation and the perils of commentary on the current, there is always the temptation to argue that IR as a discipline does not need to offer responses to the immediate. But like all other social sciences it must relate to contemporary events and concerns, if not directly then mediately, in an engaged but independent and critical way. The whole history of social science is indeed one of intellectual activity (whether or not it is taught in a university) and proceeds from a response, be it critical, outraged, or collusive, to events in the real world. IR is not and should not be any different. Economics began as a reflection on problems of trade and the industrial revolution; sociology as a response to urbanization; political science in reaction to democratization and problems of governance; geography as a reflection on the rise of a world market and of empire; psychology in response to a new awareness of mental illnesses. In the case of IR its academic origins lie in the response to World War One, as a reflection, mediate but engaged, on why the efforts of diplomats, lawyers, peace campaigners, industrialists, feminists, working-class leaders and the rest, were unable to stop the slaughter of 1914–18. The challenge facing IR, like the other social sciences, is to decide on what in the established tradition is pertinent, and where new problems are posed. There is much in Machiavelli, Kant, Marx, even Woodrow Wilson, that is relevant today; there are also developments that prompt a modicum of rethinking.

Historical overview

In February 1990, Iraqi leader Saddam Hussein, who had benefited considerably from Arab financial and diplomatic help during his earlier war with Iran, made an unexpected verbal attack on other Arab states, in particular Kuwait and Abu Dhabi, for having caused economic damage to Iraq. This campaign of criticism increased as the months unfolded, with Iraq then raising its dormant border claim to Kuwait and announcing too that it did not consider itself bound to repay money loaned by Kuwait and Saudi Arabia during the eight-year war with Iran. In July 1990 the diplomatic atmosphere worsened. The Kuwaiti royal family, believing that it could stifle a rising tide of domestic political discontent, refused to address even the more legitimate of Iraqi concerns such as those over the Rumaila oilfield;[3] and Iraq upped the stakes by demanding a number of other concessions from Kuwait. These were not forthcoming. The international community, including Egypt, were assured by Saddam that he would not invade Kuwait, but on 2 August he did so.

There then followed five months of crisis diplomacy and military build-up. Iraq did not withdraw, and on 17 January 1991 an air war against Iraq began, followed by a land offensive at the end of February that lasted one hundred hours. Iraq's forces were driven out of Kuwait but, despite a widespread national uprising against it, the Iraqi regime survived. The allied forces pulled out of southern Iraq but, in response to widespread international and public pressure, did succeed in establishing in northern Iraq a 'safe haven' for the Kurdish population, a disguised form of occupation that continues to this day. Moreover, in pursuit of the goals of the war – to disarm Iraq's capacity for mass destruction – a strict regime of disarmament and intrusive inspection was imposed, together with the maintenance of economic and political sanctions. This was the situation – without precedent in international relations – that governed the postwar aftermath.

Retrospection

At the time of the Gulf crisis and subsequent war, many claims were made as to the implications for the international system as a whole, and for the Middle East in particular. Now, in retrospect, some of these claims would seem to require further consideration and qualification.

In the first place, this war had little or nothing to do with something called 'a New International Order'. This was a phrase used by US President George Bush at the time, but he stopped using it soon afterwards; indeed the only people to go on using it were critics of US and of Western policy. Bush's 'order' was supposed to refer in part to relations between states and to the prevention of aggression, and in part to the situation within states and to the promotion of democracy. The former was a component of the war effort, the latter only secondarily so. In this sense the Western response to the Iraqi invasion was not 'new' at all, but was relatively consistent in the context of the post-1945 international system. Much was made of the issue of 'double standards' in regard to the Western defence of Kuwait, but the defence of an established sovereign state against full annexation by another state was a relatively rare event.[4] In so far as the 'new' order meant anything it referred to the situation that prevailed from 1988 and for most of 1989 in which the two great powers, formerly at odds with each other during the Cold War, sought to solve a range of Third World conflicts in which they had previously been on opposing sides. These included the Arab–Israeli dispute, and events in Afghanistan, Cambodia, Namibia, Nicaragua, El Salvador and the Horn of Africa. If one can say of these efforts that they were to some degree successful, they were not characteristic of a 'new', let alone more orderly international system for three reasons: first, because some of the problems were not liable to solution at this time and continued;[5] second, because the collapse of the USSR as a global power in 1990–91 meant that one pillar of the 'new' order was gone; and third because, with the collapse of communism and of the control, unwelcome as it may have been, which the Cold War brought to international relations, a whole range of new regional problems emerged which no amount of great power involvement seemed able to resolve. This was most notable in the cases of the Balkans and Transcaucasia.

A second general judgement on the Gulf war came from critics of the war who, rightly suspicious of the hegemonic import in the term 'New World Order' and aware that the US was now acting largely unchallenged, saw the Gulf crisis as presaging an escalation in unrestrained US aggression and intervention and marking the start of a re-established US hegemony over its allies.[6] Here, whatever the justice of their particular judgements on the US role in the Kuwait crisis, the critics mistook the broader direction of international relations. US public opinion, and Congress in particular, while in the end generally supportive of the Gulf policy, did not favour a greater international military role for the USA and, as the result of the 1992 presidential elections demonstrated, wanted to turn away from international involvements and related expenditures towards a concentration on US domestic politics. For those involved in other crises, most notably the Balkans, the problem became not *too much* but *too little* US involvement, diplomatic, military or financial. Further US military interventions in the Third World could not be ruled out, but the removal of the Cold War context and the rising alarm about domestic issues made the US less, not more, interventionist. As for strengthening the US position vis-à-vis its commercial competitors, there is little evidence that Washington gained anything, beyond the $55 billion in cash to pay for the war itself, from its efforts over Kuwait. There may have been a small combat charge, a seigniorage rake-off, but in the broader pattern of things it did not amount to much.

A third broad conclusion drawn at the time was that this war represented in some sense the start of a new, or revived, global conflict between 'the West' and 'Islam', a new version of the crusades. Saddam Hussein certainly sought to mobilize Islamic sentiment behind him, calling for *jihad* and placing the Islamic credo *la Allah ila Allah* (There is no god but God) on the Iraqi flag;[7] many who warned against taking military action prior to January 1991 did so on the grounds that it could irrevocably exacerbate relations between the West and the Arab and Islamic peoples. Here, too, closer examination reveals a less neat picture. First of all, Saddam's regime was hardly in the forefront of Islamic radicalism, having fought revolutionary Islamic Iran for eight years and having persecuted the opposition clergy at home.[8] The two main rivals for leadership of the Islamic world, Saudi Arabia and Iran, both distanced themselves from Iraq, and even Iran, while unwilling formally to back the US intervention, denounced Baghdad and ensured that its followers took a neutral stance during the war. There was a considerable amount of pro-Iraqi sentiment in the Arab world and elsewhere, but this had as much if not more to do with nationalistic opposition to a Western military intervention in a Third World area as it had to do with religion. Pro-Iraqi sentiment was probably as high in pre-dominantly Hindu and increasingly anti-Islamic India as it was in, say, Egypt or Algeria. On the Western side, loose talk of a new war with 'Islam' is, as will be discussed at greater length in chapter 4, largely nonsense, if not the self-interested exaggeration of arms salesmen and defence experts. The 'West', in other words the developed democracies, does not as such *need* an enemy, be it in communism, Islam or anything else. If there is a Third World threat today it is much more likely to come from rising industrial powers in the Far East and Latin America than in the Islamic world. It is often forgotten, too, that for much of the 1980s when the USA, and more specifically the CIA, were involved in their largest ever covert operation it was in support of Islamist forces in Afghanistan.

Finally, the Gulf war was seen at the time as a turning-point in the history of the modern Middle East. Subsequently, it has even been claimed that the war was the most important event since the collapse of the Ottoman empire.[9] The particular ways in which it was new, or marked a new era for the region, were not at first sight clear. It certainly was new in the coalition it produced: for the first time the armies of Arab states seriously fought another Arab state and, despite decades of rhetoric about American influ-ence, this was the first time US forces had in any significant way engaged in real combat in the region. The war also marked a further step in the decline of an effective, political, pan-Arab nationalism. If it seemed to boost a generalized sense of grievance in the region, there were in fact many other reasons for this, notably the critical socio-economic conditions within states. How-ever, some of the expectations raised at the time were not borne out: the Iraqi regime, although weakened, did not fall; the Pales-tinians, although apparently alienated from both Gulf Arabs and the West by their sympathy for Iraq, were soon and most unex-pectedly involved in the Madrid peace process negotiations. As far as the Arab states of the Gulf themselves were concerned, the war did bring about some political change, evident in the elections in Kuwait and in a somewhat more overt opposition in Saudi Arabia, Oman and Bahrain.[10] Yet in these states, the margin of political

freedom remained small and ruling families still shrouded the
discussion in evasive invocations of supposedly different 'Islamic',
'Arab' or 'tribal' political traditions. As with attempts to assess the
long-term impact on Iraq, it is too soon to judge the effects of the
war on the political cultures of the surrounding states. It would be
premature to regard the immediate political changes in these
countries as mere face-saving exercises. The political effects of
wars take many years to work themselves out: it is perhaps worth
remembering that the introduction of universal adult suffrage,
promised in World War One, was only achieved in Britain in
1928.

More serious, because more explosive, was the failure of the
victors to create a new system of economic or military security in
the Gulf. Iran was isolated, and soon turned antagonistic; oil prices
fell, creating greater popular rancour; the regimes and their no
wiser Western allies resorted to the oldest and most short-sighted
of security policies, namely flooding the region with weaponry
that threatened to destabilize the fragile balance and provoke
greater anxiety;[11] most important of all, the fact that the regime
of Saddam Hussein remained in power meant that there remained
the likelihood of a major future confrontation in and with Iraq.
We should not erect unreasonable criteria or expectations here:
wars do not, as Michael Howard has reminded us, tend to solve
problems; they may only prevent things from getting worse. The
Gulf war would seem, in regional terms, to bear this out, though
with one major and most unexpected further consequence: it gave
the impulsion to both Washington and Israel – and also, through
a desire to end their isolation, to the Palestinians – to engage in
meaningful negotiations, first in Madrid and later in Oslo. One
cannot yet predict that this will lead to a lasting solution, but at
least something has been initiated. On the issues of regional
security and oil, however, the worst lessons seemed to have been
learnt, and unnecessarily so.

Analysing the war

Turning to the war itself, there are a number of issues on which
more accurate assessment may now in retrospect be possible. Four
key issues in particular serve to show how our thinking can change

over time. These are: the causes of the Iraqi intervention, the issue of diplomatic alternatives to war during the five-month interlude, the character of the war that was fought, and the post-war policy of the allies towards Baghdad.

Assessment of why Iraq invaded Kuwait was central to public debate at the time because it became intertwined with discussion of the rights and wrongs, to which this chapter will return. It was, for example, argued that the arming of Saddam Hussein by the West in the past implied complicity with his regime and meant therefore that it was inadmissible now to oppose him. Alternatively, it was claimed that the failure to give him clear warning, in particular through the US ambassador in Baghdad's meeting with him on 25 July, meant that the West had in some way or other led him into a trap. Neither of these is a very substantial argument. Prior support does not invalidate later opposition, and there is a world of difference between a guarded diplomatic exchange, with the ambassador acting under instructions, and a conspiracy or green light.[12] Yet it is important to look at the motives for the Iraqi invasion. Saddam gave, at various times, four reasons: that there had been a popular uprising in Kuwait requesting help from 'brotherly' Iraq; that Kuwait had damaged Iraq's economic interests by taking oil from the Iraqi part of the Rumaila oilfield and exceeding its OPEC quota, thus lowering the price of oil; that the border between the two states was wrongly drawn; that Kuwait itself had no legal status and was, historically, part of Iraqi territory, its nineteenth province. That these arguments were contradictory did not stop Baghdad from making them. Yet other motives were almost certainly present, and would have included Iraq's need to offset its rising internal debt of up to $80 billion by seizing the assets of Kuwait; the impasse in which Iraqi politics had found itself as a result of Iran's failure to make concessions after the August 1988 ceasefire; Saddam's fear that the US and USSR were conspiring to remove him, as (he assumed) they had Ceausescu in Romania some months before; and the opportunity for Arab leadership and domination of the Gulf which the disarray over Palestine and Iran's prostrate military condition provided. There is no reason to think any one of these factors was decisive, and the decision to occupy Kuwait, based on a long-standing claim and with contingency plans for occupation well in place, could have been taken at the last moment, as equally could the decision to invade Iran in September 1980.[13]

Whatever calculations were involved, the invasion was not the decision of a madman, and it draws attention to something almost wholly ignored in the discussion of the war, namely the political background within Iraq. Indeed throughout the crisis there was virtually no discussion in the media or the serious press of what kind of country Iraq was, what its long-run political strategies were, and, not least, of the history and ideology of its ruling body, the Arab Ba'th Socialist Party.[14] (Failure to discuss this aspect would be comparable to neglecting the ideology of communism when assessing Soviet foreign policy.) The nature of Ba'thism, with its dramatic idea of the Arab nation, its cult of war as the purgative fire, its glorification of *sharaf* or honour, its obsession with the strong man, the knight or *faris* on horseback, who will deliver the Arab nation, and its explicit valorization of *al-qiswa* (harshness) as a tool of government control, tells us much about this war and its outcome. In assessing the broader motives, most commentators have inclined towards emphasis on the internal, economic causes of Saddam's gamble. Such an approach may need to be balanced with an equal emphasis on the international dimension, and particularly on Iraq's war with Iran. Indeed if there is a moment when the Kuwait crisis can be said to have begun it may lie, not in the bungled negotiations of June and July 1990, or in Saddam's address to the Arab Cooperation Council in February 1990, but in June 1989, on the death of Khomeini. After the August 1988 ceasefire Iraq had blocked negotiations with Iran in the apparent hope that pressure would force Iran to concede. The mass outpouring of grief, and the swift establishment of a new, effective government team in Tehran after the Ayatollah's death, demonstrated as nothing else could have done that the Iranian regime was solid and would not submit to Saddam's blandishments. The great gamble on Iran, the assumption that Iraqi pressure could force it to submit, had failed; the new gamble on Kuwait was to take its place.[15]

The second key issue, the question of whether alternative outcomes were possible, is in many ways the most controversial of the whole conflict. An alternative was possible before 2 August 1990: Saddam thought he could get away with it, and so, in a different way, did the Kuwaiti leaders; with clearer signalling, both could have been told otherwise. Western inattention and wishful thinking, abetted by the credulousness of Egyptian president Hosni Mubarak, who was told by Saddam that no military action was intended, must bear great responsibility for what happened. A timely set of diplomatic messages, backed by a show of force, would probably have deterred Saddam. The wrong signals were sent, as much in this case as in the Korean or Falklands cases. On the other hand, and in contrast to the views of many critics of the war, it would seem that no alternative was possible after the invasion, other than simple acceptance both of Saddam's occupation of Kuwait, and hence of his military predominance in the Gulf. Those who argue against the launching of the allied offensive can certainly put the case that lives would have been saved and the appearance of a new imperialism precluded. But other consequences would certainly have followed. Saddam would have exploited his victory, half or more of the world's oil supplies would have been under his control, Kuwait would have been destroyed, and the effect elsewhere in the world would have been considerable, as no small country would have felt secure. In such states as Taiwan, Singapore, Papua New Guinea, Israel and Belize, to name but some, the lesson would have been drawn.

However, the main plank of the anti-war argument rests not on the case for accepting the fait accompli, although a few were quick to do so by comparing Saddam favourably with the al-Sabah family, but on the belief that diplomatic pressure, plus sanctions, could have resolved the crisis. Peace, went the argument, should have been 'given a chance'. Many attempts at a negotiated settlement were made, most notably in the speech of President François Mitterrand to the UN General Assembly in September. Dozens of mediators – Arab and non-Arab, and ending up with the Secretary-General of the UN – went to see Saddam. On their side, the allies more than once said they would accept a peaceful withdrawal. Others hoped that over a year or two sanctions would do the trick; they claimed that the coalition went to war too quickly. Both judgements can be contested, though such an argument must necessarily be counterfactual. On negotiations, a decent time was given, but Saddam simply refused the way out. His treatment of the last-minute mission of the UN Secretary-General –

made to wait for several hours while Saddam conversed with the leader of the Japanese Socialist Party, and then treated to a historical discourse – and the similar treatment of many other mediators, demonstrates this. Saddam's behaviour can be explained quite simply: he did not believe that the Americans would actually attack. Instead he raised objections: that his army would not allow withdrawal, that the allies, or Israel, would proceed to attack after withdrawal. These were not trivial concerns, but the main reason for the war was his belief, born of miscalculation, that no retreat was necessary. The diplomatic option was tried, and it failed. Peace *was* given a chance.

As for the imposition of sanctions, they presuppose a government willing enough, or vulnerable enough, to bend. The general implications of this will be discussed later. In this case Saddam was not willing to bend, and did not bend even with the sanctions imposed after the war when he was in a much weaker position. He knew, and knows, that his regime can survive sanctions, through belt-tightening, a boost of domestic agricultural potential, and smuggling along the long frontiers with Turkey, Iran and Syria.[16] Sanctions could not have been expected to work in five months, but that was beside the point. The point was that he did not accept the message sent by sanctions and, given the kind of political and strategic response evident from Saddam in those five months, sanctions would *never* have worked. The alternative was, therefore, either to leave Saddam in Kuwait, or go to war. Given Saddam's refusal to withdraw, there was no third way. There are those who argue that the allies, and particularly the US, were hoping they would be able to strike at Saddam. Such a consideration certainly had currency: the phrase used was that there would be 'no golden bridge', no easy way out, for Iraq. But had Saddam taken the way out that was offered, had he even effected a partial withdrawal, abandoning the populated parts of Kuwait, the allies could not, in the face of their own public opinion and of the international community, have gone to war.[17]

Turning to the third of the analytic issues mentioned, the character of the fighting, it can certainly be said that the entire confrontation was a curious kind of war. The air campaign was almost wholly one-sided and unseen by the outside world, and the land fighting lasted for a very short time, a hundred hours. In one sense, this was a war of a historically familiar kind: a colonial war, with an enormous imbalance of technology and casualties, more reminiscent of, say, the British occupation of Tibet in 1904 (when in one engagement hundreds of Tibetans died with four British wounded) than of any postwar Third World war.[18] In some respects it was novel; in military terms, it was the first war in which cruise missiles were used and the first in which tanks on the battlefield could communicate directly with headquarters in their home country via satellite. In human terms it was the first war in which Western armies had deployed women soldiers at the front line, and also the first in which Western troops in the host country had been forced to observe temperance – trucks loaded with cool beer only appearing, as if miraculously, when the forces crossed into Iraqi territory. On the scale of Iraqi casualties, some hasty perceptions proved in retrospect to be mistaken: estimates of up to 200,000 dead were later reduced to a tenth or even a twentieth of that.[19] The level of technology used was far less advanced than allied propaganda suggested – almost all of it was conventional hardware of at least twenty years' vintage. At the same time, the military impact of Scud attacks was overstated. The most vaunted elements in the US arsenal, the Patriot missile and the Stealth bomber, were far less effective than initially claimed.[20] Similarly the Scud missile attacks, while politically unnerving, were of little military significance, and on a much lower level than comparable Iraqi attacks on Iran in the 1980–88 war.[21] At the same time allied intelligence about Iraq, although gathered in almost ideal conditions, was faulty, not least in grossly underestimating the number of Scuds possessed by Iraq.[22]

So far, some issues have been raised on which an element of retrospection and hence proportion may be possible, and where the general tenor accords with the earlier judgement that the Gulf war was not as original as was thought at the time. There is, however, another dimension on which claims of originality and precedent may more accurately be made. This concerns not the war, but its aftermath. Saddam's regime survived but was faced after the war with two forms of external pressure of a novel kind: one was the regime of intrusive arms control and inspection instituted by the UN; the other, following on the uprising within Iraq that followed the war, was the introduction of the safe haven

for the Kurds in the north which, in effect, placed about a third
of Iraq under a Western protectorate and allowed the Kurds to
exercise self-rule for the first time. Both of these, although drawing
on earlier practices and norms, were major new developments in
international relations, and constituted precedents in modern international history. The normative implications of these policies will
be returned to later. Here it should be stated that perhaps the
most important feature of this war was the form of intervention,
military and political, imposed on Iraq in its aftermath.[23]

Issues in IR analysis

So far this discussion has focused on the actual record of the war,
and has tried to isolate certain empirical issues, of assessment and
fact, that were prominent at the time. It will turn now to look at
some of the underlying and more theoretical issues, beginning
first with the analytic, and then moving on to the normative.

The analytic issues raised by the Gulf crisis read like the roll-
call of a course in IR theory: the causes of war, the functions of
war in the international system, the relation between domestic
and international politics, and between military and economic
considerations, the roles of diplomacy, signalling, misperception,
the patterns of decision-making, the construction of interstate
alliances and domestic coalitions, the functions of sanctions, the
role of the great powers, international institutions, ideology, the
media.[24]

For students of decision-making and foreign policy analysis,
there was much in this war that was familiar and stimulating.
Both sides had their share of misperception, based on the historical experience of past wars and on the workings of groups that
did not question their own assumptions. Saddam seems to have
thought the Americans would not fight because they had run away
from Vietnam in 1973 and from Beirut in 1983, the latter after 250
men were killed. He also seems to have imagined that the 'masses'
of Kuwait, whoever they were, would welcome his occupation.
From all that we know of the milieu around Saddam, contra-
dicting the boss is not a low-risk strategy, and the diplomats and
others with whom foreign envoys were in touch, and who had

some foreign experience – among them Tariq Aziz, Sa'dun Hammadi and Nizar Hamdun – were not apparently part of the inner circle.[25] But there was misperception on the allied side as well: the allies were mistaken in thinking Saddam would not invade and, later, in expecting him to withdraw under pressure. They also, as it turned out, had underestimated his military potential, including the number of Scuds and progress on a nuclear bomb. Perhaps their greatest mistake was in expecting the regime to fall after the defeat in Kuwait. Here Saddam outfoxed them all, for he led the Americans, prior to the war, into a trap which they closed on themselves. By brandishing chemical weapons, and then at the Baker–Aziz meeting in Geneva extracting the threat that he would be destroyed if they were used, he lowered the risks of war enormously: he could be driven from Kuwait or even, as he chose, withdraw most of his forces anyway, secure in the knowledge that the Americans would not pursue him. This was perhaps the fatal error committed by the allies, and forces us to ask how far, in the end, Saddam really fought to defend Kuwait at all.[26]

The issue of sanctions was also much debated both before and after the war and, as we have seen, forms an important part of the 'give peace a chance' argument. The academic literature on sanctions makes it abundantly clear that sanctions rarely work to achieve their stated goal, namely to force a government to reverse a particular policy: they did not get Ian Smith to back down on UDI, or Brezhnev to leave Afghanistan. They serve to fulfil other goals, notably that of sending a signal to the international community that a particular course of action is reprehensible. This certainly occurred in the case of Iraq, though whether sanctions alone would have done much to reassure Singapore or Belize one can doubt. But what the academic literature perhaps underplays is the fact that in some cases sanctions can work not to change a policy, but to produce a change by undermining the regime as a whole in cases where a government is already vulnerable to popular challenge. Examples of this include the sanctions against the Mosaddeq government in Iran in 1953 and against Allende's Popular Unity government in Chile in 1973:[27] in both cases Western sanctions contributed to economic crisis which in turn led to military coups in which more 'acceptable' regimes came to power. But the point here is that these were democratically elected and responsive governments where sanctions were much more inclined to work. Against Saddam, who had killed many thousands of his people and who was about to do so again in the face of the March uprising, such sanctions would not have worked even if they had been economically effective – which, as I have argued above, they could not have been. Saddam was not responsive to the plight of the Iraqi people.

The issue of what precisely caused the war was one of the subjects of greatest controversy at the time. It is worth restating here that there was no one single cause, and no simple explanation in terms of a single individual or accident that occasioned it. Equally, the Gulf war cannot be said to have resolved any theoretical disputes on war itself, or on broader paradigmatic debates in IR. Following Kenneth Waltz's famous discussion of the causes of war,[28] there are plausible explanations for the occupation of Kuwait that can be based on the 'images' he has identified. For Waltz, war lies in the nature of man, in this particular case in the suspicious and aggressive character of Saddam and his henchmen; war lies in the nature of the political systems, in this case in both Iraq and Kuwait (see note 3), each of which saw in confrontation a means to offset domestic political and economic pressures; and, finally, war lies in the anarchy of the international system, as revealed in Iraq's aspiration to increase its power with no countervailing security mechanisms in place to prevent it. In a similar vein, such explanations could be given for the US decision to go to war – the personality and personal history of George Bush, the domestic situation in the USA and the dynamic of world power.

Equally, all three of the theoretical approaches or paradigms that have been debated within IR over the past two decades could claim with some cause to be able to explain this war: but each also looks strained in the process. The realists would see it as an example, if in the end not a very important one, of interstate conflict and of the continued importance of security issues in international affairs. They would stress the importance of the great powers, without whom there is no international security and without whom nothing would have been done in the case of the Gulf crisis. They could at least argue that the Gulf war put an end to the transnationalist claim about great powers not being able to use force in the modern world (the oft-repeated cases of Vietnam and Afghanistan providing the evidence). Conversely, the transnationalists would stress the importance of economic factors on both sides – in impelling Saddam to invade, and in eliciting a Western response, in defence of vital economic interests around oil. Equally they would point to the importance of transnational ideologies – Arab nationalism, Islam, Third World assertion – in the conflict, and of the growing communality of interest of the developed countries who acted to defend what they saw as an international interest. For many Marxists and structuralists, the war would present no problems: it was a war between the dominant and subordinated in world politics, one motivated by the crudest of material interests, oil, and justified on the West's side by the spurious invocation of an international law and international interest defined to suit the needs of the hegemonic powers. Martin Wight's application of this revolutionary view of international law by Nazi Germany to the British and French ('successful burglars now trying to settle down as country gentlemen, making intermittent appearances on the bench') was well exemplified in this crisis: the very arguments used by Saddam to justify his action had been used by the Western states in colonial times.[29]

This would bear out Thomas Kuhn's observation that any decent paradigm, any 'historically significant' theory, can 'more or less' provide an explanation. Yet there are also what Kuhn has called anomalies here, which suggest that none of the three paradigms can have it all their own way. If the realists presuppose rationality and calculation of state interest, then they will find it very hard to explain Iraq's actions which, along with the Japanese attack on Pearl Harbor and the Anglo-French action at Suez, must count as among the major miscalculations of the twentieth century. Equally, the role of pan-Arab and Islamic ties, and of economic factors, will strain the framework of the realists. The liberal and transnationalist approach will in its turn have to revise some of the claims about the declining salience of military power in international relations, and will also have to recognize rather more than it might like that the UN acted as it did not out of some common interest or universal commitment, but because the USA cajoled, led and twisted the arms of the other members, on the Security Council in particular. China, for one, abstained from vetoing not because it upheld the principle of Kuwaiti sovereignty but because it got a pay-off, in the form of remission for the Tien An Men massacre of the previous year. Equally, the assumption implicit in much liberal and transnationalist writing that the end of hegemony and of great power domination is a good thing, and that those who challenge it are more virtuous, would seem rather dented in the case of Iraq. Terrorism, the Mafia, racist movements and ethnic cleansing are as much a part of transnationalism as the more benign processes commonly alluded to.[30]

The Marxist and structuralist approach might appear to have more to say on this question, but it too has its drawbacks. If the Gulf war was an 'imperialist' war, then the implication must be that Saddam somehow reflected a more positive and progressive trend in international politics. Underlying this judgement is not only a general conception of North–South relations, but also a view of historical development in which states like Iraq, brutal as they may be, are somehow regarded as having attained a 'higher' level of development, at least in their anti-imperialism. This teleological view of history, present in much liberal and revolutionary thought of the past two centuries, has taken a severe knock in recent years, and rightly so.[31] But even if this teleology were accepted in theory, Iraq was always an uneasy candidate for such an emancipatory role: at home it was brutal, far more so than its monarchical neighbours; in inter-Arab relations it used its oil money not to develop other states but to exploit their migrant workers, particularly those from Egypt; the ideology of the Ba'th party invoked socialism but had derived at least as much from another strand of radical European thought, namely fascism. The whole idea of a historical progression through appropriate states of liberation had taken rather a knock in Eastern Europe in 1989; such a concept was hardly in good shape to vindicate the events of 1990 in the northern Gulf.[32]

Equally open to debate within much of the structuralist discussion of the war was the question of 'imperialism' itself. Since the USA was an imperialist country, and Iraq was opposed to it, it followed that the war was an imperialist one, and hence illegitimate. But, apart from the question of whether Iraq had not also in some sense been acting in an imperialist manner, this presupposed the argument that everything imperialist countries do is historically regressive and, by extension, morally bad. This has become the mainstay of much left-wing and nationalist writing over the past two decades, but it is, as the late Bill Warren so well pointed out, at variance with the view of Marx himself, who took a more two-sided and contingent approach to the role of imperialism in world economics and politics.[33] The question which Marx rightly posed was what imperialism was directed against. In terms of values, some of the norms of developed (*and* imperialist) countries were preferable to those of the traditional societies they conquered: the subaltern has no ethical primacy. In more general terms, the briefest of surveys of twentieth-century history would suggest that, whatever the motives, even the USA has done some good things, at least by the criteria of most of those who criticized it during the Gulf war. Woodrow Wilson's support for national self-determination and US participation in the anti-Axis coalition are but two instances, and more recent US initiatives such as diplomatic intervention to prevent a Pakistani–Indian nuclear war, support for independence in Namibia and the Madrid peace negotiations could also be regarded as objectively beneficial, whatever the US motives for involvement in each case. Too often an initially historical and materialist critique of US foreign policy is replaced by an ahistorical and idealist one, whereby the USA becomes the incarnation of a timeless worldwide evil. European cultural anti-Americanism has in part fuelled this, as has the courageous but rather static critique produced by opponents within the USA.[34]

In conclusion, then, none of the three major paradigms of IR theory can be said to have emerged unscathed from this episode. What of the (candidate) 'fourth' paradigm, post-modernism? Its pretensions to explaining events, and providing an alternative, non-ethnocentric moral compass, were in relation to the Gulf war rather strained.[35] Rather more substantial was the response of another theoretical contender, feminism. Several new insights on the gendered dimension of this war, and war in general, were provided, and consideration given to the combat role of women and the images and symbols involved. Yet with feminism, as with the three more established paradigms, the war posed questions that challenged existing concepts and values as much as it vindicated their theories by example.[36]

Ethical issues

We can now turn to the normative or ethical questions raised by the war, which were also much discussed at the time. Three issues in particular highlighted some of the difficulties of established thinking on the subject. These were issues of sovereignty, intervention and just war.[37] It can also be stated here that even where the criteria were reasonably applied, public discussion in the West suffered from a strong degree of historical amnesia and self-righteousness. On the other hand, and despite many assertions about the relative 'ethno-' or 'euro-centric' character of criteria invoked in Western discussion, Iraq's own statements about the crisis did not follow an alternative set of standards. Its justifications were framed in the same terms as those of the anti-Saddam coalition and those of Western critics of the war.

The issue of sovereignty lay at the heart of the debate on the war. Iraq questioned both the validity of Kuwait's frontiers – which were, it said, artificial and colonial – and its legitimacy as a state. Equally, in both Iraqi and some Western critical discussion, the illegitimacy of the al-Sabah rulers of Kuwait was given as a reason for denying Kuwait's sovereignty. Others, from pan-Arab and Islamic but also from Western universalist positions, questioned whether sovereignty should indeed be the primary or sole normative criterion for debating international relations and hence whether even the most disinterested defence of Kuwaiti sovereignty legitimated war.[38] Finally, in the bizarre final twist to the crisis, Iraqi sovereignty was greatly infringed by the twin policies of arms control and safe haven.

The two most common arguments against accepting the principle of sovereignty in the case of Kuwait would seem to be highly questionable when looked at in general terms. Kuwait's frontiers may well have been created artificially, by colonialism or by force, but the same applies to the frontiers of most states in the contemporary world. If Kuwait was, by these criteria, an artificial and therefore illegitimate state, then so too was Iraq, the product of an Anglo-French carve-up in 1918. Moreover Iraq's historic title to Kuwait as a whole was, at best, debatable,[39] and even if it had been a strong one the resort to arms would not have been justified. Equally, the question of the legitimacy of the al-Sabah rulers is beside the point, since the legitimacy of a government or some rulers *vis-à-vis* their own people is separate from the legitimacy of a state or country *vis-à-vis* other states. (The case of Poland in 1939, presided over by an unsavoury albeit not very murderous military dictatorship, is an obvious analogy.) The only justification for deviating from this principle is the humanitarian one, in the case of a state that exercises extreme tyranny and commits acts 'that shock the moral conscience of mankind', and whose people clearly want intervention. In such circumstances an external state may intervene to restore the self-determination of that people, but this was clearly not so in the case of the Iraqi intervention in Kuwait.[40] Indeed, one of the most striking features of the whole episode, and one that must inflect any assessment of its legitimacy, is that none of the indigenous Kuwaiti population welcomed the invasion and few of the immigrant population did either. Even the leaders of the Kuwait Ba'th Party, who were summoned to Baghdad to bless the invasion, refused to do so; some such as the party leader Faisal al-Sani have not been heard of since.[41]

The issue of sovereignty has, however, been challenged in another way by this war. The intervention, or safe haven policy, introduced after the war is certainly an infringement of Iraq's sovereignty and one that sets precedents for other countries in the world. One can only imagine what a world where this was generalized would look like. Soon after the Gulf war, in Bosnia and in Somalia, related crises occurred. Here there is, in terms of established practice, a real dilemma. On the one hand, international law and not least the UN Charter place supreme value on the principle of non-interference, of sovereignty in this sense. On the other hand, the supremacy of sovereignty has been questioned in recent years. What are the consequences of the growth of the EU or of the global economy for the sovereignty of states? But also, how do legal or moral questions and in particular human rights issues collide with the principle of sovereignty? The UN itself has set up machinery, as has the EU, that to some extent overrides the primacy of states. This has been matched by a similar shift in public opinion in the developed world. There is, moreover, historical precedent for this in the ideas of Grotius or Kant about the validity of individuals as against states, and in the justification of humanitarian intervention (that is, intervention

against inhumanity) where extreme brutality has occurred.[42]
Beyond calculations of the cost and international consequences, at
least two ethical criteria suggest themselves here: the first is the
attitude to intervention of the people on whose behalf the intervention is said to occur; the second is the degree of oppression to
which they have been subjected. Neither criterion is of course
without its ambiguities and problems.[43]

There can be little doubt that in the case of the creation of the
safe haven the Kurds welcomed the move: indeed they subsequently held free elections where all candidates supported the
policy. Saddam's regime was certainly oppressive by any standards,
and what we have learnt since about the 1988 genocide of the
Kurds, Operation Anfal, only confirms this.[44] It is at least arguable
that the majority of the Iraqi people would also have welcomed
a complete US occupation, the 'Japanese solution'. Three other
issues remain unresolved here. First, how does one ascertain that
'extreme' brutality has occurred – the degree of violence, the
percentage of the population affected, in what areas of the country? Second, even if one can agree on this, how often can such a
moral right or obligation be implemented? It will, of necessity, be
selective. Third, there is the issue, present in the earlier discussion, of how far intervention is legitimate when carried out by an
interested power. The Vietnamese invasion of Cambodia in 1979
and the US invasion of Grenada in 1983 were both welcomed by
the peoples of those countries and would appear to meet Mill's
criteria on the oppressiveness of the regimes concerned. But both
invasions were condemned by one bloc or the other on the charge
of self-interest in a Cold War context. The Cold War ended, but
the issue of self-interest did not go away, as debates on Bosnia and
Somalia later showed.

The issue of motivation and interest prevails throughout
discussion of the war and intervention, and is raised most clearly
in the third of the moral issues that are the focus of this discussion. For some the very concept of 'just war' is an abomination in
that it permits discussion of war itself. But unless one adopts a
consistent pacifist position, itself a position on the legitimacy of
war, one has to engage with this category. For too many, 'justice'
is defined to suit political convenience. Many of those on the left
most opposed to the war, and to any measured discussion of its

justice, would in other contexts have defended the right of, for example, oppressed peoples to use force in wars of national liberation and revolutions. Conversely many of those who favoured the war would have denied revolutionary and nationalist movements this right. Indeed, much of the public argument on the war mixed up analytic questions of fact and probability with moral discussion. Such discussions also mixed up the distinction between *jus ad bellum*, the right to go to war, and *jus in bello*, the right conduct of the war itself. The argument against the Gulf war was, in broad terms, *both* that the allies had no right to wage it, *and* that they conducted it in an illegal or criminal way – there was no *jus ad bellum* nor *jus in bello*.

The argument on justice in going to war usually focuses on three issues: just cause, just authority and just intention. Saddam himself claimed just cause in several respects, arguing that Kuwait was *de jure* part of Iraq, that he had been invited in, and that Kuwait had harmed his interests. If the first two explanations are simply spurious, the last is more interesting because until this century it was, of course, regarded as a quite legitimate reason for going to war (Britain's occupation of Egypt in 1882, or the threats against Venezuela in 1902, arose out of debt defaults). If Saddam was not justified, it is in part because there has been a change of international norm or regime. Yet this has not changed that much, for the reason that though the recourse to war may now be unacceptable in such cases, the imposition of economic and diplomatic sanctions on a country that has harmed another state's economic interests, that has nationalized without compensation, that has failed to repay its debts or that practises unfair trading policies, is certainly still regarded as legitimate. Saddam was, in this respect, not so far out of line with international norms, although it could certainly be said that his response to the economic harm caused was disproportionate.

The question of just cause on the anti-Iraqi side hinges mainly on the issues of sovereignty and the legitimacy of the Kuwaiti government's appeal for help as well as on the UN and the issue of great power involvement. Many argued that the UN action was illegitimate because the Security Council acted at the behest of the USA: but this is to invoke an ideal criterion.[45] The UN charter itself recognizes the prominent role of the five permanent members who are, under Article 24, given prime responsibility for the maintenance of international peace and security. In the light of what has happened since, in Yugoslavia, one might indeed criticize the five members for failing to meet this obligation and thereby advocate that they forfeit their right to a permanent seat. In the case of the Gulf, there is no doubt that the USA led and cajoled the vote through the UN, but all politics, domestic and international, probably involves an element of this. The issue which is most difficult and raises the greatest questions is that of right intention.

All sorts of high-minded justifications for the war were given by the USA – protecting the sovereignty of Kuwait, restoring the al-Sabah to power, ensuring the supply of oil, protecting other countries in the Middle East among them. In reply, the critics suggested other motives: the defence of monopolistic Western oil interests, the protection of tribal oligarchies, the desire of the US to subordinate its commercial rivals in Europe and Japan, its desire to intimidate the Third World by an exemplary action, its wish to overcome the 'Vietnam syndrome' and offset the peace dividend, the need for Bush to distract attention from domestic problems, his effort to be re-elected. One can accept that *all* of these seem plausible motives, and to exclude any one of them we would need to know more than any archives or retrospective interviews and memoirs could tell us. However, this does not settle the argument, which is in the end not mainly about facts. To discuss the matter we may in fact need a more elaborated conception of what constitutes just intention.[46]

The differences between the morality of states and of individuals was, of course, one of the central concerns of E. H. Carr in his *Twenty Years' Crisis*, and it is worth bearing in mind here. First, the attempt to pin down *one* motive for any major act of foreign policy is probably always a misguided exercise. Discussion of such classic cases as the US decision to drop the bomb on Hiroshima in 1945, or of Khruschev's stationing of missiles in Cuba in 1962, is always bedevilled by this false starting-point. States, like individuals, act for a variety of motives, and one has to come to some plausible judgement not of the one 'key' motive, but of what the balance of motives was.[47] The considerations identified by critics of the US role were not the only motives of such a commitment and do not automatically discredit the war the Allies fought.[48] Second, in states, as opposed to individuals, self-interest does not necessarily disqualify the moral nature of an action, even if it looms large as a motive. Defending US security, indeed defending the stability of the international oil market, may not be such a nefarious consideration, given the political and economic consequences of this not being done. In the late twentieth century secure and reasonably priced oil is as important a component of stable democratic politics as cheap wheat was in the late nineteenth. This need not justify oil company profits, but it does suggest a general interest in oil. Third, while we need not assess morality solely in consequentialist terms, some of the evaluation of just intention has to be based on consequences, for states and for individuals. If it is accepted that sovereignty is worth defending, then the restoration of Kuwaiti sovereignty was a defensible result, as was the containment and domestic weakening of Saddam. Yet even if one argues that states do things largely for reprehensible motives, their actions may be defensible. World War Two provides an obvious example: Churchill fought it to preserve the British Empire, Stalin to protect the Soviet dictatorship, Roosevelt, somewhat less basely, to prosecute US hegemonic competition in the Far East with the Japanese.[49] Finally, and equally in the field of consequence, it has to be said that whether or not some of the baser or more self-interested motives were present in Bush's mind they proved to be unfulfilled. The US did not become more interventionist in the Third World, no significant advantages accrued *vis-à-vis* Western Europe and Japan and, of course, Bush failed to get re-elected. In these respects at least the consequences were soon shown to be rather less pernicious than originally feared.

We now turn to the even more contentious question of *jus in bello*, where Western arguments, though often valid in substance, tend to be unduly complacent. While analytically separate from the issue of *jus ad bellum, jus in bello* is pertinent to it, in that in some general way violation of the one prejudices the case for the other. Both sides stand accused of violating *jus in bello*. On the Iraqi side this was brought up in relation to the treatment of civilian populations and POWs, and the deliberate ecological destruction in the final days of the war.[50] The Iraqis certainly did treat the population of Kuwait badly, and looted and spoliated the

country, though not by any means as badly as many others in
modern times have done. There was no genocide, mass execution
or 'scorched-earth' policy. Allied POWs were beaten up and ill-
treated but none were tortured or killed. Indeed, their treatment
by Iraq compares well with the treatment of POWs by the US in
Vietnam, where torture, shooting and ejection from helicopters,
as well as the mutilation of corpses, were widespread.[51] Some of
the ecological damage Iraq was accused of, such as the flooding
of the Gulf with oil, was greatly, and possibly deliberately, exaggerated at the time.[52] But what is indisputable is that the Iraqi
troops blew up over six hundred oil fields in Kuwait before leaving,
causing great, though again limited, damage to the atmosphere
and to the territory of Kuwait itself. What was, however, most
striking about the public response to this was the lack of historical
perspective on the issue. What the Iraqis did was in the strict
sense new, but ecological crimes in war were far from new. World
War One saw the destruction of forests and land; the Vietnam
war saw the usage of Agent Orange by the USA for defoliation;
and perhaps the greatest among ecological crimes in war was the
detonation of atom bombs in Japan and subsequent nuclear test-
ing.[53] Here the claim of novelty in Saddam's criminality masked
a moral amnesia that was rather too convenient for the Western
states involved.

The charge of illegitimate practice in the war levelled against
the West – a charge that would pertain also to the issue of intention – rests upon a series of incidents in which it is claimed that
excess force was used. Among these incidents were the B-52 'carpet
bombing' of Iraqi troops prior to the ground offensive, the missile
attack on the Amariya shelter in Baghdad, the destruction of elec-
tricity generating plants and water pumping stations in Iraq which
caused protracted suffering to the civilian population, and the
strafing of Iraqi forces retreating from Kuwait to Basra. Some of
these criticisms would seem to be unfounded. In contrast to Vietnam, there was no massive bombing campaign to push Iraq 'back
to the Stone Age' or to cause mass civilian casualties, and in the
main allied targeting was selective and accurate. The Amariya
shelter was clearly a mistake, and a reprehensible one, but not
part of a broader pattern. Moreover, it was not unreasonable to
have thought it was a dual-use, civilian/military installation. The

destruction of the civilian electricity-generating plants had as its legitimate military purpose the disruption of Iraqi military communications. But it was, in retrospect, excessive and unnecessary and, from all we know, in any case failed to meet its objectives since the Iraqis had a well-developed system of landlines powered by their own small generators. The shootings on the road to Basra fell clearly within the legitimate use of force against combatants as defined in international law. Soldiers in retreat, but who have not surrendered, are not exempt from attack and never have been considered as such.[54] Equally to the point is the fact that those soldiers were returning to be used by Saddam against his own people, then in a state of imminent insurrection.[55] The logic of those who support that insurrection (not to mention those who criticize Bush for not having gone further into Iraq and ousted Saddam) is that the US president should have killed more, not fewer, Iraqi troops when they were still inside Kuwait. As we have seen, the key moment in the whole crisis was probably the realization by Saddam just prior to the start of Desert Storm that the Americans would not go after him, thus enabling him to pull his forces back from Kuwait with what were, despite the shootings on the Basra road, rather low casualties. Mistakes in the targeting and execution of the war were made by the coalition, but it is hard, given what we now know, to make a strong case that the war was illegitimate on grounds of *jus in bello*.

Much discussion of the war, on both sides, tried to use real or alleged violations of *jus in bello* to argue against a *jus ad bellum*. But this is a far less simple matter than such arguments imply. Once again we are confronted by a lack of adequate criteria: what degree of violation of *jus in bello* should be regarded as cancelling out what would, *a priori*, be a *jus ad bellum*? Did Hiroshima and Dresden invalidate the justice of the Allied cause? Do acts of assassination and terror undermine the rights of national liberation movements? Almost always violations of *jus in bello* are used, for polemical reasons, to bolster an argument that begins with *jus ad bellum*. And conversely, acts of atrocity are justified on the grounds that the overall cause is just. The conclusion would seem to be that a much more careful separation of the two is needed. Crimes *in bello* do not easily cancel a case *ad bellum*, just as a right *ad bellum* does not easily legitimate acts *in bello*.[56]

Ironically, one of the strongest moral arguments against the allied conduct of the war was not that it used excessive force, but that it did not use enough. It is one of the curiosities of the public debate on this whole conflict that many of those who most insistently voiced the charge that Bush should have gone further were the very same people who argued that he should not have gone to war in the first place.

Conclusions

In retrospect, this war that was in several respects historically unique can also be seen to have put considerable strain on some conceptions of international relations and to have involved a series of paradoxes. The Gulf war was an explosion of the oldest style of interstate military conflict, at the moment when the world was breathing a sigh of relief after the Cold War had ended and hoping that such crises were a thing of the past. The war raised the question of sovereignty and intervention in a two-headed way, first in the context of Iraq's claims to Kuwait and to leadership of the Islamic and Arab worlds, and second, in the historic and unprecedented UN and Western intervention in northern Iraq. The paradoxical argument of opponents at times seemed both to argue that war against Iraq should not have been started and that the war that was fought was invalid because it did not go far enough.

Where does this leave the study of International Relations? On the one hand, the crises and shifts of international relations challenge us to apply, revise, on occasion to overthrow our established concepts. Beyond the intrinsic intellectual discipline involved, the two great criteria for the relevance of the ideas we teach are first, the extent to which they succeed in explaining events in the world, and second, their capacity to make us refine our moral judgements about events. The Gulf war challenges us in exactly those ways; while it did not provoke the need for a 'scientific revolution' in the teaching of IR it did quite fundamentally test aspects of the intellectual system. There are elements of discomfort and anomalies in what occurred for all three major IR paradigms, as there are also for feminism and, even more so, for post-modernism. On a whole range of issues of analysis and ethics, the war provided a major challenge for IR: nowhere more so than on the ethical questions around sovereignty, the new precedent for intervention and the need to refine our conception of just intention.

This crisis also highlighted a second kind of relationship between the academic study of IR and the events of the world and the formulation of judgements and policy. In essence what we teach is highly pertinent to the handling of such crises themselves and to public debate. Such a relationship has at times been corrupt, often trivial, sometimes naive. But there can be a relationship, of independent and critical assessment – one separate from the dictates of power but not innocent or careless about them – which the academic teaching of IR can properly have. Such a relationship was certainly not foreign to writers such as E. H. Carr. If anything comes out of the Gulf crisis and the public discussion of it, it should be the realization of just how confused, short-sighted and lacking in historical, comparative or conceptual depth much of this public debate was. Who can have failed to be exasperated by the superficiality of much of the discussion of sovereignty, legitimacy, intervention and the confusion between *jus ad bellum* and *jus in bello* that marked the public debate? All social sciences have, as part of their job, the object of clarifying and improving public debate on the issues they study. In our field the degree of irrationality, rhetoric and sheer muddle-headedness is probably greater than in any other. Whatever its other failings, few can say that the issue of international relations and the crises it has provoked, and will continue to provoke, are not important for the public and the world as a whole. If nothing else, the Gulf crisis showed that those who teach and research in the field of IR have a job, indeed several jobs, to do.

PART TWO

Myths of Confrontation

4

Islam and the West:
'Threat of Islam' or 'Threat to Islam'?

Few, if any, issues in international relations have generated as much myth as that of an alleged 'Islamic threat'. Since the late 1970s, and more particularly since the Iranian revolution of 1978–79, the issue of 'Islam' and of its supposed challenge to the 'West' has become a matter of enduring international preoccupation, and one which politicians within Western European states, as well as a number of Islamic leaders, have chosen to highlight. Chapter 6 contains a discussion of how within this context a strain of 'anti-Muslimism', of hostility and aggression towards Muslim people, has arisen. Yet, as must be evident from the start, the image of an 'Islamic threat' is misleading in other ways. At the very core of this supposed challenge or conflict lie confusions: the mere fact of peoples being 'Islamic' in some general religious and cultural sense has been conflated with that of their adhering to beliefs and policies that are strictly described as 'Islamist' or 'fundamentalist'. It has been assumed, in other words, that most Muslims seek to impose a political programme, supposedly derived from their religion, on their societies.[1] The fact that most Muslims are not supporters of Islamist movements is obscured, as are the conditions under which people who are Muslims do turn to this particular option. All is far too easily ascribed to the general influence of 'Islam'. As with other political myths, the very fact that these ideas are propagated gives them a certain reality – for those whom they are designed to mobilize, but also for those against whom they are directed.

The argument that follows is one attempt to disentangle some of these issues, to show in what senses there is not and also in what senses there is a conflict between the secular, post-Christian world of Western Europe and that of the Islamic peoples to the south and south-east. If the major challenge has appeared to come from the Islamic Republic of Iran, a country with a population of over 60 million in a strategic position in West Asia, with a declared aim of 'exporting' the revolution (*sudur-i inqilab*) and a record of long-range liaison with hostage-takers in Lebanon and some terrorists in other states, the 'Islamic' menace has been perceived as taking other forms as well. Close to Europe, and in an area historically a part of the Mediterranean civilization and economy, an Islamist current has arisen in North Africa. Even closer, and under the influence of Islamist movements in their home countries, there has been some evidence of Islamist sentiment amongst the 6 million mainly North African and South Asian immigrants in Western Europe. This image of an Islamist challenge is compounded by the high level of political, domestic and interstate conflict involving the Muslim world. The Persian Gulf region has in the last twenty years seen the Iranian revolution, the Iran–Iraq war, and then the Gulf war of 1990–91. In between lie an array of further crisis points – Israel, Lebanon, Libya and, most recently and in closest geographical proximity, Bosnia.

This contemporary image of an Islamic threat receives, or is alleged to receive, additional support from three other sources. The first is a history of conflict between the world of the 'West', Christianity, and the world of Islam stretching back over a millennium. From the invasions of Iberia in the seventh century, through the crusades which began in the eleventh century, then through the conflicts with the Ottoman empire that lasted from the fifteenth century to the final collapse of that last Islamic challenge in 1918, conflict has been entrenched. Though with the 'reconquest' of Spain the Islamic forces were driven out in 1492, the Ottoman rival lasted into this century, leaving deep scars in the southern Slav countries. In the northern Slav areas, the 'Tatar Yoke' may have been thrown off in the sixteenth century, but the conflict with independent Islamic states in Central Asia and the Caucasus and with the Ottoman empire itself remained a leitmotif of Russian policy. In the collapse of established regimes and state structures in the Balkans in the

years from 1989, anti-Turkish and anti-Islamic themes were frequently articulated by those wanting to mobilize some popular
support and lend legitimacy to their actions. The Croats blamed
the Ottomans for implanting Serbs in eastern Croatia, the Serbs
presented themselves as the champions of a campaign against
Turkish–Islamic influences in Albania and Bosnia; Bulgarian
communist nationalists persecuted Turks in their countries; there
were demented rumours about Libyan, Iranian and Palestinian
paratroopers dropping over Timisoara during the Romanian uprisings of December 1989. The origins and content of these
'anti-Muslimist' discourses will be discussed in greater detail in
chapter 7.

This historic anxiety about Islam receives support from quite
another source, namely the end of the Cold War. Both in the
'West' and in the Islamic world it is claimed that in some way the
end of the Cold War, a conflict between a capitalist democratic
West and a dictatorial Soviet-dominated East, has occasioned
the creation or revival of the supposedly ancient conflict between
the Christian West and the Islamic world. Some of the analysis of
the Gulf war has rested on this thesis, arguing that the West went
to war with Saddam Hussein and built him up as an enemy, as
a substitute for the Cold War conflict with Russia. By extension,
Western European concern about the 'Islamic threat' in general,
including the issue of migration into Western Europe, is seen as
some ideological substitute for the Cold War and the confrontational disciplines it occasioned. In this perspective, the conflict
with the Islamic world allegedly reflects some inner need of Western society for a menacing, but subordinated, 'other': a linkage is
made between the traditional religious-based hostility to Islamic
society that goes back to the crusades and the need to assert a
post-communist hegemony.

Nor is this all. So far we have considered ideas about the Islam–
West conflict as they are generated in the West, and relate to or
apparently serve the interests of those who hold power in the
West – 'Christian', 'capitalist', 'rich', 'imperialist', or whatever they
may be. In so far as these ideas represent a form of prejudice,
negative stereotyping or false alarm – what in German is termed
Feindbild (an 'enemy image') – the assumption might be that they
are specific to those outside the Islamic world who espouse them.

Oppressed ethnic or social categories – Irish, blacks or Jews, workers, women or nomads – do not on the whole reproduce and mirror the prejudices about them held by their detractors. In the Cold War, when Western politicians denounced the aggressive intent of the communist East and alleged that the USSR was militarily superior, those who rejected this analysis sought to show that a different, if not opposite, interpretation was valid. For example, the USSR was not as aggressive as implied, and the West was more so; the military capabilities and expenditures of the West were in most if not all respects higher than those of the Soviet bloc.

In the case of the Islamic world, no such simple refutation of stereotypes is possible. First, in many respects, Islamist rhetoric matches that of the West not, as was the case with communism, by presenting an opposite picture, but by appearing to confirm it. A casual reading of the speeches of Khomeini, or of Islamic leaders such as the exiled Ghannouchi of Tunisia, al-Turabi in Sudan or al-Madani in Algeria, will reveal in them many of the same themes that are found in anti-Islamic propaganda in the West: the Islamist movement rejects Western values of secularism, democracy, the rule of civil law, equality between men and women, and between Muslims and non-Muslims; Islamists espouse gross racist generalizations about Jews, the 'West' and, in other contexts, Hindus; they are committed to a long-term struggle with the West, seen as decadent and aggressive, and to a militant, intransigent, conflict with the historic enemy. The leaders of the militant *Hizb ut-Tahrir*, literally 'the Party of Liberation', which was influential among Asian youth in Britain in the early 1990s, was quite clear that its goal was, through *jihad*, to convert the whole world to Islam.

This convergence or stereotypes applies above all to the two key areas of identification and definition. Whereas for decades critics of colonialism in North Africa and elsewhere had criticized the idea that the inhabitants of these areas could be defined primarily as 'Muslims', as if this was an ethnic term or a sufficient cultural definition, the Islamist movements appeared to concur with colonial myth in *rejecting* terms of national identification and differentiation in favour of 'Muslim' as a cultural/ethnic category. Khomeini denounced ethnic and national distinctions as alien: 'In Islam there are no frontiers,' he said.[2] In Britain, a variety of immigrant Muslim groups have sought to argue that there is a single 'Muslim' community, comparable to the Irish or black community. Secondly, beyond words and programmes, the record of what has occurred in a range of countries where the state invokes Islam as its legitimation appears to offer confirmation of the view that these societies are being organized on the basis of radically different principles to those espoused, and to some extent practised, in Western Europe. If this is true in conservative countries such as Saudi Arabia, it is even more so in the Islamist states of Iran and Sudan. Most important of all, the idea of a perennial conflict with the 'West', and one that could revive with the end of the Cold War, is evidently not just an invention of European or American demagogues. As communism collapsed, and with it the range of parties and movements in the Third World that associated with it, some in the Islamic world appeared to confirm Western prejudices by affirming that they would indeed replace Bolshevism as the major challenge to the West, and would do so more effectively because their challenge was inspired by God. In January 1989 Ayatollah Khomeini wrote an open letter to Soviet leader Gorbachev, urging him to abandon materialism and engage in 'serious study' of Islam.[3] The intermittent invocation of *jihad*, the very real support for some terrorist groups, the bloody rhetoric about cutting off the hands of America – all seem to lend credence to the image of an 'Islamic' threat.

The opponents and proponents of the Islamic movement were in agreement that 'Islam' itself was a total, unchanging, system, that its precepts operated over centuries, in all kinds of societies, and determined the attitudes of diverse peoples towards politics, sexuality and society. Both sides shared the view of a historically determined, essential 'Islam', which is supposedly able to account for all that Muslims say, do, and should say and should do. Khomeini, Turabi, the Muslim Brothers and the rest are as insistent on this score as any anti-Islamic bigot in the West. Whatever else, the image of a timeless 'Islam' is not just the fabrication of fevered Western minds.

Put another way, if there are myths about 'Islam', they are ones invented and propagated not just in the supposed hegemonic world of Europe and the USA, but also within the supposedly dominated and oppressed arena of 'Islam' itself. Any attempt to put this issue in perspective and to suggest ways of dealing with the complex set of questions involved will, therefore, involve the dual process of challenging ideas dominant not only in Western Europe but also in the Islamic world itself.

Disentangling the myths: initial clarifications

Regrettably, for politicians, popularizers and demagogues on both sides, the reality is far more complex than they normally imply. There are very real issues underlying the rise of Islamic movements, their relations with Western Europe and the formulation of a European policy in regard to them. These genuine concerns can only be reached by cutting away some of the jungle of misconception that normally surrounds them. No one familiar with the misconceptions can imagine that they will easily disappear or that mere identification and criticism will dispel them, not least because myths, once propounded, gain a force of their own; all the same, it is worth while to establish some basic parameters of accuracy and proportion in order to help clarify the issues.

First, a few explanatory points about the historical dimension. Probably the most common charge against Islam is that it sanctions terrorism. In answer to this, it has to be recalled that there is no necessary or historic relationship between terrorist politics and Islamic identities. As noted in chapter 1, in the nineteenth century, when terrorism in the contemporary sense emerged, it was not the Muslims who led the field.[4] More recently there has been terrorism aplenty, but no Islam, in Northern Ireland, Euzkadi, or Sri Lanka. Moreover, if intolerance and repression of differing ethnic/religious groups is the concern, then the Islamic world, while responsible for many crimes in the past and today, is by no means alone. The claim made by many Muslims that ethnic and religious minorities were treated as equals in the earlier Islamic empires is quite false, though the comparative record of these societies is in many respects still better than that of their competitors. After all, it was not the Muslim world that organized the Judaeocide of World War Two or that expelled the Sephardim from Spain. In a range of countries today it is Islamic peoples who are the victims of repression and terror – in Burma, Kashmir,

Palestine and, most recently, in Bosnia. No one can claim that it is militant Islamic peoples who are solely responsible for these crises, if they are responsible at all.

The very concept of an 'Islamic' threat is itself a chimera, and to talk of some enduring, transhistorical conflict between the 'Islamic' and 'Western' worlds is nonsense. On the 'Islamic' side, it is absurd to see Muslim countries as in some general sense menacing the West. The military threat posed by unified Islamic forces (under the Ottoman empire) has long since disappeared. Driven from the gates of Vienna and Budapest in the seventeenth century, the imperial troops evaporated with the Ottoman empire in 1918. Today the combined strength of the Islamic world is far less than that of the West, even assuming the (almost impossible) case of the different countries forming an alliance to act in unison. In reality Islamic countries have pursued individual, nation-state interests, and as often as not fought each other: Iran and Iraq, Egypt and Libya, before that Egypt and Saudi Arabia, Algeria and Morocco. Of course, an Islamic country with a nuclear device could cause great destruction, as could China or Israel, but any such usage would be small in comparison with that which its opponents could potentially inflict on it.

A further constituent of the 'threat' argument is the myth of the 'necessary' enemy. On the Western side, it is a profound if widespread mistake to think that in any general sense the West 'needs' an enemy. Of course, certain benefits arise from international and ideological/religious confrontation: arms manufacturers benefit, as do proponents of social discipline. That external challenges have a function to play within a society was indeed true in the case of the Cold War. But this does not mean that the Cold War arose as a result of pressure for such internal benefits.[5] Western society as a whole, and Western capitalism in particular, have never 'needed' an enemy in some systemic sense. On the contrary, as the liberal internationalists of the nineteenth century and Karl Marx himself saw clearly, capitalism is an expansionary force that seeks to subject the whole world to its domination and force it to imitate the West in key areas of social, economic and political activity. Its main conflictual drive is competition within itself – for profit, markets, power. Cultural and religious diversity between the US and Britain or Japan and

Germany will remain, but the system as a whole has an inbuilt drive towards homogeneity. That, if anything, is its secret. There is nothing in Western society – be it profit, market, or ideological and cultural stability – that requires an 'enemy' in the form of communism, Islam, Japan or anything else. As discussed in chapter 3, the explanation of the Gulf war in terms of the necessary 'enemy' is, on closer examination, vacuous.

Islamists and their opponents appear to agree that 'Islam' can be taken as the explanation for political and social behaviour. The idea that 'Islam' as such provides an identity, explanation and moral code for all actions undertaken by Muslims is a clear simplification. Islam, like any great religion, has a set of texts – a holy book, traditions, legal documents, learned writings – that are invoked to justify the actions of Muslims. But these texts cannot and do not explain what is done or how the interpretation is rendered for the simple reason that they contain within them a range of possibilities and possible uses. No religion, Islam included, is a set menu of moral, political and social behaviour; it offers, within some varying limits, an à la carte selection, varying with sect, time and context, if not from individual to individual. Nowhere is this more true than in regard to *shari'a* law, supposedly a guide to behaviour for all Muslims. As we shall see in chapter 6, it is no such thing.

To ask of Islam the answer to basic questions about politics and society is spurious. As on many other issues, the main texts of Islam are silent on whether it is desirable for societies to be organized around nationalism or pan-Islamism; capitalism or socialism or, for that matter, slavery; state control of the economy or private ownership. Nor does Islam tell us about the circumstances in which the state should be opposed or supported, whether there should be one state or many; whether believers should embrace modernity or tradition. Indeed, anterior answers to these questions determine the interpretation derived from the texts. Those outside the Islamic world who explain what some Muslims do by reference to the religion miss the point, as do those from within who seek to justify their particular practices by reference to it. Beyond its core doctrines[6] and a broad sense of intra-Islamic solidarity *vis-à-vis* the non-Muslim world, Islam is as variant, flexible, and open to new interpretations as any other body of

religion and thought. If those within it seek to justify their actions
by reference to a particular traditional authority, this is a choice,
not a necessity, and often conceals what is in fact an innovation
or completely new departure under the guise of a return to some
imagined past (Khomeini's theory of Islamic government was a
good example of this, as is talk of Islamic development economics
and Islamic computing). If we want to know why most Muslims
hold the views they do about economics, democracy, or the position of women, it is not Islam as such that can explain it.

The contingency of Islam – the fact that no one set of political
or social principles follows from it – is of particular relevance in
relation to two issues central to the contemporary debate. The
first is that of identity and ethnicity. It is never valid to present
'Muslim' as a term of ethnic identity. This is either a stereotypical
projection employed by those who have sought and still seek to
dominate or exclude people of Islamic origin, or it is an equally
spurious claim made by people within an Islamic community who
seek to exercise authority over a social group by advancing their
particular interpretation as the sole legitimate and authoritative
'Islam'. Other identities – social, ethnic, linguistic and national –
all play their part. There is no one Islamic people, just as there
are no peoples whose ethnic identity is defined by religion alone.

The one state that was formed on the basis of Muslim identity,
Pakistan, was itself a multi-national entity, comprising Punjabis,
Sindis, Baluchis and Pathans in the west and Bengalis in the east
(all indigenous peoples), and a sixth grouping, the *muhajirs*, who
were immigrants from India. In 1971 the Bengalis seceded on a
national basis – the only successful case of such a breakaway to
have occurred in the period between 1945 and the collapse of
communism. The remaining state, the former West Pakistan, has
increasingly come to be the site of conflict between the different
groups established there. In the creation and diffusion of contemporary identities within multi-national states, Islam, when linked
to nationalism or communal identity, can indeed play a part. This
applies as much among immigrants in Western Europe as in
established communities in West Asia and North Africa. Islam,
like culture and history, becomes a reserve on which the promot-
ers of new identities draw. But as in theological interpretation, so
in the fostering of ethnic identities, the choice and character of

identity is determined by contemporary and secular forces, and not by the religion itself.

The second issue is that of democracy. Many people in the world opposed to Islamic states – Christians, Jews, Hindus, South-East Asian Chinese – hold the view that Islam and Western democracy are incompatible. Once again we find people in the Islamic world, from the Saudi ruling family to Khomeini, advancing the same belief. One of the most common themes of Islamist discourse in the 1980s and early 1990s was the alleged failure of Western democracy. Yet to be drawn into an argument about any *necessary* incompatibility, or for that matter compatibility, between Islam and democracy is to accept precisely the false premise that there is one true, traditionally established, 'Islamic' answer to the question, and that this timeless 'Islam' rules social and political practice. There is no such answer and no such 'Islam'.

If there are in a range of Islamic countries evident barriers to democracy, this has to do with certain other social and political features that their societies share. These would include low levels of development, entrenched traditions of state control, political cultures that inhibit diversity and tolerance, the absence of a tradition of private property, and the lack of separation of state and law. These will be examined in greater detail in chapter 5. Though some of these features tend to be legitimized in terms of Islamic doctrine, there is in fact nothing specifically 'Islamic' about them.

Islamists today deny the separation of politics and religion. Anyone familiar with the teachings and practices of Islamist thinkers will be aware of a strong tendency to link religion to politics. The oft-repeated phrase, which appears to have become common in the nineteenth century, that 'Islam is religion and state' (*al-Islam dinun wa daulatun*), has traditionally served as the basis for authority, legislation and repression in many Islamic states. In contemporary debates, Islamist thinkers attack in particular the concept of 'secularism', the European-generated idea that law and politics should be separated from the church and from invocations of divine authority. This they regard as un-Islamic, and indeed as one of the sources of Western decadence. Critics within Islamic countries, as well as those outside, have contended, and justifiably so, that this rejection of the notion of secularism does preclude the consolidation of democratic institutions. As will be argued in chapter 5, democracy, apart from other preconditions, presupposes secularism, since only on that basis can a state operate according to the rule of law, respect for the rights of individuals, tolerance, and pluralism of ideas and political organization. Here we once more encounter the mutual reinforcing of stereotypes: those opposed to the Islamic world unite with Islamist thinkers themselves to deny that Muslims can separate religion from politics.

It would seem, then, that we arrive at a fundamental problem: no secularism, no democracy. There are, however, two important qualifications that need to be made, one contesting the external image of Islamic societies, the other criticizing the Islamist account. In comparative perspective, it should be noted that the problem of religion and politics is by no means specific to Islamic countries. A range of North European nationalisms, such as the Irish and Polish versions, are suffused with religion, as are virtually all those of Orthodox Christianity: Greek, Serbian, Greek Cypriot and Russian. There are certain dimensions of this problem which are specific to Islam, as the Islamists themselves proudly assert, but the division between a secularized Western politics and a religious Eastern variant is far from absolute. The emergence of what came, somewhat inaccurately, to be termed fundamentalism in the 1970s was certainly not specific to the Islamic world. In India, movements of Hindu chauvinism mobilized millions, and in the USA Christian fundamentalism has played a significant role in politics.[7] To turn to the question of international tensions, it is striking how Europe presents a picture not of a two-sided division between Christian and Muslim, but of a three-sided one between Western Christian, Eastern Christian and Muslim. The EU in its wider conception will be a community not of Christian states keeping out Turks and Tunisians, but of Western Christian states plus one anomalous Orthodox inclusion, Greece (a state which, if Brussels gossip is to be believed, most other EU members now wish they had never allowed to join in the first place). The Treaty of Rome was not so termed for nothing.

The second corrective to the idea that Islam has a unique, enduring problem with secularism comes from within Islamic tradition and history itself. For all that critics and proponents of

Islamist thinking allege, it is simply not true that Islamic societies cannot separate politics from religion. One can in fact argue an extreme case, namely that the whole history of Islam as a political and civilizational project has been dominated by realistic, political calculations. This, incidentally, was one of the arguments of *The Satanic Verses*. The lack of a unified Islamic polity for the last thirteen hundred years, and the different political uses to which Islamic authority is put, suggest that there is no one unifying politics to be derived from the holy texts. In the contemporary world, the example of a country like Turkey, once the leader of a supposedly Islamic empire, shows that there is no necessary relationship between a particular political and economic system, or indeed between religious sanction and the state, within the Islamic world. Here is not the place to give full consideration to theological possibility; suffice to say that a separation of religion and state, indeed a rejection of all worldly, political activity, is just as possible an interpretation of Islamic thinking as anything the Islamists now offer.[8]

The rise of Islamist movements and the invocation of Islam as a justification for political action do not represent some general, transhistorical phenomena; they reflect particular forces within specific societies in the contemporary world. In other words, they are a response to current problems, often of a social and political nature. Where Islamist movements arise, or where particular groups identify themselves primarily as 'Muslim', they are responding not to a timeless influence, but to the issues their societies and communities face today. Such issues include the intrusion of the state into everyday life, the evolution of legal codes, the fact of external domination (or the belief that this is a major factor), rapid urbanization, competition for educational and employment positions, cultural and social changes, not least in relation to the position of women. None of these problems is specific to the Islamic world; each, to a considerable degree, has come as a result of recent changes in these societies. If one tries to explain the rise of Islamist movements in Iran, Algeria, Afghanistan, Palestine and elsewhere, one can start by examining the problems facing the populations of these countries.[9] If, in Western Europe, communities from Islamic countries increasingly define themselves in Islamic terms, this may be not so much a reassertion of some already existing Muslim identity, as a response to the problems of immigration and status, racist prejudice, employment discrimination and alienation that they face where they now are. It is, of course, part of the self-image involved in expressing such allegations, that they claim their Muslim identity as an eternal given and a universal, pan-Islamic, adhesion. However, such claims are part of the ideology, not of the explanation.

It follows from this that the image of Islam as in some sense an international or stateless phenomenon is also misleading. There certainly have been such transnational forces, in the past with networks of Islamic scholars and sects, and today with the transmission of images, messages and texts between Muslim countries. The interaction of the Pakistani writer al-Mawdudi with the Egyptian Sayyid Qutb is one example of this. Muslims may also on some issues feel themselves to be part of a wider community, to feel solidarity with struggling Islamic groups elsewhere. But in its political form, the Islamic movement is defined and determined by national states and rival political factions. This is so in the sense, first, that it remains the goal of these movements to capture state power and, second, that if and when they do so they use Islamic doctrine to bolster the interests of those states (Iran and Sudan are no exception). Finally, these trends are national in that the particular form which the Islamist movement takes is determined by the problems that the society confronts. For example, although neighbours, Iran and Afghanistan produced very different Islamist movements. Iran's Islamism was urban-based and led by traditionalist clergy, acting through mass political mobilizations; Afganistan's was rural-based, but led by modernized intellectuals acting through guerrilla war. The implication of this for relations between Islamic states and Western Europe is evident: these movements will remain diverse, defined as they are by particular states and influenced by state interests, and will be more likely to conflict with each other, as was the case with Iran and Iraq, than to unite against the West. There cannot be a great 'Islamic challenge', not only because the Islamic states are, and will remain, much weaker than those of the West, but also because they do not represent a coherent, internationally constituted alliance. Indeed, one could take the argument further and show how, on the basis of proclamation and practice, most Islamist movements are concerned with what is going on within the Islamic world and with competition between Islamic states and parties, rather than with the outside world. It is worth recalling that Ayatollah Khomeini's rhetoric was not one calling for a *jihad* to conquer or convert the non-Muslim world, but was a cry of concern: 'Islam is in danger' (*Islam dar khatar ast*). If there is any common thread running through these movements, it lies here.

The struggle for the migrant soul

Nowhere is this sense that Islam is under threat and at risk of being corrupted more evident than in the context of the growth within the developed world itself of Islamic communities. Indeed such communities now represent a significant force in many Western countries. Conversion to Islam has not been a significant trend, except amongst blacks in the United States. In Europe a Roger Garaudy – the former French communist now a Muslim convert – and the occasional Sufi do not constitute a mass shift. The main reason for the surge in Islamic communities has been migration. In Britain, France, Germany, Holland, Switzerland, Sweden and other countries, there are now established Islamic communities born of this recent migration. Precise figures are impossible to come by, but rough indicators give the broad picture: in Britain there are between three-quarters and one million Muslims; in France, there are over three million; in Germany, the figure is believed to be around one and three-quarter million. The total for Western Europe is over 6 million.[10]

For all the differences of origin and country of residence, these communities evince some common characteristics. The first is that, while the migration itself took place overwhelmingly in the 1950s and 60s, before recession and immigration controls sealed it off, not until the 1970s and 80s did there occur the remarkable surge in religiosity, in the public demonstration of Islamic faith. This trend is evident in the number of mosques: there are over 1,000 of these in France, and the number in Britain rose from 51 in 1970 to 329 by 1985, the great majority in converted houses or flats. It is equally evident in the activities of Islamic associations and community groupings, hundreds of which exist in each major state.

The same increase in religious visibility among immigrants has also led to campaigns on issues of special importance for Muslims: the availability of halal meat, the provision of places of worship, respect for Islamic practices in education, the clothing and segregation of Muslim women.

Many of these campaigns reflect alarm about how to maintain control within the community, rather than about the threat from a non-Islamic world without. In every country Islamic leaders express concern about the degree to which the second-generation immigrants, by now up to half of the total, will continue to respect the faith. In Paris and Lyon, as in Birmingham and Bradford, the young, as distinct from the very young, are not proportionately present in the mosque. The increased religiosity of the 1970s and 80s may go some way towards reversing this, but it is too early to say. Yet some factors common to different Western European countries have certainly encouraged increased religious identification. The closing of frontiers to further immigration has reduced the degree of circulation of migrants and has therefore made it clear that those now resident are going to stay. The rise of racist attacks on Muslims – evident not only in 'Paki-bashing' in Britain but in the rise of Le Pen in France and far-right activities in Germany – has forced many in the second generation to qualify their hope for full integration. Donations and expressions of solidarity from Islamic states have also played their role, as have certain international events, such as the Iranian revolution, the attacks on Libya, the Palestinian *intifada*, and the war in Bosnia.

If these substantial Islamic communities in the West share common concerns, they are also marked by enormous differences. For this reason it is impossible to form any general picture or 'sociology' of Western European Muslims. First of all, Islam is a centrifugal religion; it has no even putative centre. The caliphate abolished by Atatürk in 1924 had long since ceased to act as an authority even for Sunni Muslims. The variety of sects and orientations that are present within the communities is a reflection of this centrifugal pattern, and fragmentation within Islam as such is compounded by the religious changes that occur in the process of emigration. While it is safe to assume that many migrants retain the beliefs of their place of origin, there is much adoption of Islamic ideas from other sources, encountered only in exile. Thus Yemeni migrants in Britain in the 1930s and 40s were organized by a religious sect, the Alawiyya, originally based in Algeria.[11] Among French Muslims of North African origin there has in recent years been considerable support for the *Jama'at al-Tabligh*, the Society of Propagation, a proselytizing grouping founded in India in 1927 and with its European headquarters in Britain. The experience of migration both confirms a desire to assert or reassert certain traditional values and exposes the migrant to new ones. The parallel with communist recruitment of migrants is striking: indeed in France many Arabs and Turks now live in former strongholds of the Parti Communiste Français (PCF). It is not for nothing that the most prominent centre of the autonomous 'French' Muslims is la mosquée de Stalingrad and that its worshippers live in the rue Youri Gagarin and the avenue Maurice Thorez.

To these religious differences are added those of a national, linguistic and political character. The 'Muslims' of Western Europe, who appear homogeneous to the non-Islamic world and to the, usually self-appointed, official representatives of Islam, also come from a variety of national backgrounds: in Britain, Pakistanis, Bengalis and Indians, but also Turkish Cypriots and a variety of Arabs; in Germany, Turks and Bosnians; in France, Algerians, Moroccans, Tunisians, Senegalese, Mauritanians and Turks. Even these 'national' labels conceal local and linguistic divisions – between Pathans, Punjabis and Gujeratis, between Kurds and Turks, between Algerian Arabs and Kabyles, and of course between the different Arab peoples. If the countries of origin differ, so too do the countries of reception. In Britain, Commonwealth immigrants were automatically granted the vote, something denied in France and Germany; on the other hand, the French government has, from the mid-1970s onwards, provided special housing for immigrants, and encouraged the building of places of worship in immigrant estates. Some French firms have provided these at the place of work. In Britain such provision for immigrant religious needs was almost inconceivable; much energy was, however, expended in conflict over an especially British issue: the school uniform.

The variety of currents and organizations within the Islamic communities of Western Europe is, moreover, compounded by the fissiparous impact of Islamic states, many of which have tried to influence the communities with financial and other inducements. At one level this takes the form of funding mosques and publications, where religious duty and state interest may coincide. Saudi Arabia has specialized in this, and through the Islamic World League in Mecca operates its own transnational organization. Since 1979 the Islamic Republic of Iran has also sought to build up a following in this way, albeit with fewer resources. Ayatollah Khomeini's Rushdie campaign was, in part, designed to strengthen his claim to be the leader of *all* Muslims. Other states use religious links as a way of maintaining administrative, and coercive, control over those from their own countries. Visas, funds, channelling of remittances, access to buildings all help to keep the migrants in line. Still others try to use the Islamic migrant communities as a way of extending what are basically secular political interests; Libya and Iraq, for example, have given money for this purpose, their 'Muslim solidarity' an extension of inter-Arab conflict. Beyond the influence of states, Islamic parties in the home countries have built up networks abroad. An obvious case is that of the *Jama'at-i Islam* of Pakistan, a right-wing group with Saudi connections that has strong support among Pakistani Muslims in Britain and organizes campaigns in both Britain and Pakistan.[12]

One final twist to this tale of fragmentation is that of the competition between Arabs and non-Arabs for primacy within Islam. The Turkish imams in France consider that their people understand more of the Quran than the Arabs,[13] and Gaddafi has denounced non-Arab influences, including the *Tabligh*, within Islam. It can be noted that there is more than a trace of this ancient cultural and religious rivalry to be found in the pages of *The Satanic Verses*, as well as in the response to Rushdie's novel.

Despite these evident diversities, the myth, perpetrated by Muslims and non-Muslims alike, is that 'Islam' and the Islamic communities represent one community, one *umma*. This has never been true of the Islamic world since the years of the first caliphs, and is certainly not true of the Muslims of Western Europe. The variety and fluidity lying behind the supposedly universal Islam promote a recurrent theme of all studies of 'Islamic' society, whether in Western Europe or in the relevant Third World countries. How far can the very designation 'Islam' provide a key to understanding the behaviour of such groups in the social and political arenas? This issue has already been addressed: for all its claims to prescribe for social and individual as well as political behaviour, the variety of practices in Islamic countries indicates that 'Islam' as such cannot explain how Muslims behave, or how they might or ought to behave. As has already been suggested, other factors outside 'Islam' must be invoked. The resort to an all-explanatory 'Islam' is therefore circular. Moreover, 'Muslims', like non-Muslims, have multiple identities, the relative balance and character of which change over time. It is one of the intriguing but elusive challenges of any analysis of different 'Muslim' communities to disentangle and chart the relation between the different identities of their members. The study of Islamic communities cannot be based on a 'sociology of religion' alone; it must, rather, involve a sociology of how religion interacts with other, ethnic, cultural and political forces.

To take the example of one long-standing Arab community in Britain, in the eight decades since they have been resident in Britain, the Yemenis, a community of at most 15,000, have been identified by a variety of terms. They have been described as lascars, negroes, blacks, Asians, Arabs, Yemenis, Muslims and Pakistanis. To these 'identities' must be added their own list of variants – whether North or South Yemeni, Shafi'i or Zeidi Muslim, supporters of one or other faction of their respective regimes, and the tribal and regional variations, Dhali'i, Yafi'i, Maqbani, Shamiri and so on.[14] In much discussion of Western Europe, this problem recurs. For example, Kepel appears to work with a dichotomy 'French/Muslim', as if the two were alternatives.[15] Such usage does not sufficiently address the question of how far the separateness and distinctness of Muslims in France is a matter of their being Muslims, or of their being Arabs, or Algerians, or identifying with some subdivision. There is very little room in such a polarity for discussion of the place of an Arab or Algerian, of identity in the lives of these people, and of how religious activities, publications and meeting places interact with the political. Equally, comparative studies of Western European Muslims tend to treat their subject-matter in too restrictedly religious a manner. Yet as is evident from the mosques of Birmingham, attendance at these breaks down almost completely along national and regional lines: in proclaiming belief in one God, Pathans, Punjabis, 'Campbellpuris', Azad Kashmiris, Bengalis, Yemenis, Gujeratis go their separate ways to prayer.[16]

Much of the discussion of Western European Muslims focuses on issues of identity in a non-Islamic world, on questions of assimilation versus separateness, and on the distinction between 'insertion', that is, finding a recognized but distinct place, and 'integration'.[17] There is no doubt that both kinds of process are at work. Many second-generation citizens from Muslim backgrounds mix with and share the values of their generation in Western European society, and come to be critical of the national and religious backgrounds they come from. This phenomenon is exemplfied by the second-generation North African writers in France, the *beurs* (slang for French-born Arab), and in Britain films like Hanif Kureishi's *My Beautiful Launderette*. Now that the doors of immigration have closed, it is harder to go back. At the same time the forces in favour of a negotiated 'insertion' have also gained ground: some through the widespread rise in religiosity in the 1970s, some through the exertions of Islamic states and organizations like the *Tabligh*. Islamic community and national organizations are now stronger and more vocal than ever before. In France they are already a political force, and they are increasingly becoming so in Britain. The 1987 manifesto, *The Muslim Vote*, signed by 24 Islamic associations, sought to lay out a set of demands for Muslims in Britain, pertaining above all to education – clothing, food, single-sex teaching, and the avoidance of dancing, mixed bathing and sex education. In France and Britain policies designed to alter the educational system on general grounds have provided occasion for Muslim parents to voice special concerns.

The dispute over *The Satanic Verses*

What this suggests above all is that for all their assertiveness the Muslim communities in Western Europe feel themselves to be under threat: it is the fear of loss of social control that animates the activities of their leaders, traditional and new. Here, of course, their concern has been shared by many of the most vocal leaders of the Islamic world, including Khomeini. Aggressive and aggrieved as they may sound, theirs is a defensive cry. This sentiment of erosion, real or imagined, underlay the reaction to *The Satanic Verses* after its publication in 1988. The novel's fictionalized account of early Islam is, in itself, regarded by many Muslims as unacceptable, but Salman Rushdie's book is as much about the Islamic experience in one Western European country, Britain.[18] It was, indeed, said of Rushdie some years ago that after writing one book about India (*Midnight's Children*) and one about Pakistan (*Shame*), he would now write one about Britain. That book then appeared and, after the initial outrage on the part of Islamic officials, it was, appropriately, the turn of British ministers to denounce its anti-racist and satirical view of the United Kingdom, not least because of its reflections on the police.[19]

Rushdie's novel speaks for one aspect of the migrant experience in turning a critical face both towards the country of origin and its traditions and towards the country of reception. The novel's challenge, its expression of the alienation of the migrants and its 'offence' to Islam, is two-sided. It is no accident that at one point Rushdie links the migrant to the blasphemer: both act a part, both run the risk of causing offence. But Rushdie's main challenge to the Islamic world, beyond his Rabelaisian account of early Islam, is to have broken away from it. Khomeini accused him of *kufr-i jahani*, 'world blasphemy', but the term *kufr* and its adjective *kafir* contain several meanings: not only atheism and blasphemy, but also apostasy.[20] It is this latter charge that is the most serious since, in writing as he did of Mohammad, of doubt, of the profane masquerading as the religious, Rushdie represented a challenge from within that embattled religious leaders, in Bradford as in Tehran, could not accept.[21]

There is certainly a strictly religious foundation for such anathemas against those charged with 'blasphemy', in Islam as there is in Christianity and Judaism. Mohammad ordered the murder of Asma bint Marwan, a woman poet who criticized him, just as in the Bible Leviticus:24 enjoins us to stone all such offenders.[22] But the question of why such injunctions from another age have been invoked here and now can only be answered by reference to current social and political concerns. All the great victims of blasphemy charges (Socrates, Christ, Galileo, Spinoza) were also charged with sedition. It is by looking to political concerns that the roots of the campaign around *The Satanic Verses* can be comprehended. Islam is 'in danger', and it is seen to be under threat not so much from without, something that has always been the case, as from the loss of belief and of submission emerging within.

What appears, therefore, to be a conflict between Islam and the external non-Islamic world is above all a reflection of a conflict within the Islamic world. The greatest consequence of the Iranian revolution has been to divide the Muslim world more grievously than ever before, and the same may well turn out to be the case with the response to *The Satanic Verses*. The reaction of some Tunisian Islamists to the Iranian condemnation of Rushdie may be indicative in this regard. They have declared that people should stop worrying about 'the British Rushdie' and instead concentrate their energy on the 'Rushdies' among their own people, by which they mean the secularizers and those proclaiming the equality of men and women.

Managing the conflict: the relevant issues

The ramifications of the Rushdie affair, and in particular the issues and interests which can be seen as underlying reactions to *The Satanic Verses* within the Islamic world, may serve to illustrate the more general point that explanations of contemporary attitudes in terms of religion, or a supposed return to the one 'true' religion, are insufficient. Three preliminary conclusions may be drawn. The issue of 'Islam' and the 'West' is more complex and more contingent upon contemporary concerns than either the opponents or proponents of Islamist politics would imply. If many of the problems – terrorism, fanaticism, an international threat – are imagined or confused, there are nonetheless very real issues at stake here, which will take many decades to resolve. Finally, these issues are, in the main, secular ones relating to the power of states, the status and treatment of migrant groups, and the balance of forces within a range of developing societies. It is all too easy to see this interaction in transhistorical terms. The conflict between communism and the 'West' lasted seventy years, or at most two hundred, from Babeuf to Gorbachev. That between Islamic movements and the West has been going on for nearly fourteen hundred years, and continues. The wall of Berlin fell after 28 years, that of Avila, built in the fourteenth century to defend the city against Arab forces, still stands. The issue endures, however, not because of some timeless religious or ideological determination, but because social problems faced by both groups continue to be expressed in the language and symbols of religious identification, amongst other points of reference. To evolve a policy to solve or reduce what is presented as the conflict between the 'West' and the Islamic world requires a dual programme: first, separate the real, material, specific and secular difficulties faced by both Islamic and Western society from their confused religious expression; then address these difficulties themselves. To sum it up, such a policy would have to be underpinned by a concept of universalism, which would include secularism, plus development.

The issue of development, understood as both growth in the economic field and democratization in the political, is a useful starting-point. Within Islamic societies themselves, Islamist sentiment and Islamist movements have developed as a cultural and nationalist response to very real contemporary problems facing these societies, and more particularly to problems that have become clearer as the first generation of post-independence regimes has come to an end. Whether in Iran, or Tunisia, Algeria, Pakistan or Egypt, the rise of Islamist movements has been directed less against direct foreign domination than against the indigenous, albeit post-colonial, state that has failed to resolve the problems of the society it rules and has exhausted its political credit. The Islamist movements, although themselves determinedly committed to taking and using state power, are above all revolts against the policies – authoritarian, secular and intrusive – of the modernizing state. This is as true of supposedly conservative, pre-revolutionary Iran, as it was of Algeria in the later days of the FLN. The inability of these states to meet either the economic expectations or the cultural aspirations of their people has provided the context in which Islamist movements have developed. The logic of this analysis is evident: that until and unless the internal problems of these countries are reduced different varieties of Islamism will retain their appeal, against the backdrop of the diverse social and political crises between the different countries. As one Algerian official commented during the 1991 crisis, the way in which Europe could best help overcome the *Front Islamique du Salut* (FIS) would be to provide guidelines on how to employ millions of young people. Moreover, the Islamist movements themselves are unable to provide answers. Deluded with empty ideas about 'Islamic economics', the 'third way' and other supposed alternatives to either capitalist or communist development, they offer in effect a run-down form of Third World populism that is even less able than its more secular antecedents – Nasserism, Peronism, the Indian Congress and so on – to resolve the problems these societies face. Their failure is explained by the fact that the situation in these countries has in many respects substantially deteriorated since the immediate post-independence period. The demographic explosion is perhaps the most obvious instance of this.

What this crisis situation must entail in policy terms is a necessarily protracted but clear-sighted attempt to help these countries resolve their problems of economic and social development, in order to provide their populations with some prospect of future economic development. There are, of course, severe difficulties here: external capital is not limitless, and there are many other claims on it, particularly from the post-communist world. Yet the Islamic world itself is, thanks to the flow of oil revenues, not short of capital. What matters is how that capital is used. The states of many Islamic countries have a record of diverting economic resources, however generated, into consumption or the purchase of arms for various forms of 'security'. Moreover, many of the countries have social and economic structures that militate against economic development. This has been particularly evident in the past decade or so with the advent of export-oriented industrialization which has led no Middle Eastern country (with the exceptions of Turkey and Tunisia) to greater economic development. If oil revenues are factored out, the economic record of these states over the past two decades is amongst the poorest in the world, matched only by parts of Africa. No one will choose to invest in these countries for manufacturing purposes while alternatives such as South-East Asia, Latin America and Eastern Europe are available. Yet until these basic problems of economic development are addressed, and until the bogus solutions of the Islamist movements are exposed, the context in which such forces can grow and attract support will persist. In the end, the only solution for the Islamic world's relations with the outside world is for it to compete, but in that domain – the economic rather than the military – that more and more constitutes the ground of international conflict in the late twentieth century.

This is the lesson which the Islamic world needs to learn – not from Europe, but from the rising economies of the Far East. If there is to be a successful integration of the Islamic countries into the wider non-Islamic four-fifths of the world, it will have to take the form of economic competition, both industrial and other, as opposed to a recourse to outdated and rather ineffectual dema-gogies, and arms. The implications of this part of the argument for Western Europe are clear: employment and equality are the prerequisites for a successful integration of the new Muslim communities. Economic exclusion and political rejection will fuel fundamentalist antagonism.

More difficult is the issue of the appropriate political response to Islamism from within Muslim societies as well as from without. On the one hand, Islamist movements could be accepted as a valid expression of the popular will of the countries where they arise and of the communities within Western Europe that are influenced by them. Pragmatically and morally, there are reasons for taking this stand. Many in Western Europe, notably in Germany, feel that a century of colonial domination should now give way to a more tolerant and neutral attitude to what occurs in Third World countries. However, such a position can also be argued to be fundamentally mistaken, the product of both misplaced guilt and post-modernist confusion which ignores the very real dangers that Islamist movements involve for everyone, not least the dangers for Islamic countries themselves. Policies that deny the equality of men and women, of Muslims and non-Muslims, which legally suppress the rights of the individual, are not matters to which Western Europe, whatever its own failings, can remain indifferent. As will be discussed at greater length in chapter 5, human rights at present give cause for concern in countries dominated by Islamist policies and will do so more and more in the future. Indeed it is a relativist appeasement to say that such issues should be ignored on the grounds of pragmatism or anti-imperialism. Moral con-siderations apart, there will continue to be political pressure from groups and individuals inside Middle East countries for greater international condemnation of human rights violations. And the influx of refugees from Islamist dictatorships – actual in the case of Iran, potential in those of Algeria or Egypt – will prevent any facile obscuring of this question.

The question of the principle of sovereignty outside Western Europe raises a similar set of alternatives: those who say that 'we' should not interfere and should 'mind own own business' are allowing the sovereignty of states (Kuwait, Bosnia) and of peoples (the Palestinians, the Kurds, the Eritreans) to be denied. Imperialist domination is not a legitimate policy for the end of the twentieth century; a firm, multilateral, always self-critical insistence on universal codes of political practice, as embodied in the conventions and documents of the UN to which all member states supposedly subscribe, definitely is. It can be anticipated that those in power in states that violate the sovereignty of their neighbours will resort to the platitudes of anti-imperialist and cultural relativist outrage to rebut external criticisms, but this must take second place to insistence by the wider international community on the universality of legal and moral considerations, and insight into the calculations and corruptions that often underlie appeals to distinctive moral principles. Abstention, agnosticism, caution, compensation for the past can be taken too far: indulging the tyrannical policies of Islamist states and movements against their own peoples and, through chauvinistic utterances and policies, against others, becomes a form of appeasement.

In practice, then, Western Europe has to evolve a two-sided, balanced policy towards the issues encapsulated in the term 'Islam'. On the one hand, there needs to be greater awareness of and hostility to the racism and general ethnic-religious prejudice that is directed against Muslim immigrants in Western European societies, and Islamic countries outside. Not least must come the recognition of how often Western Europe has permitted and indulged the oppression of Islamic peoples, whether in Palestine or in Bosnia. Beyond this it is essential that the West frames a long-term policy of economic interaction with these countries designed to assist them on the path of development. However, such a policy must not entail the indulgence of Islamist movements themselves, or of the false inclusive claims made by Islamists in the Islamic world or in the West. That the myths of the Islamists and of their opponents often coincide in postulating one single, timeless, all-pervasive 'Islam', only makes it more important to devise an approach, based on solidarity and critique, by which to assess and respond to this very contemporary phenomenon.

5

Human Rights
and the Islamic Middle East:
Universalism and Relativism

'Islam approaches life and its problems in their totality. Being a complete and perfect code of life, it holds no brief for partial reforms or compromise solutions. It starts by making man conscious of his unique position in the universe, not as a self-sufficient being but as a part, a very important part, of Allah's creation. It is only by becoming conscious of their true relationship with Allah and His creation that men and women can function successfully in this world.'

Universal Islamic Declaration of Human Rights, 1981, p. 9

'For a Muslim country, as for all complex state societies, the most pressing human rights issue is not local cultural preferences or religious-cultural authenticity; it is the protection of individuals from a state that violates human rights, regardless of its cultural-ideological facade.'

Reza Afshari, *Human Rights Quarterly*, vol. 16, no. 4, 1994, p. 249

In the international debate on human rights that has evolved over the past two decades, the Islamic countries of the Middle East have occupied a position both common and specific. On the one hand, they have articulated views that are shared by other Third World and non-Western countries and, on the other, they have defined a specific position on human rights derived from the particular religious character of their societies and beliefs. Thus, at the June 1993 Vienna UN Conference on Human Rights, and at the regional conferences which preceded it, Islamic states, including those of the Middle East, joined with Asian states in criticizing UN and Western policy for its double standards, its violation of sovereignty, its neglect of economic rights and its imposition of 'Western' values. But at Vienna, the Islamic countries also submitted the 'Cairo Declaration on Human Rights in Islam', originally propounded at the 19th Conference of Islamic Foreign Ministers in August 1990.[1] This specific Islamic position on the international human rights debate pertains both to the issue of what constitutes a 'right' (which relates to its derivation from divine, rather than human or natural, law), and to a number of more specific issues. Four specially prominent themes have been the rights of women, of non-believers, and of people deemed to be apostates, and the question of punishments.[2]

This dual relationship to the international debate has also been reflected in international, state and non-governmental reports on the human rights record of the Middle East Islamic states. While many of the practices for which these states have been criticized (most notably, the denial of political rights across a wide spectrum) are common to other countries, some pertain to specific aspects of the ideologies and laws of these countries, formally phrased as they are in terms of Muslim law and practice. Recent examples have included the treatment of non-Muslim minorities in Islamic states, the use to which a law against apostasy has been put in Pakistan, and the persecution, through judicial and extra-judicial means, of writers whose views are said to offend Islam.[3] In addition, the place of these states and societies within the international debate has excited greater resonance than it might merit because of factors such as the oil-based wealth which these states have deployed to defend their position, or the particular international attention which the Islamic revolution of Iran, and its imitators elsewhere, have commanded. An examination of the claims and practices of these states may therefore throw light on their particular ideologies and political structures as well as on the general, global, debate on human rights.

Many commentators, Muslim or other, have fallen into the habit of presenting this question as part of a broader, historical and enduring, conflict between two determinate 'civilizations', the Western or Judaeo-Christian and the Muslim. Convenient and attractively polemical as an argument based on the sense of a transhistorical conflict may be, it has little relevance to the matter in hand. Whatever the philosophical foundations for a theory of human rights, or the historical roots of our modern concept, the discourse of human rights as we express and formulate it today is a recent, post-1945, phenomenon.[4] Hence, in explaining how and why particular attitudes to human rights are articulated, we are looking above all at influences that have operated since that time, in spite of the anterior religious or ethical principles that tend to be invoked in the debate. Thus while there are some elements of Islamic tradition and literature that can be drawn on to discuss the issue of human rights, we are in fact dealing with a relatively recent set of arguments, the result of contemporary trends in the international system and within Islamic states.[5] As such the debate on human rights in the Islamic context reflects the convergence of at least five distinct processes. First, it is part of and a response to the international debate that arose with the Universal Declaration of Human Rights of 1948 and led on to subsequent, more specific codes in the 1970s and 1980s. Second, the Islamic debate reflects the way in which, partly influenced by the UN-centred debates, a broader set of political questions affecting the Muslim world have come to be phrased in human rights terms – the Palestinian, Kashmiri and Bosnian issues, and the treatment of Muslims in Western European society being cases in point. Third, the 'Islamic' human rights discourse is a response to the particular use that has been made of human rights in criticizing governments by non-governmental organizations such as Amnesty, as well as by other governments, notably the Carter administration and all subsequent US administrations, in conjunction with the UN Human Rights Commission. Fourth, the debate reflects the pressure from within Islamic states for greater democratization and respect for human rights, in the direction of an increased compliance with international codes. Finally, and quite separately, it is affected by the current that can be broadly termed 'Islamization', imposed from above by governments, and from below by mass Islamist movements. From the 1970s onwards, this tendency has sought to alter legal codes and state practice so that they conform more closely to what is deemed 'traditional' or correct Islamic practice.[6]

As this rather bald list of trends should suggest, the debate on human rights in the Islamic world has reflected a range of political concerns, often in rather marked conflict with each other. The result has been a variety of interpretations of the correct relationship between Islam as a religion and the issue of human rights. At least four distinct responses or themes from within an Islamic

discourse may be identified. The approaches they adopt are clas-
sifiable as: *assimilation*; *appropriation*; *particularism*; *confrontation*; to
which may be added a fifth approach, present within Islamic
societies and the non-Muslim world and falling outside an Islamic
discourse. This fifth could be described as the *incompatibility* thesis.
Given the nature of the discussion, on both sides, these five
approaches are often combined in a particular discourse and are
not mutually exclusive positions.

Assimilation involves denying that there is any intrinsic conflict
between Islam and the international conception of human rights.
At one level, this involves arguing for a particular, 'liberal' or
'modernist', interpretation of Islamic texts, either attributing
greater weight to the more favourable passages that conform more
easily to 'liberal' notions, or offering a less conflictual gloss on
parts that might appear to conflict with international norms.
Liberal Muslims and Western anti-ethnocentrics alike have worked
hard to produce an interpretation of Islamic tradition and law
that appears to meet international standards. In essence, such an
approach appeals most to those who wish to deny that there is a
fundamental problem about adopting an Islamic response to
human rights and seek to fend off both international criticism and
fundamentalist reaction alike.[7] Where it recognizes that the
different tendencies within Islam pose a profound challenge to
any attempt to discover a single notion of Islamic human rights,
this assimilationist approach argues for the liberal, open interpretation of holy texts, thus implying that it is realistic to expect this
reading to prevail.[8]

Appropriation involves the assertion not just that Islamic states respect
human rights, but that they do so to a greater degree than other
societies. Such an approach can take a polemical form, whereby
Western criticisms of human rights records are rejected by counter-attack, to demonstrate that in the West the rights of women,
minorities or old people are in fact neglected.[9] In a less conflictual
form this appropriation arises in the context of growing state and
non-governmental interest in human rights: Islamic countries have
made their contribution, as much as they have on other emerging
'global' issues like development, anti-racism and ecology. Through

the usual channels of conferences, declarations and the like, they have sought to articulate a distinctive 'Islamic' view of human rights, showing how Islamic theory and practice can enhance and enrich the universal norms articulated in UN documents. The assumption is that only Islam can provide a full guarantee of human rights. One notable example of this is the Universal Islamic Declaration of Human Rights (UIDHR) formulated in 1981 by the Islamic Council, a London-based body with Saudi backing, which in its preamble states: 'A universal order can be created only on the basis of a universal faith and not by serving gods of race, colour, territory or wealth. The ideal of man's brotherhood seeks and finds its realisation in Islam.'[10] The 1990 Cairo Declaration of Human Rights is another such case. In both cases, rights are derived from divine revelation and the equality of humanity is presented as an equality before God. While in many respects the wording is similar to that of UN documents, these 'Islamic' codes make clear that all interpretation of rights is to be found within *shari'a* law. In addition, as Ann Mayer has pointed out, there are frequent and significant divergences between the Arabic and English versions of such texts.[11]

If the first approach has produced a literature stressing the compatibility of Islamic and Western practice, and the second has claimed a superior, Islamic interpretation relevant to the whole world, neither of these approaches has proved adequate to the task of responding to international criticism from the UN, the US, and non-governmental organizations such as Amnesty and Middle East Watch. Instead Islamic states have found it necessary to invoke a thesis based on *particularism* – the cultural and historical specificity of their societies – in order to reject external criticism of their human rights record. The specificity of 'Islamic' society has also been stressed in response to those opponents and critics from within Islamic countries who have, by arguing the existence of a widespread aspiration for universal standards, called for greater conformity with international practice and criteria. The response of rulers to such demands has been to argue that, in various ways, their societies are 'different' by dint of tradition and belief. Such responses do not involve an outright rejection of international criteria, codes or criticism, but seek to deflect them through this somewhat defensive stress on specificity. Saudi Arabia, the longest-established of the Islamic states, provides a clear example; its well documented restrictions on women, or on believers in religions other than Wahhabi Islam, are defended as expressions of a particular, distinct way of life. The Saudi regime does not say that women should not drive cars anywhere, or that other countries should not allow some freedom of religious expression, but only that in Saudi Arabia these are not appropriate. Equally, when announcing the establishment of a council or *shura* in 1992 King Fahd stressed the particular Islamic character of his country which, on the basis of religious tradition, provided the legal and constitutional system appropriate to it.[12] In a subsequent interview he stated: 'The democratic system prevailing in the world does not suit us in the region ... Islam is our social and political law. It is a complete constitution of social and economic laws and a system of government and justice.'[13] Iran has, for its part, defended its legal codes on the grounds that these are part of the culture of one billion Muslims. The generalized Islamic defence of the call for Salman Rushdie to be killed rested on a similar, apparently particularist, argument.

This stress on specificity has, however, been greatly boosted by the spread of Islamization, separate from but coincidental with the changes in the international climate. While adopting arguments similar to those who advocate particularism, the Islamists have generally taken a much more militant, and usually 'anti-imperialist', approach that confronts the perceived reality of Western domination, rejecting all-pervasive Western culture and advocating fundamental changes to the law. This approach then can be described as being based on *confrontation*. In particular, the Islamists reject concepts of secular law, as instituted both by colonial regimes and their modernizing, post-colonial successors, and wish to replace existing legal systems with the divinely sanctioned codes of *shari'a*. Far from stressing any compatibility with international standards, or claiming a common core of values, this trend has sought to reject all non-Islamic conceptions of law and right. The *shari'a* should then provide the basis for all legislation, including that pertaining to human rights, within the contemporary world. This tendency is, therefore, also part of a much broader rejection of the secular, modernizing and universally legitimated programmes of Middle Eastern and other Islamic states.

A fifth approach stressing *incompatibility* assumes, simply, that for anyone committed to some variant of the universal codes on human rights there *is* an inescapable conflict with 'Islam'. 'Islam' is seen here as a combination of traditions, practices and discourses; and human rights have to be defended against attempts either to deny that they conflict with 'Islam' or to subordinate them to Islamic states and Islamist movements. This does not constitute the claim that Islamic belief, in strictly religious terms, is incompatible with human rights, but rather that for a combination of reasons 'Islam' as an actually existing set of political and social ideas does entail such an incompatibility. Most commentators are loath to argue this line, given the practical conclusions which would result and the charges of ethnocentrism, imperialism and prejudice which they would face. Yet such an argument can be found in at least four variants. The simplest is *textual* and simply involves quoting significant and authoritative sections of the Quran and related documents to show that Islamic tradition is on any plausible interpretation in conflict with internationally recognized codes.[14] The second variant of the incompatibility thesis argues that, whatever the texts say or do not say or can be interpreted to say, the political culture of Islamic society and thinking is such that it is inherently illiberal, authoritarian and totalitarian. This may be justified on the grounds that Islam in general has this character, or merely that, while a liberal and internationally compatible interpretation of Islam is theoretically conceivable, given the form in which Islamic discourses are articulated in the contemporary world, the outcome is bound to be authoritarian and illiberal.[15] This relates to an argument of political instrumentality which concludes that an examination of those states or opposition movements that invoke 'Islam' and the 'Islamic' conception of human rights will invariably unmask them as instrumentalists using such policies to acquire and consolidate their hold on power. For example, the apparently pious or sincere return to a tradition in fact turns out to be a tool to help legitimize a political struggle. Of course, in Western society too the issue of human rights cannot be straightforwardly divorced from such questions of interest either. We must always ask the question of whose interests the articulation of human rights is serving, and then examine the relation of those interests to the instrument that most commonly denies human rights, namely the state. Indeed, as Reza Afshari rightly emphasizes, the starting-point for any discussion of human rights in the Islamic world, as theory or policy, is the modern dictatorial state.[16]

Finally, underlying all discussion of religions and socio-political matters there is the issue of *secularism* and the question of whether any attempt to reconcile the claims of religion over the social and political sphere is not bound to fail because the rights appropriate to this sphere can only be established and guaranteed in a context where religion is excluded from public life. Secularism is no guarantee of liberty or the protection of rights, as the very secular totalitarian regimes of the twentieth century have shown. However, it remains a precondition, because it enables the rights of the individual to be invoked against authority and because it is associated with a broader 'culture' of individualism and toleration, which are themselves prerequisites for the respect for human rights. Thus, whatever the texts, the religious culture and the nature of the political forces involved, the whole attempt to evolve an 'Islamic' position on human rights is doomed. The only response is to promote and await – no doubt for many years to come – the secularization of Muslim societies. As this chapter will go on to argue, the only foundation for a conception of human rights can be the secularized derivation of natural law that underpins the Franco-American discourse present in the Universal Declaration of Human Rights and similar documents. While tactical accommodations and distortions may be possible, and often advisable, no derivation from any religion is ultimately possible. This may be a dismal conclusion, but it has at least the merit of stating the case quite clearly.

Despite its appeals to tradition and Islamic law, the Islamic debate on human rights can be seen as a relatively recent phenomenon, in effect a composite of responses to the different and in some ways conflicting pressures of the modern world, and the product of both international, exogenous, processes and of shifts within Islamic countries themselves. At first sight, their claims on human rights may appear to be another case of what has come to be termed 'cultural relativism'.[17] They argue that, by dint of historical condition and cultural–religious particularity, a different code of human rights is applicable to their countries, and that they therefore cannot be said to fall under the jurisdiction of universal codes as drawn up and interpreted by non-Muslim bodies. The implication of arguments to this effect from the Muslim side is that we are dealing here with a set of equal, but incommensurable, moral and legal systems and that it is improper for those outside the Islamic world to criticize or assess Muslim theory and practice. Outside the Muslim world, states and non-government bodies have often accepted this relativism, for reasons of diplomatic and economic interest which dictate that little or nothing be said to discomfort Muslim states, or out of a broader concern about the possibly 'ethnocentric,' 'eurocentric', and 'imperialist' character of external judgement. In international forums other, non-Muslim states may join with the Islamic countries in resisting universalistic critiques and codes on the grounds that they somehow embody 'Western' prejudice and hegemony. Indeed at Vienna, and in the regional conferences preceding it, it was the Asian states more than the Islamic ones who voiced this view. The combination of these various pressures towards relativism has produced a situation of apparent polarization, in which the claims of one region aspiring to be universalistic are set against those of another region voicing a strong particularism, without apparent possibility of resolution.

An alternative universalism

The argument that follows is one attempt to disentangle this debate, and to cast some light both on the claims of Islamists with regard to human rights, and on the broader issue of relativism in this sphere. It will begin by looking at the suggestion that the Islamic response to the human rights debate is a form of cultural relativism, and showing that in many ways this argument is a simplification. Then it will examine some substantive issues underlying this apparent polarization, and what lies behind the conflict between Islamic and universal codes. The chapter will conclude with some reflections on the critique of universalism, based on the Middle Eastern experience.

In writing on the question of Middle Eastern and Islamic responses to the human rights issue it is certainly tempting to contrast a Western, universalistic approach to the Middle Eastern, particularist one. Much writing on the subject, by Muslims and non-Muslims, operates with such a set of generalities, implying that the Islamic approach is comparable to the historicist or communitarian one found in Western thinking according to which there are no universal values, but only ones generated by and therefore specific to particular ages or communities.[18] Yet, on closer examination, this is itself a simplification and can serve to confuse rather than shed light on the issues at stake. In the first place, if current statements and policies are anything to go by, there is no one 'Middle Eastern' or 'Islamic' body of thought on this question. Attempts, declamatory or benign, to identify an 'Islamic' position are as misguided as those seeking to produce a single 'African' or 'Asian' one. There are over fifty Muslim states in the world, with a variety of legal and political systems, and there is no single body, political or religious, that speaks for the Muslim world as a whole. The Muslim religion itself is not only highly fragmented, but operates, in contrast to Christianity, without even a purported theological and legal central authority. What we have are a range of bodies, some political, some juridical and some academic (such as the al-Azhar University in Cairo), which interpret law and tradition as they see fit and which appeal to all Muslims to follow them.

While many aspire or claim to speak in the name of all Muslims, none do. There is, for example, a world of difference between the position of Saudi Arabia, on the one hand, with its promotion of a conservative 'Islamic' code of rights, and that of Tunisia, which has been in the forefront of the battle *for* universal rights and which even proposed to the pre-Vienna 'African' conference a denunciation of the threat to human rights posed by religious fundamentalism. In confronting the claims made by governments, individual writers or organizations, one has to take account of their specific context and not assume that they speak for one 'Islamic' world or tradition, or that theirs is the only possible or legitimate interpretation of the religion. We are dealing with a diversity of views and interpretations, not a single body of thought.

This variety is all the more evident if one takes not just those who claim to speak for the Islamic world, or in the name of 'Islam', but the full range of those who live, work and express themselves in Muslim countries. There are many who reject, to a greater or lesser extent, the formulation of legal, political and human rights issues in Quranic or *shari'a* terms at all. For over a century, there have been those in the Islamic world, variously classified as liberals, modernizers and secularizers, who have sought to develop legal and political bodies of thought based on secular values, or who have inflected and interpreted the religious traditions to give maximum expression, in the given political context, to secular values. The claim that those invoking the Quran and *shari'a* in some way represent or speak for the Islamic world as a whole is thus false. Turkey has gone furthest in secularizing its law, but for much of the twentieth century most states in the Islamic world have sought to develop legal codes and political systems based wholly or largely on secular principles. The spread of Islamization and the rise of Islamist groups over the past two decades has put such states on the defensive, but it remains quite inaccurate to claim that all opinion on such issues currently being aired in the Middle East is part of some common 'Islamic' or 'Middle Eastern' approach. Claims of this kind, of course, are made by states who wish to monopolize opinion on these questions. On the issue of human rights, those who are the victims of regimes speaking in the name of a legitimating 'Islam' (be this in Iran, Saudi Arabia or the Sudan) have often invoked universalistic principles precisely because they contest the very legitimacy of the regimes that are repressing them.[19] In other cases, opposition to Islamization has come from those who want a more moderate, liberal interpretation of Islam.[20] The debate on the Islamic character of law and the constitution in revolutionary Iran pitted clerical and other Islamist forces against those, many of whom had been involved in years of opposition to the Shah's regime, who sought a secular approach to these issues. The latter were, in time, silenced by repression justified in the name of Islam. Indeed, as those concerned with human rights in these states so often point out, what the victims of Islamic states and societies repeatedly ask for is not a different, better or more authentic interpretation of Islamic law, but the consistent application of international, universalistic principles.

Moreover, if one examines the arguments of self-proclaimed Islamic states then it can be shown that culturally relativist positions are generally avoided altogether. What is indeed striking about so much of the rhetoric emerging from such regimes, and from writers in the Islamic tradition, is that, with varying shades of explicitness, they articulate arguments in universal terms. Confrontations over foreign policy between the Islamic and non-Islamic worlds are most frequently discussed in terms that have little to do with religion or culture. Some themes often reiterated are heard throughout the Third World and focus on redistribution of wealth, equity in international trade and so forth. Other arguments pertain to the Islamic world, and to the Middle East in particular, but not simply for reasons of cultural variety. Thus the most frequent substantive argument used against Western, particularly US, policy in the region has been that it is consistently based on 'double standards'. The USA is said to expound the principle of self-determination of peoples, while denying it to Palestinians and Kashmiris; to condemn Muslims for violations of international law, while permitting continued Israeli occupation of the Palestinian lands taken in 1967; to call for democracy in communist states, while denying it in such countries as Algeria or Saudi Arabia; to condemn one group of nationalist militants as 'terrorists' while encouraging others as 'freedom fighters'; and, most recently, to argue that the sovereignty of states should be upheld while denying a Muslim state, Bosnia, the right to self-defence. The underlying principles behind this are not relativistic at all, and cannot be compared to the historicist or communitarian principles articulated elsewhere.[21] On the issue of double standards and historical responsibility, the critique emanating from the Muslim world has considerable validity – but this validity is a function of the force of arguments based on solidly universalistic principles.[22]

The same applies to the very terms used to articulate critiques of the Western position. In the first place, many rebuttals of Western human rights criticisms start by arguing that states with an imperialistic record, past or continuing, have no right to criticize Third World states. In effect, this argument is invoking a principle, implicit or explicit, that those who voice human rights criticisms should themselves be countries with a morally defensible record in this respect. The validity or correct application of this argument may vary, but like many of the other views expressed by Muslim states it has nothing particularly to do with Islam. Secondly, in rebutting external criticism, Islamic states (like other states which find themselves the object of such criticism) frequently resort to counter-attack, publicly highlighting the human rights violations by Western states, and indeed the general moral decline of Western society as it relates to crime, relations between the sexes, treatment of the aged and so forth. Beneath what appears to be a plea for difference lies a moral critique of the West expressed, with greater or lesser degrees of explicitness, in universalistic terms. Thus the Iranian foreign minister Ali Akbar Velayati, speaking at the UN in 1993, attacked the West for seeking to impose its values on the Islamic and Third worlds, but then linked this to the moral crisis in the West arising from unlimited freedom. He made the comment that 'some Western countries intended to impose on other societies their own social and ethical decline, to which they themselves confess, within the attractive package of human rights'.[23] In responding to the report of the UN Human Rights Commission that was highly critical of Iran, Iranian officials and press did not reject the UN principles: rather they claimed that the West was manipulating the UN's human rights process for political ends, and that those who were criticizing Iran in the name of human rights were busy violating them in such places as Bosnia and Palestine. Iran's Foreign Ministry reply was a defence of its commitment:

> Based on the supreme teachings of Islam, the Islamic Republic of Iran considers respect for human rights and the lofty character of mankind in all material and spiritual dimensions as a fundamental duty for all governments. According to this belief, the Islamic Republic of Iran, without paying attention to any propaganda hue and cry, will continue its efforts to strengthen the principles which guarantee support for the rights of all citizens ... As the majority of the countries of the world stressed in the course of the international conference on human rights [i.e. Vienna], the only way to lend real support to human rights and promote such principles throughout the world is to end the practices

of having double standards and exploiting human rights issues for political objectives. This process should be accomplished by open, independent and impartial international mechanisms.[24]

The Iranians and Chinese have made much of issues of selectivity and violation of sovereignty in their rebuttal of UN Human Rights Commission reports. Again, whatever the rights and wrongs of this position, it has little to do with religion or specificity.

Most importantly, however, even where the critique is phrased in terms of Islamic tradition or *shari'a*, and where it is claimed that a different set of moral and legal principles should be applied, a relativistic approach is not adopted. Indeed the claim that a particular principle is derived from Islam contains within it, explicitly or implicitly, its own universalism. Islam is a religion without ethnic or regional particularism, one that aspires to encompass all of humanity and which regards other religions and traditions as, comparatively, inferior. The *da'wa*, or call to submit to God, the basis of Islamic faith, is made to all mankind. Hence, given that the truths of Islam must be applicable to all humans, be they believers or not, any position articulated in Islamic terms is itself universalistic. To imply otherwise – that in a culturally relativist vein what Muslims believe is no better or worse than what non-Muslims believe – would be a violation of the faith and of its core doctrine.[25] A consistent Islamic position is the very opposite of that contained within communitarian Western thinking, since the latter implies that the values of different communities can be held to be equal. By contrast, if there is a conflict between 'Western' and internationally established codes of conduct and those of Islamic states it is not a conflict between universalism and particularism, but between two apparently divergent and contradictory forms of universalism.

Myths of 'tradition'

So far the argument has accepted, or implied, that there is a body of thought, unitary or diverse, which can be termed 'Islamic' and which does constitute an alternative for those states and bodies opposed to Western principles and codes. Such indeed is the argument both of Islamists themselves and of many outside the

Islamic world for whom 'Islam', 'Muslims' and indeed *shari'a* provide the basis for explanations of social and political behaviour and the terms around which to conduct the debate on human rights.[26] Elsewhere this book has touched on the various reasons why such terms are abstractions, reifications that obscure more than they illumine, often being used in ways that reflect highly politicized considerations of power by self-proclaimed Islamic authorities or those they oppose. Suffice it to say that, while on some questions the weight of Islamic tradition is identifiable and distinct, much of what passes for Islam and its associated codes and traditions is a particular, contemporary and arbitrarily formulated set of views, or local tradition dressed up as authoritatively 'Islamic'. Good examples of the latter are traditions of 'tribal' honour in Afghanistan and Pakistan, and the practice of clitoridectomy or female circumcision found in parts of Africa and Arabia. Neither has anything to do with Islamic doctrine, and the term 'Islamic' is applied to them merely to denote that they are part of the established (male-dominated) way of life. Equally without Quranic basis is the policy implemented in a number of Muslim countries that bans women from being judges. What we are dealing with is not an established, perennial tradition, whether legal or otherwise, but a set of discourses and interpretations that are created by contemporary forces and for contemporary needs.

As already argued, we have to look behind the assertion of a transhistorical body of thought, supposedly both legitimate and explanatory, and examine how in the conditions of the modern world a specific tradition has been codified and implemented. Over the past two decades diplomacy and liberal good will alike have allowed the discussion of human rights to work with such categories as 'Islamic', 'African' and 'Asian' codes of human rights, but in each case this involves a simplification, naive when not manipulative.[27] To reach this conclusion in the Islamic case we shall examine first the issue of *shari'a* law, the supposed code to which Islamists would have their societies 'return', then the broader issue of Islamism's relationship to the contemporary world and its supposed opposition to modern and secular forms of thinking, and then the origins and purposes of Islamic political movements themselves. What we discover is not so much a clash of cultures or civilizations as the pursuit of power, political and social, in the conditions of the late twentieth century. Above all, we are certainly not dealing with incommensurable values or activities that preclude moral and legal judgement.

The starting point for much discussion of 'Islam' in relation to Western concepts of human rights is *shari'a* law, which is assumed to constitute the legal and constitutional basis of Muslim societies. This claim is itself derived from the argument that *shari'a* is a divinely given code which is quite sufficient for Muslims and which brooks no emendation or contradiction by subsequent secular, legal or philosophic considerations. However, the claim that *shari'a* is such a basis for law is contestable even in the terms in which this claim is made by Islamists and other Muslims. The only parts of the Islamic traditional texts that are sacred are the Quran itself, which is said to be the word of God, and the *Hadith*, or sayings of the Prophet Muhammad as subsequently codified.[28] In the Quran, of the 6,000 verses only around 80 are concerned with legal matters and most of these concern marriage, inheritance and punishment. The term *shari'a*, literally 'path' or 'way' (the root is the same as for the conventional Arabic term for a street, *shari'*), did not initially denote a legal code at all. The interpretation of this divinely sanctioned material and its elaboration into a set of comprehensive legal codes is known as *fiq'* (literally 'understanding', hence jurisprudence), and it is this humanly evolved and variously codified body of legal material that has come to prevail in Muslim society under the misapplied term *shari'a*.[29]

Thus what is today invoked as an unchangeable and sacred body of text is, even in Islamic terms, nothing of the sort. As the Syrian writer Aziz al-Azmeh has written:

> Islamic law is not a code. This is why the frequently heard call for its 'application' is meaningless, most particularly when calls are made for the application of *shari'a* – this last term does not designate law, but is a general term designating good order, much like *nomos* or *dharma* ... Calls for the 'application of Islamic law' have no connection with the Muslim legal tradition built upon multivocality, technical competence and the existence of an executive political authority which controls the legal system. It is a political slogan, not a return to a past reality.[30]

This corrective can equally be applied to Islamic discourses on human rights. Great effort has been put into finding the foundations of a theory of rights in Islam, and in claiming that such a theory can be derived, indeed only derived, from divine revelation. But this claim is quite bogus: Islam, like other religions, has no doctrine of rights, and the imposition of a human rights discourse on selective quotes from the Quran and the *Hadith* is an ahistorical and artificial, if politically attractive, venture. Most Islamic tradition has been concerned with obligation to God and to the ruler. Those elements that indicate a different direction, such as the Quranic line that 'there is no compulsion in religion', are quite inadequate to the task of serving as the foundation for a human rights doctrine: they are flimsy at best and easily overridden by other, more authoritarian, elements.

This critique of the established, univocal, given character of Islamic law may be applied more generally to the concepts of 'Islam' and Islamic tradition. In common with all movements invoking tradition and various forms of essence, Islamic states and Islamist movements claim that there is one true body of thought that legitimates and guides their thought. Thus with varying degrees of emphasis, Muslims contrast their tradition based on derived legitimations with secular Western traditions.

These recent discourses on human rights are, on closer inspection, variants of a contemporary political project. On the one hand, the texts themselves are responses not to 'tradition' but to an international, largely Western, set of developments, and mix elements plucked out of Islamic tradition with the concerns of these international discussions. As Ann Mayer has written: 'the authors [of Islamic human rights schemes] lack any clear theory of what rights should mean in an Islamic context or how to derive their content from the Islamic sources in a consistent and principled fashion. Instead, they merely assemble pastiches of ideas and terminology drawn from two very different cultures without determining a rationale for these combinations or a way to reconcile the conflicting premises underlying them.'[31] On the other hand, while text and policy can never be simply reduced to each other, it is legitimate to enquire as to the political purposes and past records of those advancing particular human rights interpretations. This applies, not least, to those areas where ideas of human rights become highly relevant, namely the construction and maintenance of Islamic political systems. Behind claims to transhistorical and divinely sanctioned legitimacy lie projects for the acquisition and maintenance of political power in the late twentieth century. These may vary, as between tribal oligarchies (Saudi Arabia and other Gulf states), military regimes (Pakistan, Sudan, Libya) and clerical dictatorships (Iran), but the mechanisms and goals of all these projects are eminently comprehensible in secular terms and comparable to those of other contemporary political systems.[32]

Responses to the human rights pressures identified above can be seen not as disembodied or theological interpretations of a holy text, but as *political* responses, in a context where power is being promoted domestically and internationally. States have embraced Islamist discourses above all where this has served to consolidate power at home or to promote the state's interests *vis-à-vis* other Muslim states or the West. The history of human rights in all societies, Muslim and Western, is one that reflects such pressures and interests. It is not the result of an abstracted thought process, even if much thought has gone into it, but of determinate social and political conflicts within societies, some of which gain and some of which lose power.[33] The response of Islamic states, and of non-governmental groups within these societies, is similarly a discourse which reflects considerations of power as well as of principle. Indeed, such considerations of power deny any regime or religious body the claim to moral or cultural particularism. It is here, moreover, that it becomes relevant to look at the record of these states: to compare their claims to respect human rights with the reality. The philosophical and legal assessment of Islamic texts on human rights, which show the limits of such interpretations, is more than reinforced by the actual record which shows that Islamic states have been systematic violators of human rights, even by their own restricted criteria. Projects such those as in Pakistan and Sudan to 'Islamize' law are calculated and instrumental initiatives by regimes to consolidate their own power, both by silencing critics and social groups targeted by these laws, and by mobilizing support from sections of the population who may be sympathetic to such changes. The arguments advanced in international forums to repel external criticisms may be seen as similarly instrumental and manipulative attempts to mobilize domestic support and ward off independent criticism.

Clarifications and policies

The argument so far has sought to question the way in which the debate between Muslim and Western thinking on human rights is often presented as centring upon two conflicting, incommensurable sets of ideas. Given this essential difference, an acceptance of cultural diversity or relativism is regarded as the only appropriate response. However, not only does Islamic thinking itself reject any such relativism, but the tradition or 'culture' behind this supposed particularism turns out to be diverse and, in many respects, contemporarily constituted. The conditions under which Islamic fundamentalism and Islamization projects have arisen, and their human rights record, suggest the need for a critical assessment of what lies behind their discourses.

To argue this, however, does not amount to denying either that there is some legitimacy in the discourses on human rights emerging from Muslim countries, or that the issue of 'culture' is to some extent relevant to discussions of human rights. The rejection in Islamic thinking and discourse of human-rights-based interpretations does draw attention to underlying problems in the existing body of thought on this question: the conflict between a universal, in the Kantian sense cosmopolitan, body of thought on human rights and the claims of states to be sovereign;[34] the shaky philosophical and moral foundations of any body of thought based on a concept of 'rights'; and the uncertainty, in all codes, as to the conditions under which rights generally conceded may be curtailed. Islamic critiques home in on all three of these issues, which are much debated in human rights literature, and use them to their own advantage.

There are other issues raised in Islamic discourses on human rights that merit attention from the international community and have been highlighted by the rhetoric and practice of Muslims. One is the subject, discussed previously, of double standards – the fact that Western states, and to some extent Western NGOs, have been selective in the way in which they have applied criteria of human rights and democracy in international relations. One need not accept all, or any, of the claims about an international policy of discrimination against Muslims (be it in Palestine, Kashmir or Bosnia) to accept that Muslim people have, in many countries, been victims of such selective treatment. But to accept this is, of course, to reinforce, not deny, the importance of universal standards. The critique of double standards itself presupposes a claim for equal entitlement and treatment, and as such, a critique conducted in these terms relates to the *policies* of Western states and NGOs and not to the substance of human rights legislation. Equally, criticism of double standards is by no means specific to Islamic countries, but has also been heard from movements in South Africa, Latin America and on occasion Eastern Europe. They form, in other words, part of a general recognition of the selectivity of Western foreign policy from the 1970s onwards. In light of this a recourse to particularism or exemption is no solution: a more rigorous and universal application of human rights legislation certainly is. There is, however, substance to the issue of origin: the fact that, despite all claims to the contrary – be they Islamic, Confucian, Gandhian or other – the international codes of human rights arose in Western societies and were codified and promoted largely by Western states and NGOs. That these states and societies for centuries dominated and exploited the world, and still seek to maintain a discriminatory hold on the international system, makes all such claims to have originated and promoted high ethical standards in the international field much the weaker. Again, however, this very real moral problem does not in itself mean that particularist, let alone 'Islamic', conclusions have a higher claim. Logically, there is no reason why the *origin* of a set of moral or legal principles should be equated with its *validity*, in regard to human rights, any more than in regard to democracy, or economic development, or natural science. This claim, of a delegitimizing hegemonic origin, is the fallacy at the root of all discourse against 'eurocentric', 'ethnocentric' and related thought.[35]

Historically, all critique derived from origin rests on a fundamental misconception: that of the unity of the 'West' itself. Islamist rhetoric is all too prone to perpetuate this error. Far from there having been, or being, a monolithic, imperialist and racist 'West' that produced human rights discourse, the 'West' itself is in several ways a diverse, conflictual entity, which developed precisely through a whole history of internal contests for power and influence. The notion of human rights was not the creation of the states and ruling elites of France, the USA or any other Western power, but emerged with the rise of social movements and associate ideologies that contested these states and elites. Human rights expressed, and continues to express, the possibility of political change and progress, not some global, pseudo-emancipatory conspiracy.[36]

There is a third possible area in which those in 'the West' should listen to Islamic discourses: the critique of Western society itself. While much of this critique is highly polemical and deeply prejudiced against the world of *jahiliyya* ('ignorance', the Quranic term for pre-Muslim societies) and corruption, not all of it is. On issues of crime, the exploitation of women, care of the aged and cohesion of the family there is plenty for Western societies to be self-critical about, even if they doubt the motives and question the record of those who articulate the criticisms. Yet, once again, if there is truth in these criticisms it arises not from the superiority of Islamic thinking or social practice, but from the attention that is being drawn to the failure of those who promote human rights to live up to their own universal and secular standards.[37]

The issue of 'cultural relativism' – the acceptance that there are distinct, historically constituted cultures of equal ethical and political worth – itself invites, and requires, much closer examination than it is often given. Certain objections are of a general character: a moral objection will show that even if something is indisputably 'traditional', this is hardly a sufficient reason for accepting it as desirable or ethically valid; a historical objection will argue that what passes for 'tradition' is highly selective, if not in fact a recent creation;[38] and a social objection will demonstrate that the definition, reproduction and use of tradition is as often as not a form of ideology in the hands of those in a society with power. Beyond these objections we face the question of what is meant by the term 'culture' itself. In the context of this debate, at least three different issues have become intertwined. In origin, the concept of cultural relativism referred to the indisputable reality of the variation of social practices and values, including ones pertaining to law, between societies. This is, in itself, an observation without ethical import, leaving open the question of whether one culture is better than another, or whether they are of equal worth. Even when such ethical judgements are introduced, we are still faced with the question of whether *all* differences between societies are of equal value, or only some. It would be perfectly consistent to argue that on many issues (such as those of language, eating utensils, traffic regulations, physical gestures, cooking practices) the variation between societies is of no ethical significance, but that on others pertaining to the treatment and equality of human beings, some trans-cultural ethical standards are applicable. In other words, cultural relativism of the ethical kind applies in some situations and not in others. How far this can go in the legal field I am not competent to judge, but there are self-evidently great variations in legal culture and practice between countries with broadly similar human rights conditions, suggesting that a degree of legal relativism is also possible. Moreover, the majority of people in all cultures accept some validity for universal criteria: very few people would argue that torture, starvation, infanticide and slavery are to be treated at the same level as greeting customs or festival arrangements. The key question about cultural relativism is where to draw the line and where not to, rather than whether a line is to be drawn at all.[39] By dint of the international system, and the criss-crossing of moral and indeed cultural discourses, we are to some degree in a common ethical universe in which an absolute 'cultural relativist' position is untenable. If, as is often argued, attempts to produce moral codes on the basis of an irreducible, internationally recognized minimum have not yet succeeded, this does not gainsay the principle that some such elements are so acknowledged.

Behind this issue, however, lies another more intractable question that goes to the heart of the debate on human rights in Islamic states. To what extent does culture play a role not in defining, but in supporting and maintaining human rights? Accounts of human rights in Western society explain this, broadly, in one of two ways. Either a particularist view is taken to argue that only in Western, generically Christian, society could human rights and democracy arise; or a specific but potentially universal view is adopted which argues that for human rights to be respected, and indeed for democracy and the rule of law to be maintained, there are certain cultural prerequisites, involving individualism, tolerance and a general respect for legality. These two positions are not exact alternatives since, among other things, the term 'culture' is used in different senses. There would, however, seem to be much evidence, historical and circumstantial, for the latter view. The question then to be asked of Islamic societies is whether, and how far, such cultural preconditions exist. Moreover, if they do not, the reasons for their absence must be addressed. At the very least this suggests that there can be no examination of the human rights discourses in Islamic countries without a broader, concomitant examination of 'cultural' pre-conditions.

Here, of course, we encounter the argument advanced by Islamists as well as by those hostile to Muslims, that there can be no human rights, no democracy, no rule of law in Muslim societies because of 'Islam' itself. (This is an extreme version of what has above been termed the 'incompatibility' theory.) By invoking a timeless and all-pervasive Islam, such a claim invalidates itself, both because 'Islam' is itself such a varied, multivocal system, and because the actual record of Islamic societies, contemporary and historical, shows among them a great variety in the extent to which the state has, by universal standards, violated the rights of its subjects. But, unfortunately, this is not the end of the story for, as identified earlier, there are other variants of the 'incompatibility' thesis based on text, culture, instrumentality and the absence of secularism. It can be argued that the difficulties which Islamic societies have with the concept of human rights are explained by the combination of these factors together. Any longer-term solution must, therefore, involve addressing each in turn.

The issue of text has received greatest attention, vast effort being devoted to promulgating 'Islamic' codes or to providing different interpretations of Quranic and prophetic sentences. A great deal can be done to produce a more liberal, modern, human-istic interpretation of these texts, and this is the great hope of the liberal interpreters of Islam and of their non-Muslim supporters. The fact remains, however, that with all the reinterpretive energy in the world, some of the texts pertaining to women, non-Muslims and apostates cannot be fudged.[40] Texts are not, however, the main reason for the difficulties with human rights: in this sense Islam is not the issue. What is far more intractable is the *political and social context of interpretation*, the manner in which texts are conventionally interpreted in the contemporary social and political conditions of the Islamic world. The 'meaning' of a holy text is, therefore, not wholly, but largely, a contingent matter. The option of simply rejecting texts is not open, given the claim to divine origin, but that of neglect sometimes is (Quranic injunctions on, say, slavery have certainly been rejected).[41] However, to assume that a liberal, modern interpretation will be derived from these texts is to assume a very different political and social climate in the Islamic world. The authoritarian, patriarchal, obscurantist interpretations that currently prevail are inimical, in terms of broad political and legal culture, to any more liberal interpretation. While the hopes of those within and without the Muslim world for a more liberal reading are laudable and have already shown their theoretical and practical potential, they can at times ignore context in favour of text.

The issue of cultural context relates directly to the third constituent of the incompatibility thesis, namely that of instrumentality or, stated more bluntly, the relation of state to society. In sum, states in the contemporary Islamic world, like their predecessors, have denied the autonomy of society and of the legal and other constituents of a human rights practice. As has been well demonstrated by Simon Bromley, this dictatorial practice which is often ascribed to 'Islam' has other more secular and changeable roots, for the modern state has as much to do with oil, repressive technology and interstate war as with any cultural continuity.[42] But the fact is that in a context where states deny civil society and where, among other forms of demagogy, they seek to promote their own spurious human rights rhetoric, the development of respect for human rights has little hope: the objective historical and political preconditions for it are absent, and it is illusory to pretend otherwise.

The final point of collision is that of secularism itself, in other words the insistence on the exclusion of religion from public, including legal and constitutional, life. Although Islamists are keen to focus on this issue, and to denounce the influence of secularism in Western and Islamic societies,[43] 'liberal' writers on Islamic attitudes to human rights often avoid this question, preferring to hope for the triumph of human rights as far as a 'liberal' Islamic vocabulary and framework will permit. The most notable exception to this general reluctance has been that of the secularist tradition in Turkey, partially formulated by the Muslim secularist Ziya Gökalp, and implemented by Kemal Atatürk.

Discussion of secularism is all the more difficult because the Western definition and policy on it are open to criticism and less solid than might at first sight appear. Islamist thinkers often go further and argue that, in another case of misleading Western propaganda, the continuing hold of religion on Europe and the USA is not acknowledged.[44]

Despite all these difficulties, however, the issue of secularism lies at the heart both of the justification of human rights and democracy, and of the difficulties that Islamic societies face in formulating and implementing policies in this regard. Secularism is part of, but conceptually distinct from, the issues of political culture and the relation between state and society mentioned above: it involves not only the exclusion of religion, but a climate of tolerance of debate, and the application of reason to social and legal life. Without it, not only do theologically sanctioned authoritarian texts take automatic precedence but, more importantly, there is available an authority and atmosphere that denies the scope either for individual challenges to the state or for reasoned, free discussion of the concept of rights. The central issue is not, therefore, one of finding some more liberal, or compatible, interpretation of Islamic thinking, but of removing the discussion of rights from the claims of religion itself. Unless this step is taken, the multiple levels of limitation identified here – text, culture, instrumentality and religious hegemony – will prevail. It is this issue above all which those committed to a liberal interpretation of Islam seek to avoid – for very good practical, as well as philosophical, reasons.

Conclusion

The above argument may lead to some uncomfortable, but arguably unavoidable, conclusions about the contemporary debate on human rights. If it suggests that discussion on an 'Islamic' approach to human rights has often been confused, if not straightforwardly manipulative, it also suggests that there is no easy resolution of this question, given the forms of ideological domination that prevail in the Islamic states of the Middle East, and the absence of the preconditions for an effective discussion, or policy, on rights. It seems that the future will require a long-term, often dispiriting, defence of human rights and a simultaneous encouragement of those broader processes of social and political change that make rights a practical possibility. In so far as there are those within the Muslim world who do accept the implications of international conventions and practice on human rights there should be no obstacle to collaboration with them. The hope for reinforcing respect for human rights in these states rests as much with the elaboration of a liberal Islamic understanding of the issue as it does with the strengthening of secularism.[45]

The case of the Islamic countries should also encourage us to question the prevailing trend towards relativism, which is as evident in human rights discussion as in many areas of the social sciences and of moral philosophy,[46] and which is fuelled from at least three distinct sources: anti-imperialist concern about the ethnocentric nature of universal values; post-modernist rejection of any claim to rationality and universality; and philosophic doubts about the validity of asserting universal entitlements. The first is prey to the fallacy of origin: the fact that a set of ideas were produced in one particular context says little about their subsequent authenticity.[47] The second is a debilitating intellectual fashion indulged in by people who give the impression of never having been near a human rights violation.[48] The third is, for all the solemnity of its utterance and the genuine philosophic concern it reflects, a political and legal abnegation that corresponds rather weakly to the requirements of much of humanity, a reformulation, in the conventions of late twentieth-century liberal thought, of what Nietzsche said rather more boldly a century before. There are many aspects to these forms of relativism which cannot be dealt with here. However, in so far as the case of the Islamic countries is often invoked to justify such relativism in one or all of its above variations, or to legitimate or illustrate arguments that rely upon a concept of 'tradition' or historically produced 'community', it is to be hoped that the above discussions will, at the least, indicate that 'Islam' provides no such succour. Whatever else they may be, or are interpreted to be, the Islamic discourses and practices of the countries of the Middle East are not examples of relativism, or mutually tolerant communitarianism, as those who are subjugated to their various contemporary political and social manifestations are all too cruelly aware.

6

Anti-Muslimism and Contemporary Politics: One Ideology or Many?

Hostility to 'Islam', and the notion that there exists an 'Islamic threat' external to European society, has in recent years come to acquire an additional, more inward-looking aspect, and to be directed against Muslims living in Western and other non-Muslim societies. Racism in European countries, above all in France, has taken on a more explicitly anti-Muslim character. In the USA, where Muslims are not a noticeable immigrant community, anti-Islamic rhetoric is a significant factor in political discourse; in India it has provided the mainstay of the Hindu chauvinist right.

The tone of this rhetoric is often alarmist, and encompasses racist, xenophobic and stereotyping elements. The term 'anti-Muslimism' is used here to signify such a diffuse ideology, one rarely expressed in purely religious terms, but usually mixed in with other rhetorics and ideologies. In so far as one can term it thus, anti-Muslimism is a semi-ideology, that is, a body of ideas that, like gender and racial prejudice, is often articulated in conjunction with others that have a greater potential to function independently. It involves not so much hostility to Islam as a religion – indeed, few contemporary anti-Muslimists take issue with the claim of Muhammad to be a prophet, or with other theological beliefs – but hostility to *Muslims*, to communities of peoples whose sole or main religion is Islam and whose Islamic character, real or invented, forms one of the objects of prejudice. In this sense anti-Muslimism often overlaps with forms of ethnic prejudice, covering peoples within which there may well be a significant non-Muslim element, such as Albanians, Palestinians or even Caucasians.

At first, it would appear that the prevalence of this rhetoric poses no analytic problems. It is seen by many Muslims purely as a continuation of the enduring hostility of the non-Muslim world to their religion, and is often regarded in the West as a continuation of the rivalry with the Islamic world and the threat of Muslim invasion that goes back to the seventh century. Words such as embedded, engrained, age-old and traditional come into play, along with such speculation as that recently revised by Samuel Huntington, that conflict repeatedly arises along historically established cultural 'fault-lines'.[1] For some, hostility to Muslims requires no justification because it is itself a legitimate response to the threats and the militant rhetoric that emerge from the Muslim world.

But analysis needs to go further than this. In the first place, invoking history can provide little guidance as to why and how such rhetoric is used now. Unless we argue for the existence of transhistorical ideological formations, Jungian archetypes or Blochian *mentalités* which determine our behaviour, the appeal to history is unilluminating. While (for both sides) history certainly provides a reserve of ideological themes upon which to draw, the question of why and how a certain rhetoric emerged when it did still has to be asked. This search for contingent causes also suggests that even in the present historical period there may be no single reason for the re-emergence of anti-Muslimism. The rhetoric of one country may well influence another, – Serbian stress on Muslim 'terrorism' is an obvious case in point – but while there may be elements of common determination, it may also be the case that in each particular instance rhetoric originates from different causes and serves different purposes.

This stress on contingency is directly pertinent to a second explanatory belief, common among many Muslims, that anti-Islamist prejudice is an enduring feature of non-Muslim society. In this perspective the current prevalence of anti-Muslim sentiment requires no particular explanation according to time or place. There is, and has always been, a worldwide anti-Islamic conspiracy, which manifests itself in different forms and is an intrinsic part of the global hostility to Muslims. Thus long-standing issues such as those concerning Palestine, Kashmir and the southern Philippines are all seen as part of some secular hostility going back to the crusades, and have now been joined by a new set of products of that conspiracy – Bosnia, Salman Rushdie, Nagorno-Karabagh, conflicts over veiling and education in Western Europe. The first thing to say about this approach is that it is itself ahistorical and essentialist, though it is of course only one instance of many such approaches based on transhistorical explanations and is inevitably promoted by those who claim leadership of 'victim' groups. In nationalist contexts, too, the world is full of people claiming that their people are the victims of some timeless and pervasive hostility – the Serbs and the Greeks are among the more prominent recent cases. Equally common in contexts of racial and gender conflict are analyses based on timeless and apparently determinant phenomena (which racism and patriarchy can be represented as). The same applies to the most brutal of all twentieth-century experiences, that of the Jews. The claim that gentile society is in some way intrinsically and pervasively anti-semitic is common to many writers, and the suggestion that it may not be, that it has an element of contingency and indeed variety, is often in itself seen as a concession to the racism identified.

This issue of timeless hostility is reinforced by those who justify hostility to 'Islam' on the grounds that it is indeed the Muslim world that is aggressive, has always been so, and which deserves the opposition which it has produced. The argument that in some way Muslims 'deserve' or 'provoke' the resentment they encounter rests upon two potentially reinforcing arguments. The first is psychological: that the assertion by Muslims of an all-pervasive menacing hostility is an example of projection – that is, of identification with the 'other', the non-Muslim world, of something that is in fact a *product* of the Muslim world. In other words, Islam's recurrent emphasis on *khatar*, corruption and the rest, reflects the aggressiveness of Muslims, not that of their opponents. The second argument is more concrete and contemporary, namely that it does not take one long to find, in the statements of Muslim leaders, claims of precisely the kind of confrontation, rivalry, incompatibility that the anti-Muslimists assert. Such statements have been found throughout Muslim history and are the stock in trade of the Islamists: Sayyid Qutb on the evils of Western *jahiliyya*, or Khomeini on the corruption of the West, are cases in point. More immediately, as we have seen in chapter 4, many Islamists have responded to the collapse of communism by arguing that they are indeed the successor challenge to the West, and a more long-lasting and effective one at that. Khomeini made precisely this point in his curious letter to Gorbachev in 1989; in Britain, the leader of the 'Muslim Parliament', Kalim Saddiqi, repeatedly states that the next century will be characterized by the Islamic challenge to the West. As noted in chapter 4, we are therefore, in purely ideological terms, faced with a phenomenon that is quite unlike those other stereotypical hostilities, anti-communism and anti-semitism. In the case of anti-semitism, Jews did not subscribe to the myths of the anti-semites; and in the case of anti-communism, there was certainly a communist challenge from 1917 to the mid-1980s but it did not take the form that it was often claimed to take.

Analysis of anti-Muslimism has, therefore, to take account of these complexities: it has to provide an explanation that, while aware of historical continuities, is contingent and specific; it has to show how the very real cases of anti-Muslimism have causes other than that of timeless *kafir* hostility, and it has to provide alternative explanations for cases which Islamists see as proving their point – Bosnia is an obvious example. It has to accept that Islamist propaganda often compounds anti-Muslimism, but to separate out what are legitimate issues of disagreement or rivalry between Muslims and non-Muslims from the projection of any-thing defined as 'Islamic' as part of some global, and unitary, challenge. In this particular context, analysis of Islamism and Islamist movements that brings out the contingency and variety within them, and the role of contemporary political and social factors, allows for a separation of myth and reality through the establishment of some elementary points, which would include the fact that 'Islam' is not one phenomenon but many, that the Islamic states have not posed a strategic threat to the West since the seventeenth century, and that the issues underlying current unrest are ones of development and political change.

Equally, an analysis of anti-Muslimism provides the context for developing what can be a discussion, or dispute, between Muslims and non-Muslims over issues that are genuinely in dispute and in which morals, traditions and interpretation vary. The worst that such an analysis could do would be to argue that there were no issues at stake, or that all criticism of the Islamic religion, whether doctrine or practice, is itself based on prejudice.

The following analysis is an attempt to clarify the current origins and character of anti-Muslimism, with the intention of separating out those issues which are legitimately in dispute from those which are not. It addresses, but makes no prior assumptions about, the extent to which history plays a role in determining these and the extent to which there are similarities in the emergence of anti-Muslimism in different countries. This analysis leaves open the question of how far discourses that can be seen as anti-Muslim are, in cause or content, wholly or mainly directed against the Islamic religion, and how far the anti-Muslim theme is in fact deployed in contexts where it is issues of ethnicity and disputes over territory or power that are at stake, and where it may be directed against peoples who are either not Islamist in political character (such as Bosnians) or who are only partly Muslim (Palestinians, Eritreans, Albanians). Rather, the aim here is to begin with some case-studies and to address four broad questions: first, the history of anti-Muslimism in each particular context, the history being seen not principally as being cause or origin, but as thematic reserve; second, the growth of anti-Muslim rhetoric and movements over the past decades; third, the particular themes emphasized in this rhetoric; fourth, the apparent functions of this rhetoric within each country.

The term 'anti-Muslimism' is, therefore, used to cover not only hostility to the Islamic religion itself, but also to peoples who are, in whole or significant part, Muslim and who are conventionally categorized as being part of the Muslim world. Criticisms that are, on the basis of available evidence, legitimate are not covered by this term: thus critical discussions of Sudan's and Iran's human rights record, or of Quranic verses sanctioning rape in marriage or patriarchal authority over women, or of the practice of cliterodectomy or the terrorist acts of Islamist organizations, are not subjects of anti-Muslimism, although Islamists will be quick to say they are.[2] It is never easy to identify what is, and is not, the product of prejudice, but we all need such distinctions and must try ourselves to make them. To say that one Bahai, or Jewish or Armenian banker is corrupt and exploitative may, if the evidence is there, be valid; to say he is corrupt *because* he is Bahai, or Jewish, or Armenian, or to say that because one is, all are, is prejudice, as is the attempt to deny that peoples other than these are not similarly capable of corruption. Similar distinctions can, and should, be made with regard to issues raised in the context of Islam.

Orthodox Christianity: Serbia and Greece

After the rise of Islam in the seventh century, Orthodox Christianity had a moving, often hostile frontier with the Islamic world to which it progressively lost territory, leading to the fall of Constantinople in 1453 and the Ottoman conquest of the Balkans in the fourteenth and fifteenth centuries. As historians have pointed out, the challenge of Islam had important consequences within the Orthodox world. The rise of iconoclasm in the eighth and ninth centuries was, for example, a response to Islamic hostility to images of living beings.[3] But the elements of history that are most pertinent to contemporary anti-Muslimism date from the conquest of the Balkans. From this period certain central themes emerged. These included the image of the Orthodox Christian lands as the barrier or rampart between the Muslim world and Europe; the notion of the Muslims as demographically superior and as able to expand rapidly through high birth-rates and settlement; the memory of the destruction of Christian holy places by Muslims; and the sense of the trauma and pathos of conquest despite heroic opposition. In the Serbian case, much mythology and sentiment surrounds the battle of Kosovo in 1389, when the Serbian Tsar was defeated by the Ottoman armies. The River Drina which traverses Serbia was also invested with special significance because of the battles of that time. In the Greek case, the loss of Constantinople, the preferred capital of Hellenism, plays a similar role.[4] To these themes the Ottoman period added a number of others. The Muslim or Turkish rulers (the two terms used interchangeably) were caricatured as cruel and corrupt; the Turks were said to favour particular forms of brutality, including homosexual rape, against Christians;[5] and the image arose of the Muslim populations moving into previously Christian lands. A culture of resentment, paranoia and self-pity was thus generated and codified with the rise of the nationalist movements in the nineteenth century which led to the independence of Greece in 1830 and of Serbia in 1878. This culture was perhaps all the more bombastic because Ottoman rule had in fact been rather benign: Christian communities had collaborated with the Turkish regime, and relations between the three religious communities of the Balkans – Catholic, Orthodox, Muslim – were relatively harmonious. To the shame of defeat at Kosovo was added that of centuries of collusion.[6]

The rise of a new anti-Muslimism in Serbia draws, in the first instance, on the experience of World War Two, when significant Muslim support from Bosnia and elsewhere was provided to the Croatian ustasha state, with the backing of, among others, Hajj Amin al-Husseini. In postwar Yugoslavia such ideas were suppressed in the name of a new pluralism of nationalities, and in 1974 the Muslims of Yugoslavia, of whom there were around 2 million, were declared to be a third major nationality of the country, along with Serbs and Croats. Propaganda against Islam and Muslims began to emerge later, and in relation to two issues in particular. The first was the migration of large numbers of Albanians into Kosovo, especially in the post-World War Two period, and the subsequent Serbian charge that this was another case of demographic invasion which would mean the weakening of Serbian identity. The second issue centred on the trials of groups of Bosnian Muslims accused of being pan-Islamists, of receiving support from Turkey and/or Iran, and of simultaneously being in league with an anti-Yugoslav (in other words anti-Serb) exile network based in Vienna. In the 1980s, when Iranian press reports began criticizing Yugoslavia for its treatment of Muslims, and for problems relating to the building of mosques, the Yugoslav communist press increased its level of anti-Islamist propaganda.

With the disintegration of the communist regime after the death of Tito, Serbian nationalism became a more explicit part of government policy.[7] Serbian academics, mobilized by the regime, produced a history that denied the legitimacy of the Muslim communities in the Balkans – whether Bosnian, Albanian or Bulgarian – and which sought to portray Muslims as playing a central part in some perennial anti-Serb and anti-European conspiracy. One recurrent theme was the claim that the Bosnian Muslims were really Serbs who had converted to Islam for financial reasons and hence were traitors to the Serbian nation.[8] The function of this writing, directed both at Serbs and at a hopefully broader anti-Muslim European public, was to degrade and demonize the Bosnian and other Muslims, and thus to legitimize and reinforce the persecution of these peoples.[9] Above all, it served to deny the right of the Bosnians to self-determination, to their own state. Bosnia, it was claimed, was an invention of the communists in 1945. The issue of Kosovo became central to the tone of Serbian nationalism, with the press replete with articles on the threat posed by the Albanians. This was linked to the crescendo of nationalist sentiment that accompanied celebrations of the six hundredth anniversary of the battle in 1989. Serbian propaganda also began to report on the takeover and/or destruction of Christian holy places by Albanians. The issue of homosexual rape was given special prominence in two particular cases. In one instance a Serb named Martinovic was allegedly attacked by a group of Muslims on 1 May 1985 and had a bottle shoved up his rectum.[10] Martinovic became a national symbol, with poems lamenting his fate and pictures of him on the cross. The second case was that of the leader of the nationalist Serbs, the politician Vojislav Seselj, who claimed to have been raped seventeen times by Muslim policemen while under arrest in Bosnia. Both cases were embellished with propaganda about Turkey's expansionist aim to reconquer the Balkans, with Serbia now portrayed as the bulwark against the new Islamic threat, both Serbia and Greece facing encirclement.

The outbreak of fighting in Yugoslavia from 1991 saw the further development of these themes. Here it is important to note that it is not only the Serb leadership of Slobodan Milosevic and his Serbian Socialist Party (the former League of Communists of Serbia) which is responsible. While Milosevic does routinely attack the Albanian presence in Kosovo, and denounces forces which he claims are trying to fragment Yugoslavia/Serbia, his two main opponents, Seselj of the Serbian far-right Radical Party and the otherwise more centrist Vuk Draskovic of the SNO (Srpski Narodna Obnova), have gone much further than Milosevic in anti-Muslimism. Thus Draskovic made a particular point of spreading alarm about the

Islamic threat in his 1990 election campaign, and spoke of the rise of what he termed 'the ustasha janissary state'. He said he would 'cut off the hand' of anyone raising a Muslim flag. In Croatia, a Catholic country ruled not by the Ottomans but by the Austro-Hungarian empire, Franjo Tudjman has been equally vociferous in his anti-Muslimism, in addition to his well-known anti-semitism (in private, he regularly refers to Bosnian president Izetbegovic as 'the Algerian'). Of course, one of the things Croatian nationalists denounce the Turks for is settling *Serbs* in the Krajina area, four or five centuries ago. What all this would suggest is that the prevalence of anti-Muslimism in this context has at least as much to do with contemporary needs and calculations as with any historical determination.

In Serbo-Croat there is a range of words used to vilify Muslims: the most common are *turkcin*, 'Turk', and *balija*, usually meaning a violent, lazy and stubborn person.[11] A casual reading of Serbian press materials since the start of the war in Bosnia reveals a plethora of anti-Muslimist themes, some drawing on the Serbian past, others obviously drawn from available international themes: Muslims using chemical weapons, Islamist terrorists and fundamentalists pouring into Bosnia, the destruction of Orthodox churches and monasteries, drug-running from Muslim areas, the faking of human rights abuses and of starvation by Muslims, Turkish and Iranian strategic plans, German collusion with Muslims in anti-Serb policy, fundamentalist laws being applied to women in areas under the control of the Sarajevo government.[12] A graphic illustration of this sentiment was given in an interview with the Serbian Bosnian military commander General Ratko Mladic in August 1993.[13] Mladic evoked the importance of the Drina: 'This river, the Drina, is the spine of the Serb state and it will be the mother of Serbia in the future. Some forces in the West did not want the Berlin Wall, but they wanted a border along the Drina. It will never be a borderline again.' Rejecting accusations about his ethnic cleansing, he claimed that the Serbs were the victims: 'Serb mothers watched their children taken away by the *Musulmani* to become sultan's kids to be sold as slaves ... The Islamic world does not have the atomic bomb, but it does have a demographic bomb. Atomic bombs are under some kind of control. Their enormous reproduction is not under any kind of control.' Wherever Muslims go, Mladic stated, 'very swiftly one man with five or six wives creates a village. Then they build a mosque and there you have it! Gorazde is not Istanbul, not Izmir, not Ankara. The Muslims who live there are not of that soil. They were not raised there.' Mladic talked confidently about how he would blockade UN soldiers and Muslims into Bosnian towns: 'When the snow is 3 metres thick, the UN will beg us to bring them food.' By mid-1994 Mladic's forces had destroyed upwards of 800 of the 2,000 Muslim places of worship in Bosnia.

In the case of Greece, a somewhat different configuration has operated. Since 1821 and in the recurrent crises of World War One and more recent clashes over Cyprus, Greek animosity has, in particular, been directed against Turkey and, to a lesser extent, Albania, where a Greek Orthodox minority was persecuted under Hoxha's regime. Thus in Greek nationalist rhetoric the threat of Turkey is recurrent – in Cyprus, in the Aegean and, perhaps most dangerously, in the Greek-held area of western Thrace where a Turkish-speaking minority still exists. In the novels of Nicos Kazantzakis, for example, Turks are referred to as 'dogs'. More recently, Turkish influence in post-Soviet states, and the war in Yugoslavia, has aroused anti-Turkish and more generally anti-Muslim sentiment in Greece. As Radovan Karadzic, the Bosnian Serb leader, stated when visiting Athens in May 1993: 'Only God and the Greeks are with us.'

Beyond a recurrent nationalist Turcophobia, certain particular themes have contributed to this.'[14] First, the issue of western Thrace is very sensitive in Greek politics, and there is a widespread belief that the Turks, through the local minority, will try to get it back. In 1990 anxiety about this reached fever pitch when two Turkish-speaking deputies were elected to the Athens parliament: they have been the subject of nationalist vilification in the press ever since. Second, the end of communism in Albania has created friction with the new government in Tirana and unleashed chauvinism against the estimated 300,000 Albanians who have come to work in Greece, mainly as illegal immigrants. Third, the Greek Orthodox Church has become more alarmed and concerned about its position, in Greece and in other Orthodox countries, not so much as a result of Islam, but as a result of the resurgence of the Catholic and Uniate churches who claim not only souls but also property and status. As a consequence the Greek Orthodox Church has become more assertive of its religious and social position and thus, indirectly, more hostile to the Islamic world.

These themes are all reflected in the Greek press with varying degrees of intensity. Thus the right-wing nationalist press regularly carries articles on Albanian and other Muslims as illegal immigrants (*lathrometanastis*), drug-smugglers, agents of a long-standing Turkish conspiracy, and so forth. Articles argue that the region of Epirus is under 'Albanian occupation'; headlines read 'Every day three hundred new illegal immigrants arrive',[15] 'Invasion of murderers', 'Illegal immigrants, the scourge', 'Threat to our society'. Many other articles stress the Turkish encirclement, the arc that threatens Greece. Interestingly, increased Turkish influence in Central Asia is often presented not as a welcome diversion from the Balkans, but as a sign of Ankara's expansionism, a token of what is to come in Greece.

However, the extent of this anti-Muslimism should not be overstated. In Greek national mythology the (Orthodox) Bulgarians have often ranked second only to the Turks as enemies: one of the main heroes of Greek national history is *vulgarochthonos*, the killer of Bulgarians. Greece has, traditionally, had good relations with many countries of the Middle East and has projected itself as the *yefira*, the bridge, between Europe and the Arab world. In some Greek nationalist propaganda the Jews are the main enemy, and the Arabs/Muslims even pitied as victims of the Jews. While the Greek political scene is rife with anti-Turkish and now anti-Macedonian propaganda, its coverage of issues around Islamic religion and of immigration varies from the grotesque to the objective. In all of this, hostility to Islam as a religion, derived from Greek Orthodox concerns, is insignificant: indeed it is the Catholic and Uniate threats that are seen as the greatest religious problem, not the Islamic.[16] Once again, it would appear to be secular, contemporary, political concerns such as strategic influence and immigration that provide the real occasion for anti-Muslimist ideology, rather than an animosity that is timeless and religiously based.

A third country, of historically Orthodox culture, which saw the mobilization of such sentiments was Bulgaria. Here, in the dying years of the communist regime, and to bolster its falling fortunes from 1985 to 1989, the ruling party fell back on anti-Turkish and anti-Muslim racism, directed at the roughly 10 per cent of the population of Turkish origin who spoke Turkish, and at the Pomaks, a group of around 50,000 Bulgarian-speakers in the south-east of the country who had converted to Islam under the Ottomans. The basis for anti-Turkish and anti-Muslim racism already existed in Bulgaria, a legacy of centuries of Ottoman occupation and conflict with Turkey. Indeed, a study of words referring to Turks in Bulgarian found that around 90 per cent of them had negative connotations, and the Ottoman *robtstvo* (enserfment) was the target of much nationalist denunciation. In general, relations between Bulgarians and Turks within Bulgaria had been reasonably good. The Turks had been allowed to use their language, to wear their *shalvar* or 'baggy' trousers, and to celebrate *bairam* along with Bulgarian national day. However, in the 1970s and 1980s the cultural and religious rights of Muslims had been curtailed, with closures of mosques and restrictions on education. Then in 1984 the Bulgarian Communist Party went a stage further and initiated a campaign to force Turks to acquire 'Bulgarian' names, arguing that all genuine Turks had left the country in 1945 and that all those who remained were in fact Bulgarians, that is, Christians who had been forcibly converted to Islam under the Ottomans.[17] This campaign was accompanied by propaganda about the Turkish threat, about those 'who dance to Ankara's tune', about the linking of Turkish ambitions to NATO encroachment on Bulgaria's sovereignty, about a possible replay of the Turkish invasion and annexation of part of Cyprus in 1974, and about the high birth-rate among Turks.[18] In 1989, when political controls were relaxed, the regime allowed, and in many ways instigated, the mass exodus of Turks from Bulgaria to Turkey. In the space of a few months, 350,000 Bulgarian Turks fled the country. If a year later about half of those who had fled returned, the human cost and long-term poisoning of Bulgarian life remained.[19] As in Serbia, the rise of hostility to Muslims, combining religious with nationalist hostility, reflected political instrumentality in a context of decomposition and crisis. The difference was that in Bulgaria, unlike Serbia, the collapse of communism led to a reversal of this policy and to a degree of progress, within the context of political pluralism.

India

The country in the world where anti-Muslimism has made perhaps
the greatest impact in recent years, and where it is most central
to a political and ideological mobilization, is India. Here the right-
wing Hindu movement, represented by a cluster of overlapping
groups, has made the campaign for a reassertion of the Hindu
character of the country, against Muslim influence, its central
programme. This has led to rising communal violence and to an
increasingly hostile attitude to Muslims.[20] One slogan commonly
heard in recent riots runs: '*Mussulmanonke do his sthan, Pakistan aur
kabristan*' ('There are only two places for Muslims, Pakistan or the
graveyard'). This is a cry that sits with chilling disingenuousness
next to the claim that Pakistan has no right to exist anyway.
Muslims are abused as *ganda* (low status, also low caste) and as
katwa (literally, 'half-penis'). Often the Sanskrit word *mleccha*, meaning both outsider and impurity, is used. A literature of justification
and abuse has been produced by the parties involved in this
campaign. The pages of *The Organiser*, the weekly paper of the
Rashtriya Swayamsevak Sangh (RSS), are full of predictable themes:
Muslim infiltration of Hindu regions, the fate of women in Muslim
society, Pakistani support for terror in India, the destruction of
Hindu holy places by Muslims.[21]

In one sense, this is not uniquely directed against Muslims: it
is in part a campaign to turn India from a secular into a religion-
based state. Indeed many of the anti-secular themes sound similar to those heard in Islamist countries, and all non-Hindus –
Christians, Jews, as well as Muslims – are regarded as the
potential foe, as well as secular-oriented Hindus such as those in
the other political parties. It has also been argued, with some
justice, that the main line of conflict is not between Hindus and
Muslims but between communal and secular Hindus, and that
the major cause of the rise of the BJP (*Bharatiya Janata Party*) and
its allies is not the Muslim presence but the failure and corruption of the Congress Party.[22] In many ways the history of the
Congress Party is parallel to that of other post-independence
secular modernizing regimes, most notably the FLN in Algeria.
Like the FLN, the Congress Party can be said in part to have
encouraged the rise of religious parties, in this case Hindu

communalism, by adopting some of its slogans itself. But the Muslims are certainly the major target of this attack: they are by far the largest non-Hindu minority in India (110–120 out of 950 millions, or 12–13 per cent of the total). It is the centuries of Muslim conquest that the Hindus want to avenge and reverse, and the Muslim threat 'within' is linked to the threat from 'without' in the form of Pakistan. Some of the themes found in the Indian case mirror those in the Balkans: resentment at the Muslim conquests of the fifteenth and sixteenth centuries, alarm at Muslim demographic and immigration trends, denunciation of the Islamic threat to the unity of the country, reciprocal policies of ethnic cleansing and, of course, the contest for the control of holy places. On the latter issue, for example, supporters of the destruction of the Ayodhya mosque justified the action by arguing that the Muslim conquerors destroyed all the Hindu temples in northern India. In the words of one Hindu nationalist: 'Not one temple was left standing all over northern India. It was a conscious spell of vandalism. No nation with any self-respect will forgive this. They took over our women. And they imposed the Jazia, the tax. Why should we forget and forgive all that?'[23]

There are, however, important differences between the Indian and the Balkan cases. The particular history of the rise of Hindu chauvinism is linked with that of the emergence of the Muslim League from the 1920s and the creation of Pakistan in 1948. The BJP and RSS explicitly reject secularism, whereas the Serbian nationalists do not. In the long run, the potential for explosion and loss of human life are even greater in the sub-continent than in the Balkans.

The history of the rise of Hindu anti-Muslimism is linked to the development of Indian politics since World War One. This is not the place to explore the reciprocal process by which an increasingly explicit Hindu Indian nationalism interacted with an increasingly separatist Muslim faction to produce the partition of 1948. Suffice it to say that each fed on the other, but that in the event the main poles of division were between a predominantly secular Indian state and a predominantly Muslim Pakistan. However, there was from the beginning a third force, that of Hindu communalism and chauvinism, which, in its self-justifying history and ideology, mirrored the language and terms of the Muslim

League. This was, in particular, expressed in the policies and ideas of the RSS, founded in 1923. Its ideology can be gauged from the writings of M. S. Golwalkar, its intellectual inspiration and one of its main organizers until his death in 1964.[24]

Golwalkar begins from the evocation of an ideal Hindu polity, the Hindu *Rashtra*, which his party is committed to restoring. This ideal is influenced by conventional German romantic ideas of the nation, including the reverence for the original language, Sanskrit, and involves the denial of other non-Hindu peoples. When Golwalkar began writing in the 1930s this category denoted Jews, Christians and Muslims, and the Sikhs were excluded as in effect a sub-branch of Hinduism. This Hindu communalist reassertion also involves a gradual reshaping of the Hindu faith, what has been termed the 'semitization' of Hinduism. Thus what had hitherto been rather androgynous gods are turned into male warriors and one god, Ram, is given precedence over others; congregational worship is introduced; and what had previously been rather diffuse holy texts and stories are given the status of sacred books.[25]

This project of *Hindutva*, Hindu revival or, more accurately, assertion of Hinduness, is tied to a justificatory historiography.[26] India is referred to by its Hindu name, Bharat, this being the name of one of the younger brothers of Ram. The fate of Bharat is seen as having been doomed by the Muslim conquests of the fifteenth century, a process that pursued its anti-Hindu dynamic through the period of British rule and up to the creation of Pakistan. Partition, sometimes referred to as 'the vivisection of the motherland', is unacceptable: 'Our Motherland has been partitioned. Some people ask me to forget this fact. But I, for one, can never persuade myself to forget it. I would appeal to you also not to forget this tragic episode. It is an abiding humiliation for us. We have to pledge ourselves resolutely not to rest content until we have wiped out this blot.'[27] Indeed, it is striking, in reading the writings of Golwalkar, how little the British figure as an enemy at all. Muslims have continued, even after dividing Bharat, to conspire against it, flooding the country with immigrants, planning to extend Pakistan's rule, challenging Hindu domination in Kashmir and so forth. Thus Golwalkar writes: 'Alien traits found today in the life of Muslims and Christians of Bharat may be traced to history. Both these sects were imported into Bharat by foreign rulers, and throve under their patronage, as their instruments. These foreign rulers did not nationally establish the superiority of their faith before propagating it. Instead, they used terror to alienate our nationals from our ancient traditions, and used the converts to prop up their rule. A large number of people embraced these faiths out of fear or greed, and simultaneously they adopted foreign ways of life too. These faiths, therefore, symbolize our slavery.'[28] Golwalkar argues that the Muslims of the twentieth century are planning not to defend their Pakistani state, but to restore the Mughal Empire, ruling over all India. Despite his hostility to Christians, Golkwalkar has no problem in identifying with Christian resistance to Islamic forces: 'If Charles Martel had not stopped the Muslims at Tours in 732, today the entire Europe would have been under the banner of the Star and the Crescent.'[29]

The RSS remained on the relative margins of Indian politics for the first three decades after independence: it was banned in 1948 after the Congress Party alleged that one of its members had assassinated Gandhi. But in 1969 an associated cultural front, the VHP (*Vishwa Hindu Parashad*), was founded and in 1980 another party, the BJP, became a militant and increasingly successful advocate of Hindutva politics. Tied to the RSS, with its mass of disciplined and lightly armed members, or to the Shiv Sena, or army of Shiva, an even more militant group founded in 1966 on a programme of Maharashtra chauvinism, these forces acquired a major influence in Indian politics both at the electoral level and in mass actions, culminating in the seizure and rededication of the Babri Masjid, the mosque in Ayodhya where it was claimed Ram was born, in December 1992. This event was preceded and followed by clashes with Muslims in a number of Indian cities.[30]

Three themes in particular are central to this current wave of fundamentalism. The first is the call for the reconstitution of a Hindu nation. This nation is to be established on a version of Hindu values: while it is not argued that the non-Hindus should reconvert to Hinduism, it is implied that many of them were converted by force and would therefore revert to Hinduism if they could, and that in some (undefined) way they should accept Hindu cultural values. 'Let Muslims look on Ram as their hero, and the communal problems will be all over,' proclaimed *The Organiser* in

1971. Hence the rejection of secularism, similar to the claim of Islamists and distinct from that of, say, Balkan anti-Muslimists. Secondly, the national territory of the state should be reunited, with the reincorporation of Pakistan. Here there is an evident contradiction between the policy of reunification and the slogan of expulsion of Muslims. It goes without saying that all other attempts to break away, such as that of the Sikhs in the Punjab fighting for 'Khalistan', or of the Mizos and Nagas in Tripura, should also be opposed. Thirdly, there is a great emphasis on the dangers of mass Muslim immigration. In his time, Golwalkar in discussing 'Internal Threats' to Bharat, began with the Muslims who, he said, had become an even greater menace with the creation of Pakistan. Golwalkar wrote that the Muslims pursued two strategies – external aggression, from Pakistan, and internal weakening, through migration, so that he saw the settlement of Muslims in areas of Bharat as part of a planned conspiratorial process.[31] A book on West Bengal promoted by the RSS, *Paradise for Infiltrators*, evokes themes familiar in other contexts: 'West Bengal may be part of India but in reality it is like a disposable concubine of Bangladesh.' The ruling Communist Party and the Congress Party are attacked for patronizing this 'infiltration'. For the Muslims, 'everything that man needs for a civilized living is available to them at no extra cost. There are no bars against him. He can purchase land for residential and agricultural purposes, get his children admitted in schools, have ration cards issued to him, have his name entered in the voters' list and yet follow his Islamic way of life. Such are the bounties of Indian secularism.'[32]

This anti-immigrant theme was especially evident in the communal clashes in Bombay in 1992–3 and in the discourse of the Hindu leader Bal Thackeray, head of the local branch of *Shiv Sena*. Agitating in a city where 15–20 per cent of the population are Muslims, Thackeray has denounced Muslims as 'anti-nationals' and 'traitors', and referred to their districts of the city as 'mini-Pakistans'. 'My fight is against pro-Pakistan Muslims. The Pakistani extremists, the Bangladeshi Muslims and the Muslims staying in this country for years together, giving shelter to them – all these people must be kicked out. Even if he is a Hindu giving shelter to these kinds of Muslims, he also must be shot dead.' Thackeray also advocated the use of violence against Muslims, in contrast to the less aggressive construction of Hinduism: 'You have to react, you have to retaliate. I believe in constructive violence. I am not Mahatma Gandhi. If Muslims do this mischief again with Hindus, come what may, by whatever means we have, we will spare our lives.'[33] Asked what he would do with illegal immigrants from Pakistan or Bangladesh he was happy to reply: 'We will compel them to leave. After all, I am not a member of Amnesty International.'[34] When Thackeray and his *Shiv Sena* associates came to power in the province of Maharashtra in early 1995, one of their first acts was to change the name of the capital from Bombay (derived from the Portuguese for a 'Good Bay') to Devi Mumbhai, after a Hindu goddess.

If, in India, this anti-Muslim discourse is perhaps more developed than anywhere else in the world, its incidence is one that bears some relation to other movements. Hinduism gave European fascism one potent symbol, the swastika, the symbol of good fortune (*su-asti* in Sanskrit). The very ideology of *rashtra* that is promoted by the RSS is based on the application of European conceptions of nation and religion to India. It is a modern ideology, with the added element of the supposed common stress on the Aryan ethnic and linguistic heritage of those opposed to Muslim expansion. This original RSS ideology, derived from European racism of the interwar period, has now adopted some of the elements of contemporary anti-Islamism, notably the stress on Islam as the source of terrorism and the pseudo-strategic concept of a Muslim 'arc', in this case stretching from Turkey to Indonesia, within which India is located. The social and political factors that have led to the rise of the RSS, the BJP and others are also familiar from other contexts: the collapse of the power and legitimacy of the secular nationalist regime, growing social tensions in the cities, to which is added the intervention of a determined and well organized ideological force, with the support of at least some in the state apparatus and among the middle classes.[35]

The West: Europe and the USA

If the visibility of mass anti-Muslim sentiment in the Balkans and in the Indian sub-continent appeared as a relatively recent phenomenon, a feature of the latter half of the 1980s, the same could hardly be said of the developed Western world, both European and American. Here a range of anti-Muslim sentiments had prevailed for far longer, so much so that it was easy for commentators to write in terms of some underlying but enduring religious and cultural antipathy in Western Christianity, going back not just to the imperial period ('orientalism') but to the earlier confrontations of the Ottoman assault of the seventeenth century, the crusades, and the initial repulsion of the Arab invasions in the eighth century.[36] In one of the most famous polemics against Islam, the French linguist and 'orientalist' Ernest Renan declared in 1883 that it was essential for the rational, scientific, 'Aryan' spirit to conquer the irrational 'Semitic' mind of Islam.[37] For Muslims and non-Muslims alike it seemed that this confrontation was 'engrained' in the Western world, its most recent manifestations but the latest chapters in a long-running and apparently continuous story.

The elements of this continuity are not hard to find. The wars with the Islamic world, from the eighth to the seventeenth centuries, were a major preoccupation of Christian Europe. The crusades, launched in the late eleventh century by Pope Urban II, were a major defining point in medieval Europe. In the Iberian Peninsula, the very state and its identity were forged in the battle to expel the Muslims, and once this was completed in 1492 the ideology of militarized and religious offensive was transferred to the conquest of the Americas. The conquistadores saw themselves as crusaders, as did those who brought Christianity to the Baltic states in the twelfth and thirteenth centuries. Later, with the Ottoman advances of the fifteenth and sixteenth centuries, a further chapter of anti-Muslimism was written: one can, indeed, suggest that it was this experience above all which shaped European attitudes, just as it was the rise of the Mughal empire that formed Hindu sensibilities. As Norman Daniel has pointed out, this period saw the earlier image of the Muslim as 'Saracen'[38] replaced by its new all-purpose variant, 'Turk'. One famous example of this was to be found in the 'War Sermon' of Martin Luther, who in 1529 saw the Turks as realizing Biblical warnings of divine punishment, such as those relating to the Flood and to Sodom and Gomorrah.[39] One of the best-selling works of the period was that of Bartholomew Georgevich of Croatia, *Tribulations of the Christians held in Tribute and Slavery by the Turks* (1544).[40] In Austria, the racist right has used as its hero Count Ernst Rüdiger von Starhemberg, commander of Vienna during the 1683 siege.[41]

The relics of these campaigns are not hard to find in modern European culture – in the abusive uses of the term 'turk' (meaning stupid) in Dutch, in the Italian warning to children who do not behave 'Mama, i turchi!' and in the abusive term *marroquino,*in the celebration of the defeat of the Muslims in the French *croissant,* or the Viennese *kipferl,*[42] in the names of English pubs ('The Turk's Head'), and, indeed, in the national symbol of one of the emergent European regions, Corsica, which has taken the eighteenth-century flag of the Moor's head, itself borrowed from the crusades, as its symbol.[43] Certainly these themes are available for current usage, as are those, of equal historical importance, that express Muslim concern about Christian hostility. But to identify these relics and revivals is not to prove a continuity of culture or politics, let alone to prove that contemporary anti-Muslimism can be explained in terms of this past. Several considerations, beyond a general scepticism about the automatic transmission of culture and the effectivity of an archetypal substratum, would suggest otherwise.

In the first place, if we survey stereotypes of Muslims and Arabs we find that they are, like many such stereotypes, contradictory. Thus Islam, today associated with austerity and the denial of the material, was long seen as a religion of hedonism, sensuality and male pleasure – as expressed in images of the *harem* and the *seraglio.* Equally, the concept of the Arab or Muslim as militant, aggressive and active goes together with that of the Muslim as quintessentially passive, accepting and submissive before God. Strikingly, Primo Levi records that in the concentration camps the inmates whose spirit was broken were known as the 'Muslims'.[44] Secondly, it is not possible to generalize about the experience of Western states, particularly if this involves the USA. For reasons above all of geographical location, but also of differential imperial experience, the role of anti-Muslim sentiment varies from country to country. The states of the northern Mediterranean were, for centuries, far more exposed to Muslim attack than those of northern Europe. Thus not only the initial Arab attacks and occupation, but the later experience of Italy with Arab naval attacks (condensed in the term 'Saracen'), were not replicated in the north. (The one other place where this image of Arabs and Muslims as pirates was found was, surprisingly, in North America: the clash between US ships and 'Barbary', i.e. North African, ships in the early nineteenth century was to form the basis for much later imagery, not least with regard to Qaddafi). That these threats and the identities of those so threatening were confused is evident from the widespread use of the term 'Moor', a pre-Islamic, Roman term that also gives us 'Morocco' but came to combine, as in the case of Othello, Muslim identity with African origin. To these earlier differences must be added those of colonial experience. For France the encounter with Arab and Muslim North Africa was a formative experience, culminating in the traumatic Algerian war of 1954–62. Italy had a less violent but nonetheless important experience in Libya. Spain too had a major confrontation with the Arab world, in the conflicts over Ifni, the Western Sahara and, to this day, Ceuta and Melilla. These were, however, but one aspect of several colonial confrontations – notably with Vietnam, (Christian) Ethiopia and Latin America respectively.

In the British case, the confrontation with the Islamic world was far less important: true there was the occupation of Egypt and the death of Lord Gordon at the hands of the 'fanatical' Mahdists in the Sudan in 1885. Probably the most influential British encounter with Muslim society was that brought about by the presence of hundreds of thousands of British soldiers in Egypt during World War Two, out of which much contemporary anti-Arab racism emerges. But the Muslim encounter was far less important for Britain than for France. French has many Arabic words derived from the North African experience, while nearly all 'Muslim' words in English come from the Anglo-Indian vocabulary derived from a predominantly Hindu experience within which the Persian vocabulary of Hindustani played an important part. For much of the British imperial period other foes were more prominent: Irish Catholic nationalists, Hindu mutineers in India, Zionists in Palestine, Greek Orthodox guerrillas in Cyprus, Christian and pagan Mau-Mau opponents in Kenya, Chinese communists in Malaya. In several of these contexts – India in the 1850s, Palestine in the 1940s, Malaya and Cyprus in the 1950s – the Muslims were not only not the main enemy but were to a greater or lesser extent allies of, or at least partial collaborators with, the British. The result is that both in popular stereotype, and in more recent racist manifestations, hostility to Muslims as such plays a relatively smaller role. It is true that one of the main terms of abuse of South Asians is that of 'Paki', or Pakistani (it being lost on those who use the term that in Urdu, the language ˙of many Pakistanis, *paki* means 'pure'), but this is almost wholly a racial epithet, referring to skin colour and clothing, and is applied indiscriminately to South Asians of any religion, be they Muslim, Hindu, Christian, Buddhist, Sikh or Jain. In the American case almost the only images of Muslims available until the 1960s were in films – Valentino as the Sheikh of Araby, Palestinian terrorists in *Exodus*.[45] Once a set of conflicts began, however, a new abusive vocabulary developed: 'rag-' or 'towel-heads', 'camel-jockeys' (a euphemism for people who have sexual relations with camels) and so on.[46]

To this must be added, as a partial corrective, the actual history of Western–Muslim relations over the past century. This is not one of concerted or unremitting hostility. The Dutch, for example, had a long history of alliance with the Moroccans against their common foe, Catholic Spain. In Poland, too, there was, prior to the disappearance of the state in the 1790s, a tradition of alliance with the Ottomans against the common enemy, the Habsburg empire. Christian hostility to Muslims is usually proved by reference to the Spanish *reconquista*, which culminated in the fall of Granada in 1492. But this degree of hostility was particular to the imperial regime of that period, and contrasted with an earlier period of greater tolerance within Christian Spain. The history of European relations with the Ottoman empire in the nineteenth century was one of both conflict and accommodation, the latter often involving alliances between various European powers and Istanbul against other 'Christian' powers – Napoleonic France in the 1800s, Britain in the 1830s and 1850s, and later Germany. In both world wars the Western antagonists devoted considerable energy to winning over Islamic sentiment, not least because in three cases – Britain, France, Holland – Muslims comprised a considerable proportion of their subject peoples. In World War One, for example, Kaiser Wilhelm presented himself as the champion of the Muslim world. The British, ensconced in Egypt and the Arabian Peninsula, made much of their being 'friends of the Arabs', be it in the World War One alliance against the Turks, or in the arms sales deals of the 1960s and later. In the whole period since 1945 the record has been mixed: in the 1950s and 1960s, the West supported monarchical 'Islamic' polities such as Saudi Arabia against the much greater threat of socialist, nationalist and communist movements in the Third World, a policy that was to reach its culmination in the substantial CIA backing for the Afghan *mujahidin* in the 1980s. Indeed the whole picture of a 'West' unremittingly hostile to the Islamic world is rather contradicted by what occurred in Afghanistan after 1979.

These correctives may support an analysis of the growth of contemporary anti-Muslim sentiment that is rather more contingent, in terms of country and time. In terms of the past one or two decades, one may indeed distinguish between two strands of anti-Muslimism which may be termed 'strategic' and 'populist'. One is related to issues of security – nuclear weapons, oil supplies, terrorism – while the other is concerned with the presence of Muslims within Western society – immigration, assimilation, race, veiling and so forth. The two may be linked, in one generic and timeless 'threat', but the elements are rather different. Strategic anti-Muslimism dates from the early 1970s, and is above all a result of the 1973 OPEC price rises: even though these were not the result of a uniquely Muslim coalition (OPEC includes Venezuela), the 1973 rises provoked a reaction that included anti-Muslim and associated racist hostility to Arabs and Iranians. This was particularly so in the USA where, for the first time, what had hitherto been experienced as an independent economic system was exposed to a form of foreign pressure, conceived of as blackmail or threat. Then came the Iranian revolution and, for the USA in particular, the hostages crisis, which confirmed the image of the Islamic fanatic and terrorist: this rhetoric did not distinguish Persians from Arabs. Side by side with this alarm, related to oil and the hostages, was the diffusion of a set of anti-Arab prejudices emanating from the Arab–Israeli dispute. These had been identifiable since the 1940s, but became more evident from the 1960s onwards, partly as a result of the 1967 war, and then as a result of the rise of a terrorist faction within the Palestinian movement. These stereotypes were played up in the press, but were reinforced by novels such as Leon Uris's *Exodus* and *The Hajj*, and by films. In the USA in particular the composite Arab-Persian-Muslim-terrorist was established through the intersection of these influences. With the end of the Cold War another chapter was written: numerous politicians were heard to proclaim that the USA was now facing the threat of Islamic militancy, and this received partial confirmation from the Gulf conflict of 1990–91. In 1990 Vice-President Dan Quayle, in an address to cadets at the Annapolis naval academy, linked Islamic fundamentalism to Nazism and communism. The right-wing Republican candidate in the 1992 presidential campaign, Pat Buchanan, declared: 'For a millennium, the struggle for mankind's destiny was between Christianity and Islam; in the twenty-first century it may be so again. For, as the Shi'ites humiliate us, their co-religionists are filling up the countries of the West.'[47]

Press analysis played up the sense both of a transhistorical force, and of a concerted worldwide campaign: from the 1979 Iranian seizure of US diplomatic personnel, through the holding of Americans as hostages in Lebanon, to the bombing of the World Trade Centre in New York in 1993, the threat seemed to be getting closer. A television documentary, aired in December 1994 and titled *Jihad in America*, presented a dramatic picture of Islamism hitting directly at the USA.[48] Such was the strength of this anxiety that when, on 19 April 1995, a bomb exploded outside a government building in Oklahoma City, killing hundreds, the immediate response of many media commentators and of the police was that it was the work of Middle Eastern terrorists. Men of Middle Eastern complexion were sought; terrorism 'experts' pontificated on television; there were calls for pre-emptive strikes on Middle Eastern states; a wave of public attacks on Arabs and Muslims occurred.[49] The culprits were home-grown American crazies.

The culture of anti-Muslimism in the USA was distinguished in several respects from that of Europe. On the one hand, it was not to any significant extent concerned with the issue of immigration or with an internal or demographic threat to US society. This was partly because of the more variant and multicultural character of the USA, and partly because while in Europe the 'immigrant threat' was represented by Muslims (among others), in the USA (Catholic) Hispanic migrants took that role. In the USA the focus fell on what was seen as the set of security threats –

restrictions to the supply of oil, hostage-taking, terrorism – that had emerged from Middle Eastern society in the 1970s and 1980s. In Europe these issues, although present, were a less prominent focus of concern. For Europe, 1973 marked a shock, but not the one it represented in the USA, since Europe had always been dependent upon foreign imports. The hostage crisis had, for obvious national reasons, less impact in Europe. Terrorism did arouse concern, but the relatively less dominant position of pro-Israeli sentiment meant that there was not the obsession with terrorism that prevailed in the USA. Moreover, European countries had themselves had recent experiences of terrorism that had nothing to do with any Muslim force: the British with the IRA, the Spanish with ETA, the Germans with the Baader–Meinhof group, the Italians with the Brigate Rosse and the fascist counter-parts, the French with the OAS.

Strategic anti-Muslimism was certainly present in Europe, both because of the proximity of European countries to the Muslim world, and because, as in so many strategic fashions, Europe copied the USA. Thus in an article published in 1993 under the title 'Islam's New Drive into Europe', Sir Alfred Sherman, a former personal adviser to Margaret Thatcher, wrote:

> There is a Moslem threat to Christian Europe. It is developing slowly and could still be checked. But the policies of the western powers have done almost everything possible to help it grow. The factors that created the threat were: 1. totally irresponsible immigration policies in western and central Europe, which have rapidly created an increasingly militant minority of 15 million Moslems there. 2. the alienation of Turkey by the European community, which rejected Turkey's sincere efforts to join the EEC, virtually compelling it to seek identification with a Moslem world it was trying to escape from. 3. Germany's aggressive policy in the Balkans, calculated to break up Yugoslavia and Czechoslovakia, suppress Serbia and achieve hegemony in the region with Hungarian help. 4. Vatican support for this policy and the Pope's persistent court of Arab states regardless of the interests of their Christian minorities ... The gradual Moslem colonization of western and central Europe owes much to social and spiritual disorientation there ... Another factor was the decline of Christian and western values caused by the unlearning of western history, including the threat from Islam. In essence pro-Islamism – like pro-third worldism and (until recently) pro-Sovietism – are symptoms of the collapse of belief in their own values among the west's intellectuals and politicians.[50]

In similar vein Clare Hollingworth, a veteran British defence correspondent, under the title 'Another Despotic Creed Seeks to Infiltrate the West' wrote: 'Muslim fundamentalism is fast becoming the chief threat to global peace and security as well as a cause of national and local disturbance through terrorism. It is akin to the menace posed by Nazism and fascism in the 1930s and then by communism in the '50s.'[51]

A quite different element was introduced from the mid-1980s onwards with the rise of anti-Muslim sentiment as part of the anti-migrant and more generally racist sentiments in many Western European countries, tied to alarmist speculation at the end of the Cold War about the new 'Islamic' threat.[52] Thus in Europe strategic anti-Muslimism combined with popular anti-Muslimism from the mid-1980s onwards. A number of particular issues involving Muslim immigrants fuelled this: these included the dispute that broke out in France in 1989, and which was repeated again in 1994, over the veiling of Muslim girls going to school, (*'l'affaire foulard'*),[53] the campaigns by Muslim organizations in Britain in protest at Salman Rushdie's *The Satanic Verses*, and the prominence of Turks as targets of racism in Germany. The most extreme case of hostility to Muslims was undoubtedly that of France, where the right-wing *Front National* headed by Jean-Marie Le Pen openly called for the repatriation of up to 3 million North African immigrants, and stimulated a general climate of permitted anti-Arab racism.[54] During the French presidential elections of 1995, for example, in which Le Pen won 15 per cent of the vote, Le Pen sympathizers openly voiced anti-Arab views: 'My father told me: Arabs are worse than mice,' one thirty-one-year-old woman told a reporter. Another attacked the way in which those of North African origin claimed social security: 'They are French when they get their unemployment benefit, Arab when they misbehave.'[55] During one of Le Pen's election rallies in Paris a twenty-nine-year-old Moroccan, Brahim Bouarram, was thrown into the river by skinheads, and drowned: Le Pen refused to apologize, saying it was the kind of 'incident' that happened in any big city and, indeed that it might have been triggered by a provocation against the *Front National*.[56] Such was the hostility to Arabs that right-wing demonstrators denounced the main conservative candidate, Jacques Chirac, with the slogan '*Chirac à la Mecque*' – 'Chirac to Mecca'.[57]

It was striking too that in other European countries the racist right made anti-Muslimism particularly central. In Belgium the Flemish right-wing *Vlaamse Vront* blamed the country's budget deficit on Walloons and on the welfare costs of supporting Moroccans with large numbers of children. In Sweden the leader of the New Democratic Party, Ian Wachtmeister, declared in 1993: 'I must confess that in my Sweden there will not be many mosques', a statement that was followed within two days by an arson attack on a mosque. Another right-wing politician, Viviane Franzen, asked at the same time: 'How long will it take until Swedish children will be bowing to Mecca?' In Austria, the recently founded Freedom Party (FPO), and in particular its leader Jochen Haider, highlighted the dangers of mass immigration and the loss of Austrian identity: in his new year's message for 1993 he warned that Austrian schoolchildren were losing their culture, since in some classes in Vienna where there was an above-average percentage of Muslim children, crucifixes were being removed.

Anti-Muslimist sentiments of this kind can be quoted from several European countries, where they express the new racist and anti-immigrant politics that has emerged. The causes of this lie in the first place in two issues separate from Islam or Muslims – the pervasive social unease arising from the economic recession, and the rise of an anti-foreign and anti-'coloured' resentment that focuses, in many cases, on Muslims. But even here it is hard to disentangle the different elements in the prejudice. In Britain Muslim immigrants have encountered hostility ever since the first Muslims, Yemenis and Somalis, began arriving around the time of World War One. In 1919 there were widespread anti-Arab riots in several British ports: but the terms used to describe these Arab sailors – Bolsheviks, Fenians, negroes – had no special religious character, and the most specific term used of them, *lascar*, was a generic Anglo-Indian word for an Asian sailor.[58] With the large-scale migration of Muslims from India, Pakistan and Bangladesh, the term 'Paki' acquired widespread usage in Britain, but it was again not necessarily religious in connotation. It was indeed only in the late 1980s, and more particularly with the *Satanic Verses* affair and the Gulf war, that an identifiable anti-Muslimist trend emerged at the mass level in Britain. In sum, anti-Muslimism emerged throughout Western Europe in a context of broader xenophobia and economic recession: it was linked to the particular contexts of political competition in each country, yet it also had certain limits. In some cases this was due to the fact that for European far-right groups the main object of hostility remained the Jews, and in this context Muslims were, if anything, regarded as victims of a supervening Zionist conspiracy.

Israel

No relationship is more controversial or complex than that between the Islamic and the Jewish worlds, above all because of what has occurred since the mass migration of Jews to Israel in the late nineteenth century and the establishment of the state of Israel in 1948. The massacre of twenty-nine Muslims at prayer in the mosque at Hebron by the Israeli terrorist settler Baruch Goldstein in February 1994 appeared to be but the culmination of this antagonism. Here, above all, images of an eternal, transhistorical hostility prevail on both sides. For Muslims, the story seems clear enough: the Quran itself states that the Jews are the enemies of Islam,[59] and this has been vindicated by the establishment of the state of Israel and the occupation not only of Muslim lands in general but of cities and places of worship central to the Muslim faith. No wonder, it might appear, that Islamists and indeed Muslims have for the several decades past seen 'Zionism' as a central element of the anti-Islamic conspiracy and Israel as an entity created for the purpose of dispossessing and oppressing Muslims. For their part, Israeli politicians, particularly but not exclusively those of the nationalist right (*Gush Emunim*), stress the danger posed to Israel and to Jews in general by Islam, and recast the Arabs as the ancient foes of Israel, the Gentiles and, more specifically, the Amalekites of the Bible. The Bible[60] commands that these Amalekites be exterminated, just as, in a verse frequently used by nationalist settlers on the West Bank, the Gentiles should be struck down.

The relationship of Jews and Judaism to Islam has, however, been more complex than this would suggest, and remains so. First, while arguments about complete tolerance by Muslim states of Jews are exaggerated, the history of relations between Jews and

Muslims prior to the 1890s was not all antagonistic. The record of Islamic states towards Jews was, on the whole, much better than that of Christian states, and this was most evident in the acceptance of large numbers of Sephardic Jews who were expelled from Spain. On their side, Jewish writers tended not to express great hostility to Islam. With the emergence of Jewish mysticism or *kabbalism*, a strain of hostility to the Islamic religion did emerge,[61] as is evident in the writings of the thirteenth-century writer Nachmonides. The Andalucian writer Maimonides wrote critically of Jews who studied Islam, but he distinguished between Christianity, which was a form of idolatry, and Islam, which was not. He himself quotes from Muslim texts with respect, and served as personal physician to Saladin, the Islamic Kurdish leader who drove the Crusaders out of Jerusalem.[62] It can, however, be argued that until the emergence of Zionism, Jewish writers were far more concerned with Christianity than with Islam.[63] Even after the Zionist movement began, the main preoccupation of Zionists was not with the Muslim world but, given the rise of fascism, with the European states. It was only after 1948 that the Arab world became the object of clear confrontation in Jewish eyes, and then it was seen as hostile not so much because it was Muslim as because it was Gentile. Arab states such as Nasser's Egypt were, in Israeli rhetoric, compared with Hitler's Germany and regarded as another political force bent on destroying the Jews.

There were certainly elements of anti-Arab and, by implication, anti-Muslim racism and prejudice in Israel prior to 1948. From the 1890s people referred to the local population in disparaging terms, as 'donkeys' and so forth.[64] The very project of the Zionist movement explicitly involved the displacement of the local Arab (and partly Christian) population from their lands and thus contained, at least implicitly, a racist denial of their rights and common humanity. The goal of a 'land without people, for a people without land' was, therefore, anti-Palestinian. The early Zionist poet, Ben Yahuda, wrote 'How beautiful is Israel without Arabs.' But Zionist ideology was not as yet specifically or mainly anti-*Muslim*: the main ideological orientation of the European settlers who came to Israel was that they were, in addition to being representatives of the Jewish people, also in the vanguard of European civilization, against the barbarians and natives whom they found in Palestine. In this their attitude was not markedly different from that of other white European settlers in the Third World. And this 'civilizational' arrogance also meant considerable prejudice not just against Arabs but also against Oriental Jews, who were considered as uncivilized and little better than the Arabs. One account of Ashkenazi hostility to Oriental Jews illustrates this graphically: 'A whole vocabulary of racial slurs referring to the Oriental Jews became commonplace: "Khomeinists", rabble (*asafsuf*), hooligans (*biryonim*), masses (*amkha*), Moroccan cutthroats (*Morocco sakin*), cave dwellers (*shluhim*), pagans (*ovdai elilim*), fanatics (*Babe Salee*). Mordechai Gur, a Labor candidate and former Chief of Staff, warned a heckling group of Oriental Jews, *Likud* supporters, in a development town: "We'll screw you like we screwed the Arabs in the Six Day War".'[65] The term *avoda aravit*, literally 'Arab work', was used to refer to sloppy or substandard work. Nothing could be more indicative of this than the use of the term *aravit* (Arab) to refer to Oriental Jews. The term *shluhim*, 'cave dwellers', came into common usage in the 1950s as an Ashkenazi term of abuse for Moroccan Jewish immigrants who had, allegedly, been cave dwellers in their land of origin. Conversely, the early Zionists used to refer to Arabs by the most common term of abuse of all in Hebrew: *frenk*, the Yiddish word for anyone in European dress. Since the Jews wore their black dress, *kapota*, and the Arab educated classes wore Western European clothing of the period, the Arabs were assimilated to Christian gentile society.[66]

Hostility to Arabs and Muslims was therefore mixed up with a wider rhetoric of racism and hostility to Gentiles in general and to people who had originated in Arab society, be they Muslims, Christians, or Jews. The more specific anti-Arab/Muslim hostility was to develop only later, in the aftermath of the 1967 war and, even more so, in the aftermath of the Iranian revolution. After 1967, with the Israeli occupation of the West Bank and Gaza, there emerged a much stronger current of militant and nationalistic irredentism, epitomized in the settlers and the newly influential *Gush Emunim*. It was in this context that orthodox rabbis began providing a religious justification – deploying elements available in the Judaic tradition – for occupation of the West Bank and the violent displacement of Arabs. In 1968 Samuel Derlich, head chaplain for the Israeli army, wrote to soldiers that it was a *mitzvah* (religious duty), recorded in the Bible, 'to destroy Amalek'. When some army officers protested, forty other rabbis wrote to defend Derlich and to certify that his statement was consistent with *halakhah*, Jewish legal tradition.[67] At the same time, particularly from the mid-1970s onwards, the parties of the religious right, the *haredim*, were to play an important role in Israeli politics, and to propagate a more assertive and prejudicial attitude towards non-Jews as a whole, including Muslims.[68] This internal shift in Israeli politics was compounded by external events – the triumph of the Iranian revolution in 1979, with its clear hostility to the very existence of Israel, the emergence of a pro-Iranian Shi'ite movement in Lebanon from 1982 onwards, and the rise amongst Palestinians of the Islamic Resistance Movement (*Harakat al-Moqawama al-Islamiyya*, or Hamas) among the Palestinians. By the late 1980s and early 1990s it did, therefore, appear as if Israel was locked into an overarching battle with the Islamic world, a view that many Islamists, intoxicated with their visions of a worldwide Zionist and Jewish hostility to Islam, were quick to confirm.

The most extreme anti-Arab trend was, however, represented by the movement of Rabbi Meir Kahane and his *Kach* movement, which occupied a militant, violent place in Israeli politics from the early 1970s until Kahane's assassination in 1990. Kahane proffered a militant reading of the Talmud and the *halakhah*, according to which Jews were enjoined to fight non-Jews, and indeed those corrupted, 'gentilized' and 'Hellenized', Jews who did not agree with him.[69] Central to his message was the call for all Arabs to be forcibly deported from Israel.[70] Kahane wanted a law to be introduced making it illegal for any Jew to have sexual relations with a non-Jew, and for all non-Jews to be denied citizenship in Israel. 'Give me the power to take care of them [the Arabs] once and for all' he declared to a rally of supporters in Jerusalem in 1989, after a Palestinian attack on a bus in which sixteen people died. His supporters were reported as replying: 'Death to the Arabs and their [Jewish] leftist friends.'[71] Kahane's rhetoric was clear, hateful and threatening:

> The Arabs are cancer, cancer, cancer in the midst of us. But there is not a single man who is willing to stand up and say it ... I am telling you what each of you thinks deep in his heart: there is only one

solution, no other, no partial solution: the Arabs out! out! ... Do not ask me how ... Let me become defence minister for two months and you will not have a single cockroach around here! I Promise you a *clean* Eretz Israel! Give me the power to take care of them![72]

In this context, the incidence of overtly anti-Arab and anti-Muslim rhetoric has become much greater in Israel, and especially amongst West Bank settlers and the parties of the nationalist and religious right. One of the texts most frequently cited by settlers is verses 5–9 of Psalm 149, which form part of the Jewish morning prayer. This includes the lines: 'Let the praises of the Lord be in their mouth and a two-edged sword in their hand. To execute vengeance upon the Gentiles and punishments upon the nations. To bind their kings with chains and their nobles with fetters of iron.' These words are widely interpreted as legitimating attacks by settlers upon local Arabs, and find their more vernacular expression in slogans scrawled on walls: 'Only a sucker doesn't kill an Arab', 'Death to the Arabs', 'To make mincemeat of the Arabs', etc.[73] At the funeral of Baruch Goldstein, one rabbi declared: 'One million Arabs are not worth a Jewish fingernail.'[74] Such attitudes among militant settlers find their parallels in the religious establishment, and especially so among the sections of the rabbinate involved as chaplains to the army and in association with settler organizations and parties. Thus in July 1993 the head of the Public Committee for the Defence of Human Dignity, Rabbi Mordechai Yedidya Weiner, called on the government to allow the organs of Arabs killed during the intifada to be used for organ transplants, in order to dispense with the need to extract such organs from the bodies of Jews, since such extractions are deemed to be forbidden under orthodox Jewish law.[75] Earlier in the year Ovadia Yoseph, a rabbi who heads the religious party Shas, had expressed his view clearly in a sermon when he said that 'Arabs are worse than the wildest animals.' Such attitudes, while not characteristic of the statements of most Israeli politicians, are, however, those of an important minority within Israel who evidently feel that they can utter and disseminate such views without fear of contradiction, legal or political.

Those who propound anti-Muslimism within contemporary Israel, and in related sections of the diaspora, are themselves quick to resort to arguments about some enduring, eternal conflict between the Muslim and Jewish worlds. In doing this, they can easily find themes and symbols from the biblical past, and from subsequent history, to bolster their argument. From their perspective, as we have seen, Palestinians, Arabs as a whole, and indeed many in the whole Muslim world, consider Jews to be the enemies of Islam. Yet this obscures the manner in which the current usage of anti-Muslim rhetoric has developed, and distorts the longer and more varied history of Jewish–Muslim relations. The contemporary form of Jewish hostility to the Arab and Islamic worlds, and the reciprocal anti-Jewish and in many cases anti-semitic rhetorics of the Arab and Muslim worlds, reflect above all a recent and contemporary history, not the resurgence of some archaeological conflict. Thus in the rhetoric of right-wing Israelis Palestinians are attacked as 'Hitlerites' or as modern versions of the Ukrainian peasants led by Chmielnicki who killed Jews in the seventeenth century, more than as part of some eternal Muslim threat.[76] The origins of the most extreme anti-Arab racism, that of Kahane, lie more in the polarized racial politics of New York, in a fusion of anti-Nazi and anti-black confrontational themes, than in any specific engagement with the Arab or Muslim world. In Kahane's rhetoric the Arabs are but the latest bearers of the title, 'enemy of Jews'. The Middle Eastern sources of this confrontation lie in modern history, in the actions of Weizmann and Ben Gurion, Balfour and Peel, Nasser and Khomeini, rather than in the resurgence of the Amalekites or of some Talmudic ideological essence. As elsewhere, anti-Muslimism in Israel is a modern, contingent and instrumental ideology.

Conclusion

This introductory survey, necessarily schematic and incomplete, allows of no easy analysis of the genesis, content or impact of anti-Muslimism, any more than it permits of complacency about the pervasiveness and manifold uses of this contemporary ideology. In one sense the debate over ideological genesis and form is irrelevant to the most pressing political and human issue, namely the incidence of this prejudice, linked to others of race, faction and party, in so many countries. No one surveying this phenomenon, and the ease with which it is reproduced and embroidered throughout the press in political discourse ranging from the most vulgar to the most 'serious', can fail to feel concern and shame.

Yet as part of any response to it, and analysis of its relation to other forms of racism, it may be pertinent to suggest some analytic conclusions. First, while historical legacies certainly play a role – in the Balkans, in India, in Western society and in Israel – these cannot explain the incidence of anti-Muslimism today. Like all cultural residues and themes, it is their revival, reformulation and redeployment in contemporary contexts that has to be explained.

Second, it is certainly possible to identify a set of core anti-Muslim themes which are found in different contexts. Terrorism, demographic expansion, strategic encirclement, the oppression of women and dirtiness are the common preoccupations. But this does not prove the existence of a single anti-Muslimism, but rather suggests how, in addition to themes generated within a specific context, others available from the international media are deployed.

Third, without conceding to the claim that hostility to Muslims is justified by what some/all Muslims have done, it is pertinent to identify the ways in which some in the Muslim world have contributed to this phenomenon. Islamists have made claims about the homogeneity of Islam and the challenge that it represents. Such claims can seem to accord with the charges made by opponents of Islam. Equally, those opposed to Islamist movements of the present, or Islamic imperial forces of the past, have tended to reproduce and internalize the rhetoric of their foes. To reformulate a phrase of Régis Debray's, *Islam has Islamicized anti-Islam*. Both the iconoclasm of the Byzantine empire and the evolution of a Christian doctrine of Holy War were instances of this mechanism, which is working today in the transformation of Hinduism, the myth of Islam as a replacement for communism in threatening the West, and the hypostatization of 'Islam' in Western discourses.

Fourth, in none of these cases is anti-Muslimism the defining feature of the ideology or conflict in which it is deployed. It is linked to other issues – of ethnicity, colour, intra-communal conflict, administrative corruption and inter-state conflict – and depends to a considerable degree on the progression of these other processes and disputes. Such an analysis of anti-Muslimism as a 'semi-ideology' may provide little comfort to those who are the objects of such prejudice. It may, however, contribute to the formulation of a response to it, as well as to an understanding of the broader issues of prejudice, racism and ethnicity in the contemporary world. In a reformulation of the infamous question of Mao Tse-tung, 'Where do correct ideas come from?', one may ask: 'Where do incorrect ideas come from?' In this case the answer would seem to be that they do not come from an immutable, recurrent, historical archetype, nor from any essence of Western or Christian or non-Muslim society, but from a set of contemporaneous national conjunctures, in which politicians and their associate ideologues draw on themes present in history, or in the discourses of other states, for their own, current and specific, purposes. It is those purposes, not the prevalence of a world anti-Muslim conspiracy, that need addressing.

7

Conclusion:
'Orientalism' and its Critics

One of the most debated issues in the analysis of the contemporary Middle East has been that of 'orientalism', the question of whether Western writing on the region over the past century or two has been, and continues to be, distorted by a set of prejudices born of European and imperial preconceptions. This is not an issue that was first raised by Islamists, but it is one that they have readily adopted in their use of terms derived from the debate – 'eurocentric', 'ethnocentric' and 'orientalist' itself – to criticize ideas or analyses with which they disagree. The debate on orientalism also goes to the heart of the debate on Islam, because behind it lies the much broader question of what set of terms, general theories and values we should adopt in approaching Middle Eastern societies. A disentangling of the arguments around orientalism may therefore serve not only to clarify some issues of method, of *how* to analyse, but also to illuminate the question that has been most central to this book as a whole, namely the explanation of the contemporary Middle East, and not least of the Islamist movements it has generated.

The subject of orientalism therefore raises a broad and continuing debate to which many writers have contributed.[1] By way of introduction I should like to clarify how I myself have approached the study of the Middle East, not so much in order to enjoin it on others as to make explicit my position.

My point of departure is a belief, cautious but firm, in the validity of social science in general, and of the branches thereof – history, sociology, politics, economics, international relations, law, and so on – constituted by general analytic and theoretical categories, independent of specific data and situations.[2] I do not hold to the view of a strictly 'scientific' view of social science and the humanities, if by this is meant something that relies solely on quantification, prediction, supposedly rigorous methodology or hypothesis. Much of this is banal, chimerical, sterile. I do, however, think it is possible to talk of 'social science' in a looser, more comparative and historical sense, and one in which qualitative judgement and the issue of values, rather than being swept under the carpet, are made explicit, subjected to reason and criticism, and debated. It is in that perspective that I approach the study of the Middle East and of the recent debate around the question of orientalism. My prime concern is thus not the issue of methodology or approach as such, or the ramifications of discourse and ideology: these are of interest in so far as they pertain to my primary concern, the analysis of Middle Eastern countries themselves. As will be evident, I retain the now supposedly outmoded and pre-modernist view that there is such a thing as reality, and that it *is* the task of concepts and theories to analyse it, that their efficacy and values are above all to be judged in terms of how much they explain it. That is my tribe, the *Bani Tanwir*, or what might be called the descendants of Enlightenment rationality. And, as with most tribal affiliations, seeing what a dangerous world it is outside, I do not intend to forsake it.

This is an approach with an inbuilt presumption against treating any region or culture or people as particular or unique. As far as area studies in general, and the Middle East in particular, is concerned, I therefore start from a set of universal principles, analytic and normative, and would ask to what extent these can help elucidate the particular societies in question. I do not believe that it is possible to approach any society, in the Middle East or elsewhere, by starting from that society alone and charting its history, values or peculiarities in isolation from other societies. Moreover I reject the notion of starting from some supposed particularism derived from religion, political virtue, the nation or anything else. There are no special nations, no eternal missions, no mysterious unknowable humans, no particular demons – unless so proven, and on the basis of universal criteria. Comparative analysis can have its dangers, but it seems to be essential not only to see what societies share, but also to pose theoretical questions that the study of the particular may ignore, and hence be in a position to arrive at a justifiable identification of what is specific or original.[3]

Secondly, I have been shaped by the context of my own intellectual formation. I came to the study of the Middle East at a particular time and through specific channels. As a student in the 1960s, part of it spent at the School of Oriental and African Studies in London, I was interested in the way in which the societies of the Middle East had been shaped and influenced by external domination, what can still, without too much exaggeration, be termed imperialism, the forms of resistance to this that developed on a national basis and in social terms, and the ways in which economic and social factors, not least class, affected these societies. The Middle East was, in this context, part of a broader pattern of Third World revolt that took place not just in Algeria after 1954, Iraq in 1958, Yemen in 1962, and in Palestine after 1967, but also in Cuba, South Africa and Vietnam. Marxism was in a broad sense a major influence here, but, as the debates of the period showed so well, Marxism provided not a set of answers so much as a framework within which to examine these questions.[4] Marxism allowed of contrasted positions on, say, Nasserism or Zionism. As the debate on imperialism developed, epitomized in the work of the late Bill Warren, who so influenced all of us who studied under him at SOAS, it became evident that there were no simple answers to the question of the role played by foreign domination, let alone to the problem of how to address the issues posed by the new regimes in the Middle East.[5] This avenue led me to focus my study on four particular historical processes, each of which influenced the others, but which, by the very fact of being seen as part of a broader regional picture, exerted no privileged or monopolistic claim. These four were: the development and then overthrow of the Shah's regime in Iran; the Egyptian revolution of 1952 and its consequences; the growth of the Palestinian movement of national resistance and the much later emergence of a two-state settlement with Israel; the revolutions of South Arabia, and the post-revolutionary regimes in North and South Yemen.[6] In a sense it is that agenda of the 1960s which has preoccupied my analysis of the region. The questions I would ask are how forms of domination are maintained, how and why they are resisted, why states fail to maintain control, how those who come to power succeed or fail in constructing alternative domestic and international orders. I have made plenty of mistakes, but would also argue that some of my analyses have born the test of time and have made a contribution to an understanding of these questions. It is for others, not least those who have been directly involved in the upheavals of the Middle East, to provide their own evaluations.

Thirdly, I would add a more personal note, but one that can in some respects be made universal: namely personal origin. I was born and to a considerable extent brought up in Ireland, a country where some of the issues posed in the politics and social development of the contemporary Middle East are also present. I am extremely sceptical of those who think that acquaintance with the Irish question as such, or any other 'question', be it Palestine or Kashmir, thereby qualifies one to deliver judgement on different contexts. Quite a few people, including some otherwise quite sage, have fallen into that trap.[7] But I do think that there are a range of issues that emerge in the history of Ireland over the past century or two which certainly serve to attune one's antennae when dealing with the Middle East. These would include the role, destructive and formative, of foreign domination and settlement; the illusions and delusions of nationalism; the divisiveness of political loyalties based on religion; the corrosive myths of deliverance through purely military struggle; the uneasy relation of national and religious identity to democratic and gender rights; the difficulties of development when links with the external world are broken; and the dilemmas and agonies of secession and national unification. A good dose of contemporary Irish history makes one sceptical about much of the rhetoric that issues from dominant and dominated alike, not least with respect to the claims of clergymen. The ideologies of political hegemony, forced modernization and market-led development have failed in Ireland as in much of the Middle East; but a critique of imperialism needs at the very least to be matched by some reserve about most of the strategies proclaimed for overcoming it, as well as by a certain caution about the utterances of those who in discourse theory are referred to as 'the subaltern'.

The debate on orientalism

As part of the political and intellectual changes of the 1960s there developed a debate about the study of the Middle East, and more generally a critique of mainstream social science literature on the Third World from a broadly left and 'anti-imperialist' perspective which focused on its relation to power and subjugation.[8] Among the most comprehensive bodies of work in this regard are the writings of Maxime Rodinson, whose critique of European writing on the Middle East is the most measured and erudite of them all. The critique of orientalism long predates the publication of Edward Said's work in 1978. Indeed, given the kinds of work that were being produced by academics and others in the previous two decades, Said's work can be seen as coming at the end of, and to a considerable degree negating, an earlier body of debate and work, much of it stimulated by the war in Vietnam and the broader upheavals of the Third World at the time.[9] Said's work both subsumed that earlier debate and started a new one, because while much of the earlier work was framed in broadly Marxist terms and offered a universalist critique, Said, eschewing materialist analysis, sought to apply literary critical methodology and to offer an analysis specific to something called 'the orient'. The result is that the issue of orientalism, as debated in the Anglo-Saxon world over almost two decades, has marshalled relatively clear battle lines, now familiar to a wide audience. On the one hand, Edward Said's *Orientalism*, published in 1978, advanced a comprehensive critique of Western, particularly English, French and American, writing on the Middle East, ranging from the eighteenth century to the present day, and encompassing literature, history, political and other sciences. Under the influence of Said's critique, a range of work has been produced which has viewed academic and other writing on the region as, variously, eurocentric, imperialist, racist, essentialist, and so forth. On the other hand, a range of writers on the region, most notably Bernard Lewis, have rebutted Said's charge and argued for an approach which falls, to a greater or lesser extent, into the 'orientalist' category.[10]

Said's critique, beyond identifying a body of literature as 'orientalist', seeks to relate it to theories of discourse and power, especially through the work of Michel Foucault. Within this approach, orientalism is a discourse of domination, both a product of European subjugation of the Middle East, and an instrument in this process. Its constituent ideas can be explained by this origin and instrumentality, one that denies the culture and history of the subjugated peoples, and which ignores the process of resistance they have generated in response to this domination. The ideas of orientalism are functional to this project of domination, or imperialism. If Said is especially insistent on the distortions imposed upon his own people, the Palestinians, he develops a broader critique of writing on the Middle East, and indeed on the whole of the Third World, derived from this critical, Foucauldian perspective.[11]

Assessment: 'discourse' analysis and its limits

This debate has now raged for nearly twenty years, has generated plenty of words and heat and is by no means burnt out, not least as a result of intellectual developments since the mid-1970s. If the 'orientalists' would appear to have received support from the rise of traditionalist and fundamentalist movements in the region – most notably in the form of the Iranian revolution – which advocate belief in the existence of an all-encompassing, determinant and unchanging Islam that is very similar to their own, the Saidians have been reinforced by the growth, within the academy, of post-modernism with its analyses of discourse and subjectivity. Said's critique has received support from a new generation of scholars influenced by historical materialism and social and economic history, and with a more flexible attitude to discourse, time and religion in the Middle East. This latter body of scholars have rather different theoretical starting points to Said, but share a common distance from more established 'orientalist' approaches.[12]

As may already be apparent, my own position is one that falls into neither the pro-Said nor the pro-Lewis camp. This is partly for personal reasons: Said has been a friend, a man of exemplary intellectual and political courage; Lewis was a teacher at the School of Oriental and African Studies when I was a student there – I learnt a great deal from him, and amidst his writings there is much that I have benefited from and respect. But there are two other, more general reasons, why I decline to align with either side in this debate. One is the specific reason that to a considerable degree *both* fail us in what I have defined as the central intellectual task, namely the analysis of the societies in question. Lewis has avoided writing substantively on Middle Eastern societies after *The Emergence of Modern Turkey* in 1961, and even that was curiously flawed by its failure in regard to economics.[13] Said has focused on discourses *about* the region, not the societies or politics themselves.[14] The other is that on methodological grounds Lewis and Said are both open to criticism, and indeed in some respects are remarkably similar: each gives primacy to what can be termed (within different theoretical frameworks) ideology, discourse or political culture. If the orientalists do so by ascribing a causal primacy to language, attitude and religious dogma, the post-modernists do so by locating their critique and their construction of an alternative at the same discursive level. For neither of them does the analysis of what actually happens in these societies, as distinct from what people say and write about them, let alone the difficulties and choices of emancipatory projects, come first. I can therefore share neither the methodological assumptions and misleading polarization, nor the quite unnecessary personal bitterness, that has characterized the public debate on this matter.

An element of distance is all the more advisable because, on closer examination, this debate involves at least four different questions, only two of which need concern us here. One is a debate about how to evaluate writing on the Middle East and how to write about the societies in question. The second issue, which is by no means particular to the Middle East, is that of methodology in social analysis, and more specifically the rivalry between two philosophies of knowledge – a traditional linguistically and culturally based approach derived from classical studies, versus a critical approach to writing and discourse derived from post-modernism and, in Said's case, from a certain reading of Foucault in particular.[15] There is absolutely no reason why this second, in itself quite valid, issue should be debated with particular regard to the Middle East. More general questions are at stake, and not least because in this case, as indicated, there is much common ground between the two camps of the 'orientalism' debate. The third issue which has come to suffuse the whole debate is the Arab–Israeli question, with accusations of ethnic origin and political bias, phantasms about Zionist conspiracy on the one hand, and Arab nationalist 'rage' on the other. Both 'Zionists' and their opponents seem to think that having a position in this conflict offers analytic and indeed ethical advantages, something which, for reasons already stated, I would deny. *Neither Zion nor Palestine conveys any epistemological or moral privilege.* Finally, there has been a sharp dose of ill-tempered academic disputation and intolerance of a kind that is not specific to the USA and its academic and intellectual culture, but which is especially present there. We can see this in debates on issues such as the Cold War, Armenian–Turkish relations, the role of gender and race in social science: the same rancour has suffused and confused the debate on orientalism. What I would hope to do here is to place the latter two of these issues on one side, and to try to focus on and disentangle the first two, namely the question of analysing the Middle East and the implicit contrast of epistemologies.

Components of 'orientalism'

Before proceeding to Said's critique, it may be pertinent briefly to summarize some of the central tenets of the body of writing categorized as 'orientalist'.[16] The term will be used here in a broad sense as far as the social sciences are concerned, but will exclude the other – literary, travel-writing, artistic – variants encompassed by Said. 'Orientalism' can be characterized as an approach to the Middle East and specifically to the Arab world which is based on several broad premises. The first is that the study of the region requires, and can to a considerable extent be organized through, a consideration of its languages and writings. This is of course a mainstay of classical studies on Greece and Rome, and was applied to much of the Middle East in a derivative manner. It would appear that some such idea lies behind the use of the word 'Arabist', a term I take to mean that if someone has got as far as to learn Arabic, then this effort must, almost on its own, qualify him or her to make sensible statements about Arab society and politics, or even to understand something called 'the Arab mind'. Related to this is an argument, worked through by a range of commentators, that regards the study of language as a path to the study of political and social ideas. Examining the root or original meanings of words is seen as a means of arriving at an understanding of what they meant to Middle Eastern peoples and of the different meanings ascribed to words in the Islamic and Western contexts.

The second and perhaps most important element in this approach is, however, the issue of the Islamic religion or, as it is widely rendered, 'Islam'. Islam, defined by its classical texts and traditions, is assumed to be not merely a phenomenon pervading most aspects of life in the Middle East but an independent variable, an explanatory factor. Thus there is the sociology of Islam, the world of Islam, the Islamic city, Islam and madness, Islam and sexuality, Islam and capitalism and much else besides. (There is no entry in the *Encyclopedia of Islam* on Islam and alcohol, but perhaps there should be, given the importance which it has always held, and continues to hold, in the life of Muslim peoples.) [17] The appropriate volumes are entitled the *Cambridge History of Islam*, the appropriate reference book the *Encyclopedia of Islam*. Many other issues are explained by reference to what is presented as the Islamic tradition or 'Islamic society': the lack of an entrepreneurial class, the frailty of democracy, the hostility to Israel, the insecurity of boundaries, the apparent rejection of modernization, the irrationality, cruelty, even terrorism, characteristic of Middle East politics are all related to an atemporal 'Islam' or, failing that, to 'the Arab mind'.

This enduring effectivity of something called Islam is said to have one further implication. The third mainstay of the orientalist position focuses on the supposed difficulty or even impossibility of change, particularly change in a direction that is liberal and secular, following what might be referred to in broad terms as the rational democracies of the West. Those who imagine they see progress are dismissed as idealists, or fools, and the timeless recurrence of Islamic practice and belief is seen to explain why no such processes endure. Gibb's remark that social scientists, in applying their concepts to the Middle East, take an approach similar to that of Walt Disney, epitomizes this view. Like a cartoon, all is timeless, stagnant or, if Ibn Khaldun is invoked, circular. Indeed, the function of learning Middle Eastern languages is to be able to lift a curtain and so view the mysterious but unchanged world behind.

I have identified here three broad themes – language, religion, and historical change respectively – which do pervade much of the scholarly writing in the West on the Middle East. It has been argued by many, Lewis included, that this idea of an orientalist body of literature is itself a polemical fiction, a straw man invented by Said and others. There are reasons, several indeed, for questioning Said's analysis, but I would argue that a reading of much of the literature on the history, society and politics of the region will yield evidence that such ideas do occur and recur in the analysis and the language of many writers. And nowhere more so than in the works, in some other respects valuable, of Lewis himself. Thus his *The Political Language of Islam*,[18] a brilliant and learned survey of terminology in Persian, Turkish and Arabic over several centuries, remains in the end unsatisfying. It has, as its underlying premise, the claim that the original meanings of words have shaped subsequent meaning and usage, and that, within Islamic countries, or as he repeatedly and significantly calls them, 'the lands of Islam',[19] the religious origins of words determine political thinking to a special degree. What we have is a single, all-encompassing, and apparently enduring totality. Thus, beyond asserting etymological determination, Lewis goes on to imply that the members of all Islamic countries must be treated as one. In one case, he moves from arguing that Islamic *states* cooperate internationally to making statements about 'Islamic *peoples*', as if what holds for rulers holds for the ruled, and as if what occurs in one country can be stretched to include others.[20] The very title of the book to some degree begs the questions, how far *is* a political vocabulary derived from religion, how far *can* there be one timeless set of meanings? We have disquisitions on those words that suit the argument – *siyasa* (politics), *zulm* (oppression), *ulema* ('knowledgable men' of religion), *dawla* (state), etc. But other words at least as common in the twentieth-century vocabulary of what Lewis would call 'Islamic' peoples are omitted: *wahda* (unity), *hizb* (party), *harakat* (movement), *jabha* (front), *monadhama* (organization), *mantiqa* (region), *tabaqa* (class), *fillahin* (peasants), *ummal* (workers), not to mention *ihtilal* (occupation), *ta'dhib* (torture), *mokhabarat* (intelligence services), *muba'din* (deportees) and so forth. It is significant too that a whole category of words with important political and normative implications are not discussed, since they would seem to undermine the idea of a continuous or specific Islamic discourse: *Misr* (Egypt), *Iraq, Filastin* (Palestine), *Yaman* (Yemen), *al-Jaza'ir* (Algeria), even Kuwait, are simply not mentioned. It is indeed striking that I can think of no so-called Islamic state that has an Islamic name, except for the qualifying word for the Islamic Republic of Iran. This is in some contrast to the neighbours of the Islamic world which have at times had names of religious redolence – Holy Roman Empire, Bharat,[21] Zion or Eretz Israel to name but three.

A second example of the assumptions in Lewis's work is an article, as ever lucid and learned, in the *New York Review of Books*,[22] a review of Stephen Humphreys' *Islamic History: A Framework for Enquiry*. Lewis's article is a study of the ways some Islamic writers have treated history, and begins with what one can only say is a striking example of the orientalist approach: 'For Muslims,' we are told, 'history is important.' This is explained as meaning that the presentation of history plays an important role in the Muslims' view of the world. But, without doubting Lewis's claim, we can suggest two other things. First, his argument is *not* that history matters for Muslims, but that history in the sense of an accurate assessment of the past does not actually matter for them. But, secondly, if Lewis is arguing that for Muslims history is about the production and maintenance of a legitimizing set of historical myths, then Muslims are hardly unique. The same could surely be said of the Irish, the Serbs, the Hindus, the Boers, the Americans, the Japanese, and indeed almost anyone. What appears as a specific, defining, characteristic turns out to be something shared with many others. The Middle East is not so particular.[23]

The delusions of etymology

There has been much distortion in the debate on this question, but I believe we are not being unfair in identifying and criticizing the issues at the core of the orientalist position, namely language, religion and history. No one can dispute that a study of these societies involves a close and constantly invigilated knowledge of the languages they speak, and in this sense the classical approach is correct. But there are two things that do not follow from this. One is the practice of what I can only term etymological reductionism, the attempt to explain politics in terms of the meaning of words and, even worse, to explain the meaning of words in today's discourse by reference to their classical roots.[24] This is an absurdity, one well criticized by Antonio Gramsci, who showed how because we use the word disaster, literally an evil star, we are not necessarily subscribing to ideas of astrology, any more than if we use the word economics we are invoking some allusion to housework. Many people invoke the names of Jesus Christ, and of his Mother, without necessarily holding to the appropriate belief: indeed while the language, political and other, of modern English is replete with words that have a Christian origin, it is an open question whether, and how far, and for what audiences, any such theological resonance remains.[25] It is not really possible to make generalizations about Islamic usage because, apart from anything, words mean different things in different tongues. *Inqilab* means revolution in Persian, coup d'état in Arabic, and in Turkish it can mean reform. One of the great joys of studying Arabic is to open Wehr's dictionary and to see how *far* words have travelled from their original meaning. The word for economics, *iqtisad*, derives from the same root as the word *qasida* a poem. Are we to assume that poetry is a branch of economics, or the other way around? And if we take the root *qasada*, meaning to be thrifty, can we explain a supposedly 'Islamic' economic behaviour in terms of a thriftiness characterizing all Muslims? The last thing one could say about the economics of the Middle East today is that it is characterized by a high savings ratio. And what are we to make of words derived from the root *sharaka*? Does it mean a capitalist company, *sharika*, or a socialist as in *ishtirakiya*, or a polytheist as in *shirk*? Is the word *wafd*, delegation, really religious because Muhammad received the *wufud* of tribes?[26]

Very often, as we know, false etymology is used for political purposes. To offer just two banal examples: the Turk who says all people in the world are descended from Turks because the Turkish for man is *adam*; the Iranian who shouts 'death to the CIA', *marg bar siah* – making 'CIA' sound like the Persian word for 'black'. A particularly interesting example of this, already alluded to in chapter 2, came up at the time of the revolution when Khomeini began to use the word *taghut* to denounce his enemies – the Shah, and then Carter, Bani-Sadr and Saddam Hussein. In the Arab world and elsewhere, people were quick to identify this as a word derived from the word *taghiya*, meaning to be a tyrant; even Bernard Lewis advanced this view.[27] In fact it has a different origin, a word for idol, of the kind the prophets smashed, the equivalent of the Persian *bot*. Khomeini as the *bot-shekan* smashed several of these – the Shah, Carter, Bani-Sadr, and he hoped Saddam. Etymology, like genealogy, can become a servant of present concerns, not a determinant of transhistorical meanings.

The other fallacy of the linguistic approach, epitomized in the very word 'Arabist', is that knowledge of the language somehow qualifies one to know something or know a single truth about a society. An ability to parse Homer does not give one a knowledge of Ionian land tenure, or gender relations, and the same must go for Arabic. The most cursory reflection will show this – after all, all native speakers by definition know the language, but this does not mean they make sensible, rational or accurate statements about their own societies. To tie this cult of language to ideas of the Arab or Islamic mind, or to the essence of the 'Muslim' and his society, represents a flight from serious social analysis. Here again the opposites meet or converge, for it is the conceit of post-modernism – and a conceit which Said at times reproduces – that literature and its methods can serve as a means, even a privileged means, of social analysis.

The functions of 'Islam'

As discussed in previous chapters, the issue of 'Islam' as an independent variable and explanatory category is equally open to debate. Here, as we have seen, the orientalist and the Islamist go hand in hand, each stressing the essential, determinant character of the Islamic religion. Khomeini is as much of an orientalist in this sense as any German or British imperialist scholar. So too is King Fahd in saying that Muslim peoples do not want or need Western democratic principles: they prefer *shura*, *majlis*, *ijma* (consultation, tribal council, consensus) and so forth.[28] The claim that Islam has this determinant role receives greater weight from the fact that Islam claims jurisdiction over a wider range of social activity than other, comparable, religions, particularly Christianity in the Western form that most writers on the region are familiar with. This is summed up in the saying *al-Islam dinun wa daulatun* – Islam is a religion and a state.[29] But here again some distance may be necessary. The fact that proponents of the religion claim something is no reason whatsoever to accept it, any more than one accepts the statements of a nationalist. The whole proposition of an unchanging and determinant dogma that is the enduring premise of so much orientalist literature is in any comparative perspective absurd. Apart from falsifying the variety of interpretations, and legitimating power in the name of one interpretation, it has two debatable implications.

The first is that this essentialist rendering of 'Islam' leads to endless attempts to resolve issues by means of *tafsir* or interpretation, asking the bogus question of what 'true' Islam is. We have often seen this applied to the position and dress of women, or to frontiers. In the 1960s and 1970s there was discussion of what the 'true' Islamic political system was, or ought to be, with a rivalry of quotes from the Quran and the *Hadith* about capitalism and socialism. Socialists recited the phrase *al-nas shuraka fi thalath: al mai wa al kala wa al nar* ('the people share three things: water, grass, fire'), the capitalists replying with the saying, *man yakhudh baitaka aqtalhu* ('whoever takes your house, kill him').[30] Even more important is the false premise in this essentialism that we can assume a continuity of belief and meaning, an inertia over centuries. Here the words of Barrington-Moore in his *Social Origins of Dictatorship and Democracy* may be relevant:

> Culture or tradition is not something that exists outside of or independently of individual human beings living together in society. Cultural values do not descend from heaven to influence the course of history. To explain behaviour in terms of cultural values is to engage in circular reasoning. The assumption of inertia, that cultural and social continuity do not require explanation, obliterates the fact that both have to be recreated anew in each generation, often with great pain and suffering. To maintain and transmit a value system, human beings are punched, bullied, sent to jail, thrown into concentration camps,

cajoled, bribed, made into heroes, encouraged to read newspapers, stood up against a wall and shot, and sometimes even taught sociology. To speak of cultural inertia is to overlook the concrete interests and privileges that are served by indoctrination, education, and the entire complicated process of transmitting culture from one generation to the next.[31]

Those who have lived under the control of Khomeini, Turabi, Hikmatyar and their ilk will need little guidance on this matter.

Two other considerations arise in this regard. First, we can observe the contingency and variety of Islamic beliefs, and their reliance on other and identifiable factors such as states, classes, ethnic groups and so forth which use and interpret Islamic dogma for their own purposes. Second, we cannot take 'Islam' as a given. We need to come up with an explanation of *why* this idiom continues to prevail in these societies, beyond invoking the fact of the religion itself. What needs explaining is the very continuity of social forms and beliefs. Here, of course, the opponents of Islam come up with a set of arguments to show how effective Islam is: the intrusive and oppressive character of states in Islamic countries; the intolerance of dissent, pluralism, secularism and non-Muslims; and the lack of democracy; to which one can add, the spread of Islamic fundamentalism.

That essentialist explanations have a certain coherence and explanatory force no one can deny: but it would seem rather implausible that these are the only explanations and that only an invocation of Islam can tell us what is going on. Indeed, many of the phenomena identified as specifically Islamic are not unique to the Islamic world: dictatorial states, tribal regimes, fragile democracies, intolerance of minorities or of dissent are hardly the prerogative of *dar al-islam*. The same goes for religious fundamentalism: the conditions, organizational principles and rhetoric of the Islamic fundamentalists have much in common with other such movements among Christians, Jews and Hindus.

To return to the four examples of popular upheavals and political change in the Middle East mentioned at the beginning of this chapter, it would seem clear that an invocation of Islam explains very little about what has happened in any of these countries, even when political actors choose to adopt such a vocabulary.[32] I would also doubt whether Islam would tell us much about the

1990–91 war over Kuwait, or about Saddam's decision-making in
that crisis. Even more dubious is the way in which by entering
this world we may be drawn to accepting the validity of Islamist
conceptual claims: *iqtisad-i tauhidi*, or 'unitary economics', much
touted at the time of the Iranian revolution, is one example, as is
the claim that Khomeini's pronouncements on *The Satanic Verses*
constitute in the proper juridical sense a *fatwa*.[33]

Said's critique

If these are problems within 'orientalism', there are also a range
of questions which Said's main book fails to resolve. Said may not
be responsible for the use others have made of his text, but four
issues in particular permit of disagreement.

In the first place, the term 'orientalism' itself is contestable: we
should be cautious about any critique which identifies such a
widespread and pervasive *single* error at the core of a range of
literature. In philosophic terms, such an approach can be termed
the search for the expressive totality or, in more mundane
language, the root of all evil. Over the last twenty years we have
been offered many variants of this in the form of economism,
humanism, eclecticism, historicism, empiricism and so on. More
recently we have seen eurocentrism, ethnocentrism and
foundationism used as root causes. 'Orientalism' while it can be
used in a precise way, as I have tried to do above, may be open
to such a promiscuous application. Orientalism in Said's usage
acquires an almost metaphysical power to pervade very different
epochs and genres of expression; in so doing it loses analytic or
explanatory purchase.

Secondly, the category of the 'orient' is rather vague, since in
Orientalism its usage implies that the Middle East is in some ways
special, at least in the kind of imperialist or oppressive writing
produced about it. Racist or oppressive writing is found about all
subject peoples, whether they are Islamic or not, and there is
nothing to choose between them. The claim of a special European
animosity towards Arabs, let alone towards Palestinians or Muslims,
does not bear historical comparison. Such ideas of persecution rest
on some implicit yardstick, a comparative 'massacrology' in which

the wrongs done to one people are deemed greater. Such an approach is best avoided, but it may be pointed out that the fate of the native people of the Americas, whose conquest was also presented as a crusade, was far worse than that of the peoples of 'Islam'. Equally spurious is the suggestion that the hypostatization and reification of the Middle East are specific, whether such a claim is made by those writing from outside or from within. Anyone familiar with the writing on Japan entitled *Nihonjiron* and books such as Ruth Benedict's *The Chrysanthemum and the Sword* will have encountered similar themes – the special place of language studies, the search for the unchanging national character, the stress on the specificities of the Japanese mind, the search for the true 'Japanese' position on women, or on the emperor, or on flower arrangement, or whatever.[34] Russia too has had its own share of such ahistorical analysis.[35] Discussion of another 'oriental' country, China, too often lapses into this vein, with spuriously profound inferences from Mandarin ideograms or invocations of the particular wisdom of Chinese thinkers: the sayings of the latter, be they Confucius or Mao Tse-tung, usually turn out on examination to be examples of universal thinking, wise in some cases, banal or authoritarian in others. Here again external authority and internal nationalist collude to create a timeless, and particularist, discourse. Indeed, can we identify a people about whom it has not been said that 'They are like that', 'They will never change', etc.? Many people in the Middle East believe that in some way they have been singled out by the West, but in its historic or contemporary form this is an unsustainable idea. The thesis of some enduring, transhistorical hostility to the orient, the Arabs, the Islamic world, is a myth, albeit one as already indicated which many in the region and in the West find it convenient to sustain.

A third difficulty with Said's approach is the methodological assumption it makes about the relation between the genesis of ideas and their validity. Said implies that because ideas are produced in a context of domination, or directly in the service of domination, they are therefore invalid. Analogous ideas are to be found in much contemporary debate about ethnocentric and euro-centric ideas in the social sciences and elsewhere. Since Said's book was written, this theme has acquired much greater diffu-sion through cultural nationalism, post-modernism and so on. In the Middle East it can be found in the writings of Islamic writers such as Khomeini, ever calling on people to be 'alert' (*bidar*) against this corruption of Western ideas, and in the writings of many nationalist intellectuals, ranging from Anouar Abdel-Malek in Egypt to Jalal Al-i Ahmad in Iran, with his concept of Westoxification or *gharbzadegi*. Such assumptions about the genesis of ideas and their validity are, to say the least, debatable if taken not simply in the context of the Middle East or of nationalist assertion, but in the academic context of the sociology of knowledge. If I have my disagreements with the epistemological assumptions underlying the approach of Lewis and his fellow writers on 'Islam', I am equally at odds with the epistemological assumptions of Said and the post-modernists. One can do worse than look again at Karl Mannheim's discussion of this in his *Ideology and Utopia*.[36] There are many difficulties with Mannheim's work, not least his view of the free-floating intellectual, but his discussion of the relation between genesis and validity is very pertinent here. As he points out, removing some of the polemic from Marx's discussion of ideology, the fact that a particular discovery or idea was produced by a particular interest group, or context-bound individual, tells us nothing about its validity. Medicine, aeronautics or good food may be produced in such contexts of time, place, culture: they are not therefore to be rejected. The same, with appropriate variations, can apply to social science. Of course, the majority of social science ideas in the world today come from Western Europe and the US and were produced in the context of imperialism and capitalism: it would be odd if this were not so. But this tells us little about their validity. The terms 'eurocentric' and 'ethnocentric', at present far too easily bandied about, confuse a statement on historical origin with a covert assessment that needs justification in its own terms. And in one very important sense eurocentrism is a valid starting-point: the economic, social and political system that prevails in the modern world, with all its variations, including those of the Far East, *is* a European product and was spread through the combination of economic, military and political pressure known as imperialism. As Karl Marx and Bill Warren alike would have pointed out, Europe has created a world after its own image, whether we like it or not.[37]

The implications of this issue of origin for the debate on orientalism should be clear. First, much critique of Western writing on the Middle East makes the assumption that the mere fact that some ideas are produced by exploiters renders their content invalid. But elementary reflection would suggest that, apart from any possible independence or autonomy of the investigator, the very fact of trying to subjugate a country would to some degree involve producing an accurate picture of it. If you want to dominate a country, you need to know where its mines and oases are, to have a good map, to be aware of its ethnic and linguistic composition and so forth. The experts who came with Napoleon to Egypt in 1798 were part of an imperial project, but the knowledge they produced, whatever its motives, financing and use, had objective value. The same can be said, *pari passu*, about much later writing on the region. To put it bluntly: if you plan to rob a bank, you would be well advised to have a pretty accurate blueprint of its layout, know what the routines and administrative practices of its employees are, and, preferably, have some idea of who you can suborn from within the organization.

This brings me to another point where, perhaps because of professional bias, Said would seem to engage in an injudicious elision, namely in his treatment of texts produced within the social sciences and in related activities such as journalism or travel writing, and literature. Of course there are similarities and mutual influences: but while one is a necessarily fictional activity, without controls in reality or direct links to the acts of administration, domination, exploitation, the former is so controlled. To assume that the same critique of discourses within literature can be made of those within social science is questionable; it may indeed reflect the hubris, rather too diffuse at the moment, of theorists deriving their validation from cultural studies.

This brings me to the fourth, and final, area of difficulty with the critique of orientalism, namely its analysis, or rather absence thereof, of the ideas and ideologies of the Middle East itself. Said himself has, in his other writings, been a trenchant critic of the myths of the Middle East and of its politicians, and nowhere more so than in his critique of the poverty of the intellectual life of the Arab world. While the rulers have constructed numerous international airports, he once pointed out, they have failed to construct a single good library. But the absence of such a critique in his *Orientalism* does allow for a more incautious silence, since it prevents us from addressing how the issues discussed by the orientalists and the relations between East and West are presented in the region itself. Here it is not a question of making any moral equivalence between the myths of the dominators and the myths of the dominated, but of recognizing two other things: first, that when it comes to hypostasis, stereotyping, the projection of time-less and antagonistic myths, these are in no sense the prerogative of the dominator, but are also open to the dominated; and, second, that if we analyse the state of the discourse on the contemporary Middle East, then the contribution of these ideologies of the dominated has been and remains enormous, not least because those outside the region who try to overcome the myths of the orient rather too quickly end up colluding with, or accepting, the myths of the dominated within the region.[38] One of the most cogent critiques of Said, made with this in mind, was that of Sadik al-'Azm, published a decade ago in *Khamsin*.[39] If there is a condition such as *gharbzadegi* (Westoxification), there is also one which I would call *sharqzadegi* (Eastoxification), the uncritical reproduction of myths about the region in the name of anti-imperialism, solidarity, understanding, and so on. Here, of course, the myth-makers of the region see their chance, since they can impose their own stereotypes by taking advantage of confusion within their own countries and without.

No one familiar with the political rhetoric of the region will need much convincing of this tendency to hypostatization from below: a few hours in the library with the Middle Eastern section of the *Summary of World Broadcasts* will do wonders for anyone who thinks reification and discursive interpellation are the prerogative of Western writers on the region. The uses made of the term 'the West', to denote one single, rational, antagonistic force, the rantings of Islamists about *jahiliyya*, the invalidation of ideas and culture because they are, or are supposed to be, from the West, the uncritical but often arbitrary imposition of controls and customs that are supposed to be genuinely from the region, an expression of some *turath* (roots) or other, the railings against Zionists, Persians, kafirs, traitors, and so on, with which Middle Eastern political leaders happily puncture their speeches, without

apparent qualm or contradiction, or awareness that they themselves are promoting prejudice – all confirm this point. Of course,
this hypostatization is most evident in the discussion of the idea
of 'Islam' itself, for no one is more insistent on the unitary, determinant, timeless, and, in his version, orthodox interpretation of
Islam than the fundamentalist. Equally, while brave and critical
souls in the West have tried to break the usage of the term
'Muslim' as a denotation of an ethnic or cultural identity, whether
in its British or French colonial usages, the reifiers of the region
are keen to re-establish this link. In this they are joined by communal politicians in Western Europe who purport to treat all
'Muslims' as one social, cultural or even ethnic group.

Conclusion: studying the Middle East

The argument so far would suggest that the debate on orientalism
has revealed some interesting issues in the study of the region and
in the construction of academic knowledge in general, but may be
of limited use in addressing what I began by suggesting was the
main issue confronting us, namely how to analyse Middle Eastern
societies, contemporary or historical. Both camps, the orientalists
and their critics, have shied a long way away from this task,
focusing more on discourse than on the analysis of reality.

This would lead me to say that in approaching the analysis of
the Middle East the element of particularism, uniqueness or im-
penetrability has been greatly overrated. Let me mention four
issues on the analyses of the contemporary Middle East familiar
to us all: the structure of states, the prevalence of conspiracy theory
in political culture, the role of the Islamic religion, the difficulties
in establishing and sustaining democracy. It is easy to construct
analyses of each of these that locate themselves in the influence of
Islam, the workings of the 'Arab' or 'Persian' mind, or the
particular havoc wrought in the region by imperialism. But other,
less particularistic, explanations are also possible, starting from
the obvious enough point that many of the phenomena analysed
in this way are seen elsewhere in the world. The Middle East is
not unique in the incidence of dictatorships, or of states created
by colonialism, or of conspiracy theories. Every nation thinks its

own conspiracy theories are greater and more inventive than those of others, but a comparative survey would suggest this may not be so. While I would certainly, if pushed, give the gold medal to the Persians, one can find some fine examples in Latin America, in China, in Greece, not to mention the USA. It would moreover be possible to provide explanations of conspiracy theory in terms of historical and material, as well as purely cultural, features of the countries in question. If we turn to the question of the dictatorial state, and its impact not just on opposition political activity, but on economic activity independent of the state, there is no doubt that this has been an enduring feature of many Middle East states, and that, for dictators and for analysts alike, the cause has been found in those aspects of Islamic tradition that allow the state to exert such power. But this is to beg the question, since, as is equally well known, other interpretations of Islam are possible and in some countries – Turkey is an obvious example – a flourishing private sector and a degree of opposition politics exist. Any analysis of the contemporary Middle East has to confront the enduring power of dictatorship, in many cases enhanced by the flow of oil revenues to the state: there are clear, and in some cases, specific obstacles there. But it is doubtful how far a hypostatized Islam can explain this.[40]

The Middle East is not unique, except possibly in the content of the myths that are propagated about it, from within and without. The political, economic, social, cultural activities of the peoples of this region have their peculiarities and differences, as much between each other as in terms of one Middle East contrasted with the outside world. Material concerns, jokes, the pleasures of good food, and the horrors of political oppression, are theirs as much as of any other peoples in the world. The development of social science in general will never be completed, and each specific issue, or country, or incident, poses questions for it. But we are no more precluded by our concepts from understanding the Middle East, and no more limited in our ideas, whatever their origins, than in addressing any other area of the world. In normative terms, we have perhaps allowed the discussion to be too inflected by relativism and doubt as to the validity of universal standards, in the face of a mistaken, and often self-interested, critique of imperialism and Western norms. Perhaps I could sum this up by adapting a slogan: *na gharbzadegi, na sharqzadegi*, neither Westoxification nor Eastoxification. Let us therefore go beyond this unnecessarily polarized and in some ways methodologically impoverished debate and continue with the job of studying these societies. I have warned against the perils of *tafsir*, but I will end with the words from the Quran that can be easily and I hope not too arbitrarily interpreted to justify this enterprise, *wa ja'alnakum shu'uban wa qaba'ilan li'ta'arifu*: 'And I have created peoples and tribes so that they could get to know each other.'[41] That could be the motto for our, necessarily unfinished, and unfinishable, endeavour.

Notes

Introduction

1. *Arabia without Sultans* (Harmondsworth: Penguin, 1974), *Iran; Dictatorship and Development* (Harmondsworth: Penguin, 1978); with Maxine Molyneux, *The Ethiopian Revolution* (London: Verso, 1982); *Revolution and Foreign Policy. The Case of South Yemen, 1967–1987* (Cambridge: Cambridge University Press, 1990); *Arabs in Exile, Yemeni Communities in Urban Britain* (London: I.B.Tauris, 1992).

2. Samuel Huntington, 'The Clash of Civilizations?', *Foreign Affairs*, summer 1993.

3. Raymond Williams, *Keywords* (London: Fontana/Croom Helm, 1976), pp. 48–50.

Chapter 1

1. The war in Korea (1950–54) cost between 2 and 4 million lives, those in Vietnam (1945–75) upwards of 4 million. The most costly Middle Eastern wars were that of Algeria (1954–62), in which an estimated 1 million people died, and the Iran–Iraq war (1980–88), in which around three-quarters of a million people are believed to have died. The human toll of the Arab–Israeli conflict as a whole, from 1948 onwards, and including Israeli attacks on Lebanon, is believed to be between 100,000 and 200,000. The best account of casualties to the mid-1970s is Trevor Dupuy, *Elusive Victory: the Arab Israeli Wars, 1947–1974* (London: Macdonald and Jane's, 1978).

2. See chapter 7 for the discussion of this phenomenon in Edward Said's *Orientalism*.

3. See the case of the writer Kanan Makiya, whose criticisms in his *Cruelty and Silence* (London: Jonathan Cape, 1993) of the Ba'thist regime and of a widespread collusion with it among Arab intellectuals, provoked a torrent of abuse from within the Arab world, and from apologetic circles without.

4. Isaac Deutscher, 'The Arab–Israeli War: June 1967', in *The Non-Jewish Jew, and other essays*, edited with an introduction by Tamara Deutscher (London:

Oxford University Press, 1968); Maxime Rodinson, *Israel and the Arabs* (London: Penguin, second edn 1982).

5. The term 'Middle East', first used in 1902, has no precise definition, in that its boundaries are flexible from one usage to the other. In this analysis I use it to cover Iran, Turkey, Israel and 17 of the members of the Arab League including some from North Africa (Morocco, Algeria, Tunisia, Libya, Sudan, Egypt, Syria, Lebanon, Jordan, Iraq, Kuwait, Bahrain, Qatar, the United Arab Emirates, Oman, Yemen, and Saudi Arabia). The Arab League has five other members, four of whom are not strictly speaking Arab states, i.e. states in which the majority of the population speak Arabic, but which for reasons of political convenience have joined the League (Mauritania, Jibuti, Somalia, Comoro Islands), while a fifth member represents an Arab people but does not yet have a state (the Palestine Liberation Organization).

6. For good background studies, see David Gilmour, *Lebanon: The Fractured Country* (Oxford: Martin Robertson, 1983), and Helena Cobban, *The Making of Modern Lebanon* (London: Hutchinson, 1985).

7. For greater detail on the question of the origins of the war, see Fred Halliday, 'The Iranian Revolution and International Relations: Programme and Practice', *Millennium*, spring 1981.

8. For two studies that do seek to escape the polarities of internal and external, see Fawaz Gerges, *The Superpowers and the Middle East, Regional and International Politics, 1955–1967* (Boulder: Westview Press, 1994), and Simon Bromley, *Rethinking Middle East Politics: State Formation and Development* (Cambridge: Polity Press, 1994). The former argues for a contingent relationship of international and regional in assessing the foreign policies of regional states, the latter challenges any simplistic reduction of the history of state formation to external 'imperialist' or internal 'Islamic' factors.

9. See E. H. Carr, *The Bolshevik Revolution* (London: Macmillan, 1952), vol. 3, for a survey of early Bolshevik policy in the region.

10. George Antonius, *The Arab Awakening* (London: Hamish Hamilton, 1938), provides the standard Arab nationalist account of this period.

11. See Fred Halliday, 'Revolution in Iran: Was it Possible in 1921?', *Khamsin*, no. 7 (1980).

12. From the large literature on this subject, see Maxime Rodinson, *Israel and the Arabs*, Pamela Ann Smith, *Palestine and the Palestinians: 1876–1983* (London: Croom Helm, 1984), and, for an alternative account, Walter Laqueur, *A History of Zionism* (London: Weidenfeld and Nicolson, 1972).

13. For a British liberal history of this relationship, see Christopher Sykes, *Cross-Roads to Israel* (London/Bloomington: Indiana University Press, 1965).

14. See Maxime Rodinson, 'Arab Views of the Arab–Israeli Conflict', in *Cult, Ghetto and State* (London: Al Saqi Books, 1983).

15. For background on the individual states of the region see Peter Mansfield, *The Middle East, A Political and Economic Survey*, 5th edn (London: Oxford University Press, 1980).

16. On the social effects of the conflict, see Pamela Ann Smith, *Palestine and the Palestinians*.

17. Alistair Horne, *A Savage War of Peace* (Harmondsworth: Penguin, 1978).
18. See Fred Halliday, *Arabia without Sultans* (Harmondsworth: Penguin, 1974), for a history of the nationalist revolution in South Yemen.
19. Ibid.
20. Britain and the USSR had jointly occupied Iran in 1941, as part of their anti-Nazi alliance, and in the course of this occupation autonomous Kurdish and Azerbaijani Turkish republics were established in the Soviet zone. The USSR did finally withdraw its forces in March 1946, leaving its Iranian allies to face the repression of the Shah's forces.
21. See the excellent collection from *Khamsin* journal, edited by Jon Rothschild, *Forbidden Agendas: Intolerance and Deviance in the Middle East* (London: Al Saqi Books, 1984), and Beth Barron and Nikki Keddie (ed.), *Women in Middle Eastern History: Shifting Boundaries in Sex and Gender* (New Haven, Ct.: Yale University Press, 1992).
22. On state formation, see especially Bromley, *Rethinking Middle East Politics*, and Roger Owen, *State, Power and Politics in the Making of the Modern Middle East* (London: Routledge, 1992).
23. The best analysis of the revolution is given in Ervand Abrahamian, *Iran Between Two Revolutions* (Princeton: Princeton University Press, 1982).
24. This argument on the social contingency of Khomeini's movement is well developed in Sami Zubaida, *Islam, the People and the State* (London: Routledge, 1989), and Ervand Abrahamian, *Khomeinism* (London: I.B. Tauris, 1993).
25. That Israel has colonial origins and retains a colonial relationship with the Palestinians does not entail, as most Arab nationalism purports, that therefore the Israelis have no right to their own state. As Rodinson among others has clearly shown, the Israelis now constitute a distinct nationality, with the right to their own state: but this does not legitimate the denial of Palestinian statehood. Dozens of nations have colonial origins.
26. Roger Owen, 'Arab Nationalism, Arab Unity and Arab Solidarity', in Talal Asad and Roger Owen (ed.), *The Middle East* (London: Macmillan, 1983).
27. Khalid Khistainy, *Arab Political Humour* (London: Quartet, 1983).
28. Hossein Mahdavy, 'Patterns and Problems of Economic Development in Rentier States: the Case of Iran', in M. A. Cook (ed.), *Studies in the Economic History of the Middle East* (London: Oxford University Press, 1970).
29. For good historical and ethical discussion, see Conor Gearty, *Terrorism* (London: Faber and Faber, 1991), and Walter Laqueur, *Terrorism* (London: Weidenfeld and Nicolson, 1977).
30. See Asad and Owen, *The Middle East*, for discussion of these dimensions.
31. The Arab world has retained a greater number of monarchies than any other region of the world. As of 1995, eight of the 22 Arab League rulers were still monarchs.
32. Thomas Naff, 'Hazards to Middle East Stability in the 1990s: Economics, Population, and Water', in William Lewis and Phebe Marr (ed.), *Riding the Tiger, The Middle East Challenge After the Cold War* (Oxford: Westview Press, 1993).

Chapter 2

1. Karl Griewank, *Der neuzeitliche Revolutionsbegriff* (Weimar: Herman Böhlaus Nachfolger, 1955), ch. 1.

2. Author's conversation with Abol-Hasan Bani-Sadr, Auvers-sur-Oise, France, August 1981.

3. Thus Radio Ahvaz, broadcasting in Arabic on 1 September 1980: 'This awaiting universal Islamic state will demolish all tyrannical thrones built on the corpses of the oppressed. The sword of justice will claim all charlatans, agents, and traitors.' See my 'Iranian Foreign Policy Since 1979: Internationalism and Nationalism in the Islamic Revolution', in Juan Cole and Nikki Keddie (ed.), *Shi'ism and Social Protest* (London: Yale University Press, 1986).

4. One exception is the nineteenth-century Shi'ite writer Mullah Ahmad Naraqi, an exponent of the *Usuli* school, which did emphasize the powers of juridical authorities in Islam. But Naraqi did not extend this to include full political power, as Khomeini was later to do (Said Amir Arjomand, 'The State and Khomeini's Islamic Order', *Iranian Studies*, vol. XIII, nos 1–4 (1980), p. 154). What is striking is that Khomeini does not invoke the precedent of those conservative writers who opposed the secular constitution of 1906. Indeed, while he exhibited an initial tolerance of the 1906 Constitution, he seems later to have regarded the whole period of the Constitutional Revolution as an embarrassment.

5. This point has been well made by Mohammad Ja'far and Azar Tabari, 'Iran: and the Struggle for Socialism', *Khamsin*, no. 8, 1981.

6. Sami Zubaida, *Islam, the People and the State* (London: Routledge, 1989).

7. Ervand Abrahamian, *Iran Between Two Revolutions* (Princeton: Princeton University Press, 1982), pp. 530–7.

8. For a guide to the earlier role of the clergy in Iran, see Nikki Keddie, *Iran: Religion, Politics and Society* (London: Frank Cass, 1980), and her *Religion and Rebellion in Iran: The Iranian Tobacco Protest of 1891–92* (London: Frank Cass, 1966). Strictly speaking Islam does not have a clergy in the sense of an ordained body of men, but in this text I have used the term 'clergy' interchangeably with the word *ulema*, literally 'those who know', the standard Arabic Muslim term, and the word *mullah*, the word normally applied to Shi'ite clergy in Iran. Iranians themselves tend not to use the word *mullah*, but to talk of the *akhund*, a slightly derogatory term for an ordinary clergyman, or of the *ruhaniyat*, the body of religious personnel. Higher-ranking clerics are called *mujtahids*, meaning that they have the authority of *ijtihad*, independent judgement on holy matters, whilst the highest ranking are called *ayatollah*, literally 'sign of God'. For a general discussion of Iranian terms for the clergy, see Roy Mottahedeh, *The Mantle of the Prophet* (London: Chatto & Windus, 1986), pp. 231–2. Given the absence of any established hierarchy, the designation *ayatollah* is a result of promotion and reputation within the Islamic institutions. Prior to the revolution it was a term confined to a small number of clergymen, of whom Khomeini was neither the senior nor the most learned. The term *Imam*, applied to Khomeini, represents a verbal inflation, but is an honorary title

and, at least officially, does not indicate any claim to his being one of the line of Twelve Imams who the Shi'ites believe are the true followers of Mohammad.

9. The Iranian revolution has generated a widespread analytic literature. See, *inter alia*, Nikki Keddie, *Iran and the Muslim World, Resistance and Revolution* (London: Macmillan, 1995); Farideh Farhi, *States and Urban-based Revolutions* (Urbana: University of Illinois Press, 1990); Mohsen Milani, *Iran's Islamic Revolution: From Monarchy to Islamic Republic* (Boulder, Colorado: Westview Press, 1988); Mansoor Moaddel, *Class, Politics and Ideology in the Iranian Revolution* (Oxford: Columbia University Press, 1993); Misagh Parsa, *Social Origins of the Iranian Revolution* (New Brunswick: Rutgers University Press, 1989).

10. We do not yet have the detailed information necessary to establish who were 'the faces in the crowd' that made the Iranian revolution, that is, a precise evaluation of the social forces behind the revolution. While it appears, from the very size and superficial appearance of the demonstrators, that members of all social groups participated, it is much less clear what the proportions were. Some initial indications are given in Farhad Kazemi, *Poverty and Revolution in Iran* (London: New York University Press, 1980). He suggests that it was second-generation migrant industrial workers, not the poorest inhabitants of shanty towns, who participated most in the revolutionary protests. The poorest sections were still outside the social networks that would have drawn them into the demonstrations of late 1978. For an important, earlier study of this issue, see Ervand Abrahamian, 'The Crowd in Iranian Politics, 1905–53', in Haleh Afshar (ed.), *Iran: A Revolution in Turmoil* (London: Macmillan, 1985).

11. The demonstrations in the last months of the Shah's regime, involving up to 2 million people in Tehran, and several million more in provincial towns, were the largest protest demonstrations in human history. States have mobilized larger numbers in supportive marches – as in China's Tien An Men Square – but such crowds have never before been seen in an oppositional context.

12. The terms 'modern' and 'traditional' have been subject to considerable criticism. Their use here does not denote acceptance of a more general picture of social development as being conceivable in terms of a unilinear progression from one to the other. They are used here in a more figurative sense, to distinguish characteristics of Iranian society associated with its past from those resulting from the changes of the last decade.

13. No full account of the revolution has yet been written, but surveys are included in Abrahamian, and in Nikki Keddie, *Roots of Revolution* (London: Yale University Press, 1981). Also of interest are Robert Graham, *Iran: the Illusion of Power*, second edn (London: Croom Helm, 1979), Mohammed Heikal, *The Return of the Ayatollah* (London: André Deutsch, 1981), and L. P. Elwell-Sutton, 'The Iranian Revolution: Triumph or Tragedy', in Hossein Amirsadeghi (ed.), *The Security of the Persian Gulf* (London: Croom Helm, 1981). The best eyewitness account is Paul Balta and Claudine Rulleau, *L'Iran Insurgé* (Paris: Sindbad, 1979). On post-revolutionary developments the outstanding study is Shaul Bakhash, *The Reign of the Ayatollahs* (London: I.B. Tauris, 1984).

Bakhtiar's own account is given in his *Ma Fidelité* (Paris: Albin Michel, 1982). See also my interview with him in *MERIP Reports*, no. 104, March–April 1982.

14. Robert Graham provides invaluable analysis of many aspects of the economic change; see also my *Iran: Dictatorship and Development* (London: Penguin, 1979), and the references contained therein. On rural conditions, see Eric Hooglund, *Land and Revolution in Iran, 1960–1980* (Austin: University of Texas, 1982). A general economic overview is given by M. H. Pesaran, 'Economic Development and Revolutionary Upheavals in Iran', in Haleh Afshar (ed.), *Iran: A Revolution in Turmoil*.

15. The merchants of the Tehran bazaar were particularly incensed in 1976 when the municipal authorities proposed to build a new urban highway that would have passed through the middle of the bazaar area.

16. American Ambassador William Sullivan complained bitterly of the Shah's indecisiveness, a characteristic foreign observers had noted during the crisis of the early 1950s. Roger Cooper, a British journalist who met the Shah in September 1978, reported that the monarch flatly refused to believe there were any slums in Tehran, a fact evident to the most casual observer. Some pertinent observations are given in Fereydoun Hoveida, *The Fall of the Shah* (London: Weidenfeld & Nicolson, 1980).

17. The army chief-of-staff, General Qarabaghi, was allowed to retire to his home and later went into exile. More mysterious was General Fardust, the former chief of the Shah's private intelligence service, who reportedly became head of SAVAMA, a new state security organization.

18. Theda Skocpol, *States and Social Revolutions* (Cambridge: Cambridge University Press, 1979), pp. 14–18. Skocpol's own reflections on the Iranian revolution are in 'Rentier State and Shi'a Islam in the Iranian Revolution' in *Theory and Society*, May 1982, reprinted in Theda Skocpol (ed.), *Social Revolutions in the Modern World* (Cambridge: Cambridge University Press, 1994). She points to the sociological weakness of rentier states and the mobilizing potential of Shi'a Islam as special factors enabling the Iranian revolution.

19. Ibrahim Yazdi, Foreign Minister of the Islamic Republic, in interview with the author, Tehran, August 1979.

20. An important comparative perspective on the 1979 revolution is given by the Mosaddeq period, when secular nationalism and a mass communist movement predominated: see Richard Cottam, *Nationalism in Iran* (Pittsburgh: University of Pittsburgh Press, 1964). The clergy at that time gave some support to Mosaddeq, but turned against him in 1952 and did not oppose the 1953 coup. Khomeini never mentioned Mosaddeq's name in a positive light and argued that his fall was a result of his abandoning Islam.

21. For discussion of this issue see Said Amir Arjomand, 'Shi'ite Islam and Revolution in Iran', *Government and Opposition*, vol. 16, no. 3 (summer 1981), Edward Mortimer, *Faith and Power* (London: Faber, 1982), ch. 9, and Hamid Algar, 'The Oppositional Role of the Ulema in Twentieth Century Iran', in Nikki Keddie (ed.), *Scholars, Saints and Sufis* (Berkeley: University of California Press, 1972). Also indispensable is the work of Akhavi, cited in n. 23 below.

22. Muslim radicals find confirmation in certain verses of the Quran which

are supposed to reinforce their orientation: for example, 'We willed that those who are being oppressed would become the leaders and the rightful inheritors of the world' (sura 28, verse 5); and other verses promising a speedy punishment for those who oppress. Khomeini's word for 'oppression', *zulm*, is the conventional Islamic word for tyranny.

23. An extremely shrewd and careful discussion of these points is contained in Shahrough Akhavi, *Religion and Politics in Contemporary Iran* (Albany, NY: State University of New York, 1980). Akhavi demonstrates the contingency of Islamic thought and hence the availability of a wide range of equally valid 'interpretations'. On Islam as a state religion under the Safavids, see I.B. Petrushevsky, *Islam in Iran* (London: Athlone Press, 1985), ch. 13.

24. A careful study of the organization and curricula of the Qom *madrases* in the mid-1970s is given by Michael Fischer in *Iran: From Religious Dispute to Revolution* (Cambridge, Mass.: Harvard University Press, 1980).

25. Akhavi, *Religion and Politics*, pp. 126–7. He quotes one reforming *mullah* who denounced *avam zadigi*, the effects of mass mindlessness, and said it was better to be affected by 'floods, earthquakes, snakes, and scorpions' than to be subject to the will of the masses on matters of reform.

26. Some of the theorists of Islamic revolution have developed a concept of a just or unitary society, based on the Islamic concept of *touhid*, or unity of God and man. These writers include the lay theoretician Ali Shariati and former President Abol-Hasan Bani-Sadr. But it does not seem that Khomeini ever accepted this concept, and he laid much greater stress on the need to implement the rules of Islamic jurisprudence.

27. In the post-revolutionary period Khomeini was officially described by three titles: Imam, Leader of the Revolution, and Founder of the Islamic Republic. These three sources of his legitimacy represented religious authority, the aura of success, and the programme he sought to implement. His frequent designation as 'Imam of the Islamic Nation', where 'nation' is a translation of the word *umma*, illustrates the ambiguous character of the constituency he was meant to represent: Iran or a wider Islamic world?

28. Khomeini's main writings are contained in *Islam and Revolution*, translated and annotated by Hamid Algar (Berkeley: Mizan Press, 1981).

29. The charge of being a *mofsid fi'l arz* ('spreader of corruption on earth') is one common charge in such cases. The other is that of being *mohareb be khoda* ('declaring war on God'). If concepts of legitimacy are essential in mobilizing populist coalitions, so too are concepts of denying legitimacy to the other side. Khomeini's favourite term for the Shah was *taghut*, a term usually derived from an Arabic root meaning to tyrannize. In fact, *taghut* has a different root, meaning idol or a false god. In later terminology Khomeini was referred to as the *bot shekan*, the 'Idol Smasher', with the Shah as the first idol to be broken, Carter the second, Bani-Sadr the third, and, it was hoped, Iraqi leader Saddam Hussein the fourth. *Bot* is a Persian language equivalent of *taghut*. His use of other sources is well illustrated by another term of abuse: *kravati* (someone who wears a tie).

30. In particular, the writer Al-i Ahmad, whose work *Gharbzadegi* ('intoxica-

tion with the West') was very popular among university students in the 1970s. Although the son of a *mullah*, Al-i Ahmad himself was rather anti-clerical in his writings. For an account of his ideas, see Mottahedeh, *The Mantle of the Prophet*, pp. 287–315.

31. On Ali Shariati see Fischer, *Iran*, Keddie, *Roots of Revolution*, and Mangol Bayat-Phillip, 'Shiism in Contemporary Iranian Politics: The Case of Ali Shariati', in Elie Kedourie and Sylvia Haim (ed.), *Towards a Modern Iran* (London: Frank Cass, 1980). Shariati too was quite anti-clerical, and is regarded by most religious authorities as an unlettered upstart. His writings fall into the mainstream of Third World cultural and nationalist writings of the 1970s. He died in London in 1977. See his *On the Sociology of Islam* (Berkeley: Mizan Press, 1979).

32. One exceptional element in Khomeini's populism was his use of irate paternalism, as he threatens to chastise and punish his followers. This is of course partly a note of Quranic punitiveness which will be familiar to his audience, but contrasts with the rhetoric of other secular populists. In a speech in August 1979 he declared: 'When we broke down the corrupt regime and destroyed this very corrupt dam; had we acted in a revolutionary manner from the beginning, had we closed down this hired press, these corrupt magazines, these corrupt parties and punished their leaders, had we erected scaffoldings for the hanging in all the major squares, and had we chopped off all the corrupters and the corrupted, we would not have had these troubles today.' But he goes on: 'I beg forgiveness from almighty God and my dear people.'

33. See Keddie, *Religion and Rebellion*, pp. 27–8, where the Muslim reformer Malkam Khan discusses how to justify modern principles in Quranic terms.

34. Skocpol, *State and Social Revolution*, pp. 19–24, outlines a theory of the international dimension of revolutions on which I have drawn here.

35. For the earlier decades of the century see the classic E. Brown, *The Persian Revolution* (London, 1909; reprinted London: Frank Cass, 1966); for the early 1950s see Kermit Roosevelt, *Countercoup* (New York: McGraw Hill, 1979), a vivid account of the American and British roles in preparing the 1953 coup that reinstalled the Shah.

36. Hossein Mahdavy, 'Patterns and Problems of Economic Development in Rentier States: the Case of Iran', in M. A. Cook (ed.), *Studies in the Economic History of the Middle East* (London: Oxford University Press, 1970), and Homa Katouzian, *The Political Economy of Modern Iran, 1926–1979* (London: Macmillan, 1981).

37. Skocpol stresses the growing autonomy of the state as another central feature of the revolutions she describes. While in my view she overstates the disassociation of ruling class and state apparatus, she none the less indicates a feature of revolutionary situations which contributes to explaining why, at a particular time, an existing state is overthrown. See n. 18 for her application of this thesis to Iran.

38. According to his post-revolution memoirs, the Shah ignored the growing crisis in his country and focused uniquely on the role of the US mission to

Iran in the last days of his reign: Mohammad Reza Pahlavi, *The Shah's Story* (London: Michael Joseph, 1980).

39. William Sullivan argues that some accommodation with Khomeini might have been possible in early 1979, but that this was excluded by an unrealistic 'hard line' being pursued by Brzezinski, the President's National Security Adviser, in 'Dateline Iran: the Road Not Taken', *Foreign Policy*, Washington, no. 40 (Fall 1980), and his *Mission to Iran* (New York: Norton, 1981). The best accounts of US–Iranian relations are in Barry Rubin, *Paved with Good Intentions: The American Experience in Iran* (New York: Oxford University Press, 1980), and Gary Sick, *All Fall Down, America's Tragic Encounter with Iran* (London: I.B. Tauris, 1985). See also my discussion of variant US accounts in *MERIP Reports*, no. 140, May–June 1986.

40. Text of Khomeini's letter to Khamene'i in *BBC Summary of World Broadcasts* part 4, 8 January 1988. For analysis see: J. Reissner, 'Der Imam und die Verfassung', *Orient*, 29, 2, June 1988. Khomeini's theorization of how an Islamic state can, for reasons of state interest, override religious precepts has an ironic relevance to the Rushdie affair: Iranian and other defenders of the death sentence on Rushdie claim that Khomeini's condemnation of Rushdie to death cannot be overridden because it is necessitated by religious principle. Application of Khomeini's *maslahat* principle would suggest that, if Iranian political leaders thought it was in their interests to do so, they could cancel the death sentence. That they do not do so is not because of some religious compulsion but because, within the politics of the Islamic world, it is still profitable for them to maintain their stance.

41. On Iranian foreign policy since 1979 and the place within it of Islamic themes, see my 'Iranian Foreign Policy Since 1979' in J. Cole and N. Keddie (ed.).

42. The concept of *zuhd* or austerity, often associated with forms of mysticism, was important in Khomeini's rhetoric and welded conveniently with the anti-consumerism of Third World populist and revolutionary ideology. In some ways Khomeini's use of anti-imperialist *zuhd* was analogous to the usage of the concept by the Imam of Yemen who in the 1950s declared that Yemen would prefer to be poor and independent than rich and dependent. How far the Iranian, or Yemeni, people were committed to such austerity was, and is, another matter.

43. On the broader politics of the *Satanic Verses* affair, see ch. 4, pp. 125–27 below. In addition to any general religious concerns, the Iranian authorities may have taken offence at the novel's account of the Imam in exile in London, all too recognizable as a fictional portrayal of Khomeini's stay in Paris in late 1978 and early 1979 prior to his return to Tehran. 'The curtains, thick golden velvet, are kept shut all day, because otherwise the evil thing might creep into the apartment: foreignness, Abroad, the alien nation. The harsh fact that he is here and not There, upon which all his thoughts are fixed … In exile no food is ever cooked: the dark-spectacled bodyguards go out for take-away. In exile all attempts to put down roots look like treason; they are admissions of defeat.' – Salman Rushdie, *The Satanic Verses* (London: Viking, 1988), pp. 206, 208.

44. On later developments, see Anoushiravan Ehteshami, *After Khomeini: the Iranian Second Republic* (London: Routledge, 1994). Some have queried the validity of the term 'second republic' on the grounds that it overstates the discontinuity between the Khomeini and post-Khomeini periods; but the case for using the term is certainly defensible, given the important constitutional changes that followed Khomeini's death with the formation of a presidential system.

45. In a speech on the tenth anniversary of the revolution Chief Justice Musavi-Ardebili listed eleven achievements of the revolution: in addition to fostering revolution and Islamizing laws, these included Iran's independence, improving conditions in the villages, safeguarding the national economy, developing self-reliance in industry, promoting agricultural production ('Iranian Chief Justice outlines Islamic Revolution's Achievements since 1979', *BBC Summary of World Broadcasts*, ME/0075/A/4-6, 15 February 1988).

Chapter 3

1. The analysis presented here, originally given as an E. H. Carr memorial lecture at the University of Aberystwyth in 1993, draws on a wide range of discussions held during and after the Gulf war, both in the UK and in the USA. I am particularly grateful to the participants in the one-day seminar 'The Gulf War and International Relations' held at the International Relations Department of the LSE on 16 June 1992: Faleh Abd al-Jaber, Michael Donelan, Lawrence Freedman, Efraim Karsh, Christopher Hill, Ken Matthews, Michael Rustin, Steve Smith, Paul Taylor. Several publications by them are referred to in subsequent notes.

2. Amongst the multitude of books on the crisis, the following are amongst the most informative and judicious: Lawrence Freedman and Efraim Karsh, *The Gulf Conflict 1990–1991, Diplomacy and War in the New World Order* (London: Faber and Faber, 1993); Ken Matthews, *The Gulf Conflict and International Relations* (London: Routledge, 1993); John Bulloch and Harvey Morris, *The Origins of the Kuwait Conflict and the International Response* (London: Faber and Faber, 1991). Freedman and Karsh are especially good on Western decision-making, Matthews on the analytic implications for IR. My own, initial, analysis is given in 'The Crisis of the Arab World – the False Answers of Saddam Hussein', *New Left Review*, November–December 1990, no. 184, reprinted in Mica Sifry and Christopher Cerf (ed.), *The Gulf War Reader* (New York: Random House, 1991), and in 'The Gulf War and its Aftermath: First Reflections', *International Affairs*, April 1991.

3. On the calculations and miscalculations of the Kuwaiti royal family, see my interview with opposition leader Ahmad al-Khatib, *The Guardian*, 19 January 1991, and the report on later investigations by the Kuwaiti parliament into the matter, 'Kuwait's MPs turn on rulers who failed them', *The Guardian*, 5 May 1995.

4. Post-1945 history has several instances of states being annexed by more

powerful neighbours, but *at the moment at which they became independent*: Palestine, partitioned by Israel and Jordan in 1948–49, Western Sahara and East Timor in 1975, Bosnia in 1992. Tibet in 1949–50 was a possible further candidate in that one can assume it would have organized itself to acquire international diplomatic recognition, following the British departure from India in 1947, if a little more time had elapsed.

5. Thus the conflicts in Afghanistan, Angola, Mozambique and Cyprus all defied such international resolution.

6. For representative views, see Sifry and Cerf (ed.), *The Gulf War Reader*; John Gittings (ed.), *Beyond the Gulf War, The Middle East and the New World Order* (London: Catholic Institute of International Relations, 1991); Victoria Brittain (ed.), *The Gulf Between US* (London: Virago, 1991); Haim Bresheeth and Nira Yuval-Davis (ed.), *The Gulf War and the New World Order* (London: Zed Books, 1991). Among the most cogent critics of the war was Noam Chomsky, whose analysis is in both the Sifry and Cerf and Bresheeth and Yuval-Davis volumes.

7. On the Islamic dimension, see James Piscatori (ed.), *Islamic Fundamentalism and the Gulf Crisis* (Chicago: Chicago University Press, 1991); Gilles Kepel, 'La carte islamique de Saddam Hussein', *Le Monde*, 11 January 1991; Jean-Michel Dumay, 'La "guerre sainte" comme arme idéologique', *Le Monde* 20–21 January 1991; Fred Halliday, 'The Fractured umma: Islamist Movements, Social Upheaval and the Gulf War', *The Oxford International Review*, summer 1991; George Joffe, 'Middle Eastern views of the Gulf conflict and its aftermath', *Review of International Studies*, vol. 19, no. 2, April 1993. For a position opposed to Saddam Hussein from within an Islamic perspective, see Ghazi Algosaibi, *The Gulf Crisis, An Attempt to Understand* (London: Kegan Paul International, 1993).

8. On the Islamic opposition to Saddam, see Hanna Batatu, 'Shi'i Organisation in Iraq: al-Da'wah al-Islamiyah and al-Mujahidin', in Juan Cole and Nikki Keddie (ed.), *Shi'ism and Social Protest* (New Haven: Yale University Press, 1986).

9. Bassam Tibi, *Conflict and War in the Middle East, 1967–91* (London: Macmillan, 1993), p. 165.

10. Roger Hardy, *Arabia after the Storm: Internal Stability of the Gulf Arab States* (London: Royal Institute of International Affairs, 1992); Mary Ann Tetrault, 'Kuwait: The Morning After', *Current History*, no. 91, January 1992; Fred Halliday, 'The Arabian Peninsula in the Aftermath of the Gulf War', *Viertelsjahresberichte* (Friedrich Ebert Stiftung, Bonn), no. 133, September 1993.

11. On postwar arms flows to the area, see Saferworld Foundation (Bristol, UK), *The Middle East Peace Process and the Arms Trade: A Fatal Contradiction?*, August 1992; and Yahya Sadowski, 'Scuds vs. Butter: The Political Economy of Arms Control in the Arab World', *Middle East Report*, 177, vol. 22, no. 4, July/August 1992.

12. Transcript of the April Glaspie interview in Sifry and Cerf, pp. 122–33. The mixed signals contained in this interview lie at the heart of several critiques of US policy, notably that by Pierre Salinger and Eric Laurent, *Secret Dossier, The Hidden Agenda Behind the Gulf War* (London: Penguin, 1991).

13. We have no first-hand evidence, written or oral, on Saddam's decision-making, and a final judgement would have to wait until any such material were made available, an unlikely eventuality. For a perceptive surmise about Saddam's impulsiveness in invading Iran, see al-Khalil, *Republic of Fear*, pp. 271–2.

14. On Ba'thist ideology, and the role of the Syrian nationalist Satia' al-Husri in transmitting European fascist and nationalist ideas to the Arab world, see al-Khalil, *Republic of Fear*, and the biographical work *Saddam Hussein: A Political Biography* by Efraim Karsh and Inari Rautsi (London: Brassey's, 1991). A comparable case of the neglect of the ideological dimension of a Middle Eastern leader, with regard to Khomeini and his view of politics and international affairs, was the lack of any commentary throughout his life on the importance of Persian mysticism, or *irfan*, in his outlook. Yet the terminology, nuances and self-image of Khomeini are incomprehensible without reference to this. See the biography of Khomeini by Baqer Moin (London: I.B. Tauris, forthcoming).

15. One indication of this shift in Iraqi thinking after June 1989 comes from the information on arms purchases revealed by the Matrix-Churchill affair: a year of relatively slack demand after the 1988 ceasefire gave way to a much more determined pace of arms procurement in the last part of 1989 and early 1990.

16. Within a year of the end of the war Iraq had, in addition to legal exports of 75,000 barrels per day to Jordan, been able to organize a smuggling trade with its neighbours, including the export, in road tankers, of up to 250,000 barrels of oil a day, especially to Turkey and Iran. Total income from these exports was in the region of $1 billion, compared to export earnings of $15–20 billion before the war. While greatly reduced, these earnings nonetheless provided the regime with some revenue (*International Herald Tribune* 16 February 1995).

17. A further argument against the war was that of some Americans who said it was not in the USA's 'national interest' to go to war. Whatever its domestic merits, this paid scant attention to the international issues involved. For one, remarkably silly, example see Stephen Graubard, *Mr Bush's War* (London: I.B. Tauris, 1992).

18. For the battle of Guru, in which 600–700 Tibetans died, out of a total force of 1,500, with only some minor wounds on the British side, see Peter Fleming, *Bayonets to Lhasa* (London: Rupert Hart-Davis, 1961), ch. 11, and the eye-witness account of the *Daily Mail* correspondent with the expedition, Edmund Candler, *The Unveiling of Lhasa* (London: Edward Arnold, 1905), ch. 6. In the run-up to the engagement Candler writes: 'I doubt if ever an advance was more welcome to waiting troops than that which led to the engagement at Hot Springs. For months, let it be remembered, we had been marking time' (p. 101).

19. On revised figures for Iraq casualties, see *The Independent*, 5 February 1992, and John Heidenrich, 'The Gulf War: How Many Iraqis Died?', *Foreign Policy*, no. 90, spring 1993. At the time of the war both US and Iraqi officials

lent credence to the idea of higher casualties, for opposed political reasons – the former to intimidate Iraq, the latter to emphasize the perfidy of US action.

20. 'The Gulf war revisited: Armchair generalship', *The Economist*, 2 May 1992. On the broader assessment of US military capabilities and the dated character of the 'hi-tech' war, I am particularly grateful to Kevin Michaels, MSc student at LSE, 1990–91. As Michaels pointed out, the balance of civilian to military technology has shifted dramatically over the past decades: the latest technology is not now that of the military, but in the civilian field – available in any high-street personal computer shop.

21. 308 Scuds hit Iran in that conflict, as against 72 used in the Gulf war, the former causing the deaths of over two thousand people. See Farhang Rajaee, ed., *The Iran-Iraq War: The Politics of Aggression* (Gainsville: Florida University Press, 1993).

22. Part of the problem was the confusion between launchers and the larger number of missiles. *The Military Balance 1989–1990* gave the number of *launchers* as 36 Scud B with a, presumably smaller, number of the Abbas and Husayn variety. It later transpired that Iraq had 890 Scud *missiles* (*International Herald Tribune*, 26 March 1993). For an overall assessment, see House of Representatives Committee on Armed Services, Subcommittee on Oversight and Investigations, *Intelligence Successes and Failures in Operations Desert Shield/Storm*, 103 Cong. 1 Sess, August 1993.

23. On the arms control regime, see Rod Barton, 'Eliminating Strategic Weapons: the Case of Iraq', *Pacific Review*, August 1993.

24. See Ken Matthews, *The Gulf Conflict*, for further discussion.

25. Personal communication from a foreign minister of an Arab state who visited Iraq on several occasions during the crisis.

26. The issue of whether the allies did nonetheless try to kill Saddam by hitting a bunker in which he was present is unclear, but intuition would suggest they did. For one version of such attempts, using a specially designed new 5,000-pound bomb, see U.S. News, *Triumph without Victory* (New York: Random House, 1992), pp. 3–6.

27. Or, in an extreme case, South African sanctions against land-locked Lesotho in 1986: a week after the sanctions were imposed, a coup removed the offending government in Maseru. Similarly, in 1993 Russia cut off energy to Lithuania, Estonia and Ukraine and quickly obtained policy concessions.

28. Kenneth Waltz, *Man, the State and War: A Theoretical Analysis* (New York: Columbia University Press, 1959).

29. Martin Wight, *International Theory, The Three Traditions*, ed. Gabrielle Wight and Brian Porter (London: Leicester University Press, 1991), p. xv.

30. For further discussion, see my *Rethinking International Relations* (London: Macmillan, 1994, forthcoming), ch. 1–4.

31. See, on this, my 'An Encounter With Fukuyama', *New Left Review*, no. 193, May–June 1992, and *Rethinking International Relations*, ch. 3 and 10.

32. Occasionally framed in terms of the popular, anti-imperialist, character of Ba'thism, and the social 'gains' it had achieved, this progressivist or stagist argument was more commonly found in an alternative form in refer-

ences to the 'feudal', 'semi-feudal', 'backward' 'tribal' regimes of Kuwait and its associates. What these latter terms meant, however, was that on some unspoken scale of historical advance and moral probity, Iraq was somehow more 'advanced'. A variant was contained in the phrase 'oil-rich Kuwaitis', as if having a per capita income of, say, $12,000 forfeited one's right to self-determination.

33. Bill Warren, *Imperialism Pioneer of Capitalism* (London: Verso, 1981).

34. It is here that the analyses of Noam Chomsky, relevant in some other respects, are questionable.

35. On the liaison between discussion of the war and post-modernism, see Christopher Norris, *Uncritical Theory: Postmodernism, Intellectuals and the Gulf War* (London: Lawrence and Wishart, 1992). For an example of German 'critical theory' turned to anti-war usage, in the finest prose of the Frankfurt School, see Helmut Thielen (ed.), *Der Krieg der Köpfe, Vom Golfkrieg zur neuen Weltordnung* (Bad Honnef: Horleman, 1991).

36. Cynthia Enloe, 'The Gulf Crisis: Making Feminist Sense of It', *Pacific Research*. On alternative invocations of women's role, 'Saddam Husayn Awards Medals to Women: Says Their Role More Important Than Men's', *BBC Summary of World Broadcasts*, part 4, 7 March 1992.

37. Among the more nuanced examinations of the ethical issues involved, see Michael Walzer, preface to the second edition of *Just and Unjust Wars* (New York: Basic Books, 1992), and Ken Matthews, *The Gulf Conflict and International Relations*, ch. 5–7, who are broadly in support of the war, and the articles by Michael Rustin and Gregory Elliott in *Radical Philosophy*, no. 61, summer 1992, who elaborate cases against. For a more one-sided defence of the war, in traditional Catholic terms, see James Sturner Johnson and George Weigel, *Just War and the Gulf War* (Washington: Ethics and Public Policy Center, 1991); for comparable critiques, see materials in Sifry and Cerf (ed.), *The Gulf War Reader*; Gittings (ed.), *Beyond the Gulf War*; Brittain (ed.), *The Gulf Between us*; and Bresheeth and Yuval-Davis (ed.), *The Gulf War and the New World Order*.

38. Peter Gowan, 'The Gulf War, Iraq and Western Liberalism', *New Left Review*, no. 187, May–June 1991, contains a powerful argument against the primacy of sovereignty and the application of this to the Kuwait crisis. For a defence of the 'legalist paradigm' on state sovereignty, but one that permits opposition to this particular war, see Michael Rustin, 'Justice and the Gulf War'.

39. See the excellent study by Richard Schofield, *The Kuwait-Iraq Boundary Dispute* (London: Chatham House Papers, 1992).

40. Kuwait was neither a liberal democracy nor a sanguinary dictatorship. One of the best descriptions is, perhaps surprisingly, that of Mohammad Heikal in *Illusions of Triumph* (London: HarperCollins, 1992), where he remarks: 'Despite their drift towards authoritarianism, the al-Sabahs were not oppressive and in some ways their rule was fairly enlightened, spreading wealth more evenly than most countries and allowing more self-expression than might be expected.' (p. 148).

41. It was argued by some critics of the war that any assessment of the

popular response to the Iraqi invasion should include the non-Kuwaiti population as well. That the Kuwaiti regime discriminated against non-Kuwaitis is
indisputable, but this is not the same as asserting a general political equivalence of all those within a country at a particular moment: no society in the
world would accept that. Certainly Iraq did not, with its brutal treatment of
tens of thousands of its own citizens accused of Persian connections and expelled in the early 1980s, and of Egyptian migrant labourers. Iraq's claim to
be liberating the non-Kuwaitis may have won support amongst a minority of
Palestinians, but their treatment of non-Arab immigrants was swift and brutal,
resulting in the expulsion, soon after the invasion, of hundreds of thousands
of Asian workers.

42. Michael Walzer, *Just and Unjust Wars*, ch. 6.

43. For general discussion of this issue, see Rosalyn Higgins, 'Intervention
and International Law', in Hedley Bull (ed.), *Intervention in World Politics*
(Oxford: Clarendon Press, 1984); Adam Roberts, 'Humanitarian War: Military
Intervention and Human Rights', *International Affairs*, vol. 69, no. 3, 1993.

44. Kanan Makiya, *Cruelty and Silence* (London: Jonathan Cape, 1993), and
Middle East Watch, *Human Rights in Iraq* (New Haven: Yale University Press,
1990).

45. Paul Taylor and A.J.R. Groom, *The United Nations and the Gulf War 1990-
91: Back to the Future?* (London: Royal Institute of International Affairs,
1992).

46. For a classic discussion of the complexity underlying any claim of
causation and intention in law, see H. L. A. Hart and A. M. Honore, *Causation
in the Law* (Oxford: OUP, 1959).

47. See Walzer, preface to second edition of *Just and Unjust Wars* (p. xix):
'But mixed motives are normal also in international politics, and they are
morally troubling in wartime only if they make for the expansion or prolon-
gation of the fighting beyond its justifiable limits or if they distort the conduct
of the war'. If anything, the less savoury motives of George Bush led him to
curtail the war and unwarrantedly narrow its aims.

48. It is on this issue that my disagreement with Michael Rustin turns. Of
course, the motives of Bush included many unsavoury ones, but this fact alone
does not preclude a *jus ad bellum*.

49. In all discussion of consequences, the issue of time is important: if, ten
years later, Saddam and his regime were to be ousted, and a democratic and
peaceful regime established in Iraq, then the war would look rather more
acceptable. But these are not judgements we can make now, so we have to
base our assessment on what has already happened.

50. Adam Roberts, 'The Gulf War and the Environment', *The Oxford International Review*, vol. 4, no. 3, summer 1993.

51. On the mutilation of enemy dead by US forces in Vietnam, see Michael
Herr, *Despatches* (London: Picador, 1979), p.161. On the starving to death of
over 700,000 German POWs after World War Two, see James Bacque, *Other
Losses* (Toronto: Stoddart Publishing, 1990).

52. There are two uncertainties surrounding the spillage of oil from tankers

and pumping stations. First, it is not clear that all of this was a result of deliberate Iraqi action – some may have been the result of allied bombing and/or artillery attacks. Second, media coverage was designed to play up the consequences of the slick, implying, wrongly as it turned out, that it would go beyond Bahrain and permanently destroy the Gulf's fish stock. See Joni Seager, 'Operation Desert Disaster: Environmental Costs of the War', in Bresheeth and Yuval-Davis (ed.), pp. 235–6.

53. During the Indochina war an estimated 11 million gallons of the defoliant Agent Orange were dumped on South Vietnam, affecting 2 million hectares of forest. 170,000 hectares were also turned into craters. See Peter Korn, 'Agent Orange in Vietnam: The Persisting Poison', *The Nation*, 8 April 1991.

54. On this, see Matthews, p. 166, and Jackson, p. 349.

55. On the insurrection, see the articles by Faleh Abd al-Jaber and Isam al-Khafaji in *Middle East Report*, no. 176, May–June 1992, and Kanan Makiya, *Cruelty and Silence*.

56. Public discussion of the war often appeared to invoke a third dimension of morality, what may be termed *jus in nuntio*, i.e. the obligation to present facts fully, fairly and accurately and to avoid derogatory, racist or misleading images of the enemy. A barrage of criticism during and after the war rested upon the charge that allied governments, and the media, had engaged in various forms of propaganda and news control. See, for example, Douglas Kellner, *The Persian Gulf TV War* (Oxford: Westview Press, 1992), and John Fialka, *Hotel Warriors, Covering the Gulf War* (Washington: Woodrow Wilson Press Centre Press, 1992). Post-modernism extended this to identification of hegemonist and other obnoxious discourses *vis-à-vis* Iraq. All this may have been true, but it was beside the point: first, because such disortion is an inevitable accompaniment of war and can hardly be adduced as a factor in evaluating its legitimacy; second, because if the allies violated *jus in nuntio* the Iraqis certainly did so as well.

Chapter 4

1. There are some problems with applying the term 'fundamentalist' to Muslim movements, but with necessary caveats it can legitimately be so used. Nikki Keddie has argued that the term 'Islamist' is probably the most accurate, distinguishing Islamic religious belief from 'movements to increase Islam's role in society and politics, usually with the goal of an Islamic state' – 'The Islamist Movement in Tunisia', *Maghreb Review*, vol. 11, no. 1, 1986, pp. 26–39. The argument often made, by both Islamists and their opponents, that the term 'fundamentalism' cannot be applied to Muslims since they are all, by definition, fundamentalists is silly: fourteen hundred years of Islamic history, and the variety of interpretations of the religion existing in the world today, show that a strict application of one set of classical doctrines to political and social life is not common to all Muslims.

2. The Islamic saying *la hudud wa la sudud*, 'no barriers and no boundaries', is often adduced to make this point.

3. 'Khomeini's message to Gorbachev', *BBC Summary of World Broadcasts*, ME/0354/A/4–6, 10 January 1989.

4. See ch. 1, pp. 35–6.

5. I have gone into this in greater detail in my *Rethinking International Relations* (London: Macmillan, 1994), ch. 8.

6. These consist of the five *arkan* or pillars (the profession of the one God, prayer, pilgrimage, alms, fasting).

7. For comparative analyses, see Martin Marty and Scott Appleby (ed.), *Fundamentalisms and the State* (Chicago: University of Chicago Press, 1993); Gilles Kepel, *The Revenge of God. The Resurgence of Islam, Christianity and Judaism in the Modern World* (Cambridge: Polity Press, 1994) and Hava Lazarus-Yafeh, 'Contemporary Fundamentalism – Judaism, Christianity, Islam', *The Jerusalem Quarterly*, no. 47, summer 1988.

8. The prime example of this within modern Islamic thinking is Ali Abd al-Raziq (died 1966), who challenged the link between Islam as a faith and any particular form of government. The linking of Islam to politics was, in his view, the road to despotism and authoritarianism. (See Hamid Enayat, *Modern Islamic Political Thought* (London: Macmillan, 1982), pp. 82-88.) Islamic fundamentalisms, and particularly the Egyptian variants, are to a considerable degree a reaction against the ideas of Ali Abd al-Raziq.

9. I would give as examples of literature that does this, Sami Zubaida, *Islam, the People and the State* (London: Routledge, 1989); Nikki Keddie, *Iran: Roots of Revolution* (London: Yale University Press, 1981), Michael Gilsenan, *Recognizing Islam* (London: Croom Helm, 1982), Edward Mortimer, *Faith and Power* (London: Faber, 1982), Bassam Tibi, *The Crisis of Modern Islam* (Salt Lake City: University of Utah Press, 1988), Fred Halliday and Hamza Alavi (ed.), *State and Ideology in the Middle East and Pakistan* (London: Macmillan, 1988), Aziz al-Azmeh, *Islams and Modernities* (London: Verso, 1993). In another perceptive and wide-ranging survey, Nazih Ayubi, in *Political Islam: Religion and Politics in the Arab World* (London: Routledge, 1991), has, while writing *within* the 'contingentist' framework, sought to examine the specific cogency of cultural and doctrinal elements in Islamism.

10. Gilles Kepel, *La Banlieue de l'Islam: Naissance d'une religion en France* (Paris: Seuil, 1989); Tomas Gerholm and Yngve Georg Lithman (ed.), *The New Islamic Presence in Western Europe* (London: Mansell, 1988); Jorgen Nielsen, *Muslims in Western Europe* (Edinburgh: Edinburgh University Press, 1992); Philip Lewis, *Islamic Britain. Religion, Politics and Identity among British Muslims* (London: I.B. Tauris, 1994); Ceri Peach and Gunther Glebe, 'Muslim Minorities in Western Europe', *Ethnic and Racial Studies*, vol. 18, no. 1, 1995.

11. See my *Arabs in Exile: Yemeni Communities in Urban Britain* (London: I.B. Tauris, 1992); and Richard Lawless, *From Ta'izz to Tyneside* (Exeter: University of Exeter Press, 1995).

12. John Rex in his essay on Birmingham in Gerholm and Lithman (ed.), *The New Islamic Presence in Western Europe*.

13. Kepel, *La Banlieue de l'Islam*.
14. See my *Arabs in Exile*.
15. Kepel, *La Banlieue de l'Islam*.
16. Daniele Joly in Gerholm and Lithman (ed.), *The New Islamic Presence*.
17. Kepel, *La Banlieue de l'Islam*.
18. Malise Ruthven, *A Satanic Affair* (London: Chatto & Windus, 1990); Lisa Appignanesi and Sara Maitland (ed.), *The Rushdie File* (London: Fourth Estate, 1989).
19. The widespread denunciation of *The Satanic Verses* by people who had never read it was part of a familiar pattern. Those familiar with Irish history will recall the nationalist 'outrage' at J.M. Synge's play, *The Playboy of the Western World* in 1904. A more recent case was the Chinese communist mass campaign of denunciation in 1973 against the documentary film on China, *Chung Kuo*, by Michelangelo Antonioni. Each was a case of orchestrated indignation that mobilized people who were deemed to be insulted by a work they were also deemed unsuited to judge for themselves.
20. There is no exact Muslim equivalent to the Christian concept of blasphemy, the term used in the Greek New Testament to describe the charge on which Christ, who claimed he was the King of the Jews, was tried and executed – from the Greek *blapto*, to harm, and *pheme*, speech. The Koranic terms *kufr* and *shirk* (literally 'sharing' or denying the oneness of God), and *ilhad* (literally 'digression' hence 'apostasy'), are used interchangeably to cover atheism (the denial of divine beings in general), apostasy (rejection of one's particular religion), heresy (the assertion of beliefs contrary to the orthodox faith) and insult to the divine being (this latter being the core meaning of the Western term 'blasphemy'). Note, however, that in Islamic tradition all pertain to the Muslim's attitude to Allah, not to the Prophet, the latter being only a human being, in contrast to the Christian concept of Jesus as both man and God. However, in South Asian Islam in particular, the figure of the Prophet is invested with a special sanctity and alleged insults to him are thus treated as forms of *kufr* and so on. For one elucidation of the background, see Rudolph Peters and Gert J.J. de Vries, 'Apostasy in Islam', *Die Welt des Islams*, vol. XVII, nos. 1–4 1976–77.
21. 'Question: What is the opposite of faith?
    Not disbelief: too final, certain, closed. Itself a kind of belief.
    Doubt.'
    The Satanic Verses (London: Viking, 1988), p. 92.
22. 'And this was the word the Lord gave Moses: Take the blasphemer beyond the confines of the camp; let all those who were listening lay their hands on his head, and let the whole people put him to death by stoning. Tell the Israelites this: The man who curses his God will be held to account for it; he blasphemed the Lord's name, and he must die. Be he citizen or stranger, he must be stoned by the whole people; death for the blasphemer.' *The Holy Bible* (London: Burns & Oates, Macmillan, 1957), p. 109.

Chapter 5

1. Entered in Vienna Conference documents as A\CONF\57\PC\35.

2. Ann Mayer, *Islam and Human Rights* (London: Westview Press, 1991), provides the most thorough survey of these. A fifth issue, the rights of ethnic minorities, is also pertinent here, since Islamic states have tended to deny the need for any specific recognition of these, on the grounds that all Muslims share a common identity. Nationalist regimes in Muslim, as in other countries, have said the same thing of their own peoples – Turkey being, until very recently, a clear example of this.

3. On the Pakistani apostasy law, see 'Islamic Vigilante Justice', *International Herald Tribune*, 18–19 June 1994.

4. For background, see John Vincent, *Human Rights and International Relations* (Cambridge: Cambridge University Press, 1986), and Jack Donnelly, *Universal Human Rights in Theory and Practice* (Ithaca: Cornell University Press, 1989).

5. For one exploration, see James Piscatori, 'Human Rights in Islamic Political Culture', in Kenneth Thompson (ed.), *The Moral Imperatives of Human Rights: A World Survey* (Washington: University Press of America, 1980).

6. 'Islamization' refers to policies of governments designed to alter law and social life in accordance with Islamic doctrine; 'Islamism' refers to political movements, of a mass populist kind, that challenge established, more secular, states.

7. Muslim feminists, such as Naawal al-Saadawi and Fatima Mernissi, have often adopted this position, whether out of conviction or tactical calculation, and have sought to show that a specific interpretation, or *tafsir*, of the relevant texts can produce a case of gender equality.

8. Kevin Dwyer, *Arab Voices. The Human Rights Debate in the Middle East* (London: Routledge, 1991), and his 'Universal Visions, Communal Visions: Human Rights and Traditions', *Peuples Méditerranéens*, no. 58–59, January–July 1992, pp. 205–20, provide rich studies of the varying interpretations of Islamic tradition within the Arab debate. One of the most far-reaching attempts to produce such a liberal interpretation is to be found in the work of Abdullahi Ahmed An-Na'im, *Towards an Islamic Reformation: Civil Liberties, Human Rights, and International Law* (Syracuse, NY: Syracuse University Press, 1990). An-Na'im is a follower of Sheikh Mahmud Mohammad Taha, a proponent of a humanistic approach to Islam who was executed in Sudan in 1984.

9. Thus at a German–Iranian colloquium in 1992 an Iranian participant replied to criticism of non-Muslims in Iran by attacking the record of Western European states towards Muslims and other immigrants, while other Iranian participants pointed to treatment of political refugees and the supply of arms to Third World dictators: Heiner Bielefeldt (ed.), 'Die Menschenrechte zwischen Universalitätsanspruch und kulturelle Bedingtheit', *Tagung des Deutsch-Iranischen Gesprachskreises* 21–24 September 1992, Orient-Institute, Hamburg. This kind of counter-offensive has also been a stock-in-trade of the Chinese response to US criticism.

10. *Islamic Council: What it Stands For,* 'Universal Islamic Declaration of Human Rights' (London: Islamic Council, 1982), p.11.

11. On the UIDHR, see Mayer, *Human Rights* pp. 86–9.

12. 'King Fahd's Statement on Introduction of New Statutes', *BBC Summary of World Broadcasts: Part 4: The Middle East,* 3 March 1992, ME/1319 A/1-2.

13. *International Herald Tribune,* 25 March 1992.

14. As in various Quranic statements on women, e.g. that women are a 'tilth' (*harathun*) to which men may go 'whenever and howevever they so wish' (a point used by clerical authorities in Egypt to justify rape in marriage) (sura 2, verse 223), that men are a degree higher than them (sura 2, verse 228), that men are in charge of women and should admonish them (sura 4, verse 34), that in law women count for half of men (sura 2, verse 228), in addition to the unequal rights of divorce, men's right to polygyny, etc.

15. For three cogent versions of this, see Sami Zubaida, 'Human Rights and Culture Difference: Middle Eastern Perspectives', in *New Perspectives on Turkey,* Fall 1994, no. 10, pp. 1–12; Reza Afshari, 'An Essay on Islamic Cultural Relativism in the Discourse of Human Rights'; and Bassam Tibi, 'Islamic Law/*Shari'a,* Human Rights, Universal Morality and International Relations', both of the latter in *Human Rights Quarterly,* vol. 16, no. 2, May 1994. For a comparable argument on the *cultural* obstacles to individualism, rationality and modernity within Islam, see Darius Shayegan, *Cultural Schizophrenia* (London: Saqi Books, 1992). Tibi's own argument is developed further in his *The Crisis of Modern Islam* (Salt Lake City: University of Utah Press, 1988). A broader onslaught on the religious and anti-modernist political culture of the Middle East, from a radical Palestinian nationalist standpoint, is Hisham Shirabi, *Neo-Patriarchy* (Oxford: Oxford University Press, 1988). All of these (Middle Eastern) writers will no doubt be dismissed as 'ethnocentric', 'orientalist', 'essentialist', 'reductionist', etc. by those who disagree with them.

16. Afshari, 'Islamic Cultural Relativism'.

17. For definitions, see Vincent, *Human Rights,* pp. 37–8, and Mayer, pp. 9–11.

18. Vincent, *Human Rights,* pp. 28–30.

19. Thus in Iran, such opposition groups as the Kurdish Democratic Party of Iran, the Liberation Movement of Iran of former premier Mehdi Bazargan, and the range of monarchist and left-wing groups all speak in a secular, universalistic, language. Even the supposedly 'Islamic' opposition of the *Mujahidin-i Khalq* formulates its critique, beyond a few token quotations from the Quran, in secular terms. This is also true for the large body of Iranian writers and poets, let alone lawyers, who have opposed the dictatorship of the Islamic Republic. Opposition groups in Saudi Arabia have ranged from the secular left to Islamic organizations. A recent, hybrid, group, now based in London is the Committee for the Defence of Legitimate Human Rights, where the word 'Legitimate' is *shari'i.*

20. For one example see the study of Khomeini's first prime minister, later committed opponent, Saeed Barzin, 'Constitutionalism and Democracy in the Religious Ideology of Mehdi Bazargan', *British Journal of Middle Eastern*

Studies, vol. 21, no. 1, 1994.

21. A striking example of the use of universalistic arguments in an attack on Western positions discussed at greater length in chapter 3 was that of Saddam Hussein's Iraq and the occupation of Kuwait in 1990. While much of the international comment on this event, in the Arab world and elsewhere, looked at the differing cultural and religious perceptions of Iraqis and Westerners, Saddam himself framed his position in straightforward universalistic terms: Kuwait as a state had no historical legitimacy, Kuwait had damaged Iraq's economic interests, a popular uprising inside Kuwait had invited Iraqi forces into the country, the divisions of the Arab world were artificial, creations of colonialism. These arguments may, individually, have been debatable and, taken together, have appeared somewhat inconsistent, but culturally specific, or particular or unintelligible to non-Arabs or non-Muslims, they were not.

22. It may also be noted that much of the criticism of the West in this regard is based on the denial of *collective* or *group* rights, namely those of national or religous groups, rather than on the denial of *individual* rights.

23. *BBC Summary of World Broadcasts: Part 4: The Middle East,* 16 October 1993, ME/1821 MED/5-6.

24. *BBC Summary of World Broadcasts: Part 4: The Middle East,* 19 November 1993, ME/1850 MED/1.

25. Of the five *arkan* or 'pillars' of Islam, the first and pre-eminent, *shahada,* or 'witness', involves the believer in uttering the words: 'There is no God but Allah, and Muhammad is his Prophet.' This brooks no contradiction or relativization.

26. Vincent, *Human Rights,* pp. 42–4, is an example of this.

27. A front-runner for the claim to be the *most* confected of such 'traditions' is that of 'Confucianism', now the state ideology in Singapore, Korea and Taiwan. Beyond vague injunctions to obey parents and subordinate women there is nothing in the 'tradition' at all.

28. It is important to remind Christian audiences that, in contrast to Jesus Christ, Muhammad was a human being, without divine nature.

29. Azmi Bishara, 'Islam and Politics in the Middle East', in Jochen Hippler and Andrea Lueg (ed.), *The Next Threat. Western Perception of Islam* (London: Pluto Press, 1995), p. 93. See also Norman Anderson, *Law Reform in the Muslim World* (London: The Athlone Press, 1976), pp. 3–10, where *Shari'a* is described as 'an amorphous volume of partly contradictory doctrine, to which lip-service, at least, was invariably given and which came to stand, like a sentinel, to bar the path of progress' (p. 10). Thus did 'road', like many other official ideologies, become the road-block.

30. Aziz al-Azmeh, *Islams and Modernities* (London: Verso, 1993), pp. 12–14.

31. Mayer, *Islam and Human Rights,* pp. 53–4.

32. Ervand Abrahamian, *Khomeinism;* Sami Zubaida, *Islam, the People and the State* (London: Routledge, 1989); Fred Halliday and Hamza Alavi (ed.), *State and Ideology in the Middle East and Pakistan* (London: Macmillan, 1988).

33. Zubaida, 'Human Rights'.

34. But note the observation of Boutros Ghali at the Vienna Conference that if a particular version of sovereignty was an obstacle to human rights then that sovereignty was that of a bygone era.

35. I have gone into this in greater detail in chapter 7.

36. Zubaida, 'Human Rights'.

37. For a spirited rebuttal of 'Asian' rhetoric on the superiority of their societies, see Philip Bowring, *International Herald Tribune*, 2 August 1994.

38. Even if it can be proved that some particular practice or value or legal prescription is indeed 'traditional' in the sense of having been upheld over a long period of time by a particular community, this need not necessarily entail that it is beyond reform, criticism or outright rejection. Some of the practices at least that have been classified with some foundation as traditional would surely revolt even the most hardened relativist. The argument, on moral grounds, should at least be open here. Equally, such invocations of tradition are open to a critique on the basis of history, in that they deny what all studies of 'tradition' contemporarily received show, namely that traditions are themselves modern creations – selections, instrumental reproductions, often inventions concealing contemporary purposes behind the invocation of a time-honoured, and incontestable, continuity. In practical terms there are many examples of this from the Muslim world – the various forms of 'modest' dress now prescribed for Muslim women are an obvious case. So too are many of the ideological components of Islamism: these are neither traditional nor so contrasted with the 'West' as is often supposed, but reflect rather a combination of modern political themes with elements, themselves selectively identified and interpreted, of religious tradition. As many students of the rhetoric and political practice of Islamism have shown, these are, as much as anything, variants of Third World populism grafted onto elements of Islam, mass mobilizations aiming for political power, with the goals, instruments and much of the rhetoric of other, more secular, late twentieth-century movements.

39. The argument advanced by John Rawls, on the tolerance of societies that are illiberal but 'well-ordered', raises as many questions as it resolves – 'The Law of Peoples', in Stephen Shute and Susan Hurley (ed.), *On Human Rights* (New York: Basic Books, 1993).

40. On this, see Mayer, *Human Rights*.

41. I am grateful to Deniz Kandiyoti for this point.

42. Simon Bromley, *Rethinking Middle East Politics: State Formation and Development* (Cambridge: Polity Press, 1994).

43. See, for example, M. al-Ahnaf and others, *L'Algérie par ses islamistes* (Paris: Karthala, 1991) 'L'hérésie laique', pp. 100–17.

44. Evidence of this is provided by the fact that the Queen of England is the head of the Anglican church, that no Jew has ever been president of the USA, that Muslim schools and holidays are not ranked on an equal footing with Christian, etc. But these criticisms themselves presuppose a universal principle.

45. Secularism has, as much as anything, meant tolerance or legal neutrality *as between* different religions; but what is advocated here is a matching

tolerance – of free speech, diversity, even renunciation – *within* religions. I am especially gratefuly to Kevin Boyle for this point.

46. Alasdair Macintyre, *Beyond Virtue* (London: Duckworth, 1984), Stuart Hampshire, *Innocence and Experience* (London: Penguin, 1992), Raymond Plant, *Modern Political Thought* (Oxford: Blackwell, 1991), ch. 9.

47. I have gone into this in greater detail in chapter 7.

48. It may, however, be worth noting the lifelong practical commitment of Michel Foucault to human rights causes. See David Macey, *The Lives of Michel Foucault* (London: Vintage, 1994), especially ch. 8, 'South', which recounts Foucault's courageous, and, for him, dangerous support for human rights in Tunisia: no trace of relativism, or anti-imperialist non-intervention, in this instance.

Chapter 6

1. Samuel Huntington, 'The Clash of Civilizations?', *Foreign Affairs*, summer 1993.

2. In this context, the writer Salman Rushdie does not qualify as a proponent of 'anti-Muslimism', whatever his critics may say: as discussed in chapter 4, Rushdie satirized the early history of Islam, but did not incite or promote prejudice against living Muslims. Indeed one of the several strands in his book is a critique of British racism towards immigrants from (partly Muslim) South Asian societies.

3. Judith Herrin, *The Formation of Christendom* (Oxford: Basil Blackwell, 1987).

4. Contingency is rife in these areas: the Croatian Roman Catholic propaganda about the need to defend 'European' values was directed against the Orthodox Serbs and cast them as the Oriental 'Byzantines'. (I am grateful to Gabriel Partos for this point.)

5. This was also a common perception among enemies of the Ottoman empire in Western Europe during World War One, not least the British intelligence officer T.E. Lawrence. However, British medical examination of Turkish prisoners captured during that war failed to show any above-average incidence of sexually induced disease.

6. For a brilliant evocation of the multi-ethnic history of Bosnia, see the novel by the Serbian writer Ivo Andric, *The Bridge Over the Drina* (London: Harvill, 1994). As this shows so well, animosity, suspicion and occasional killing there certainly was, but at the same time a degree of coexistence and tolerance prevailed for much of the last few centuries. Andric himself at one point seems to give support to the image of an eternal, and particularly Bosnian, animosity: 'Everything else was flushed away in that dark background of consciousness where live and ferment the basic feelings and indestructible beliefs of individual races, faiths and castes, which, to all appearances dead and buried, are preparing for later far-off times unsuspected changes and catastrophes without which, it seems, peoples cannot

exist and above all the peoples of this land.' (pp. 173–4). The rest of his novel, and the history of Yugoslavia, not least the record of intermarriage in the post-1945 period, are in conflict with this perennialist, and particularist, theme. For the alternative case, although laid out in unduly partisan terms, see Robert Donia and John Fine, *Bosnia and Hercegovina, A Tradition Betrayed* (London: Hurst and Company, 1994).

7. Misha Glenny, *The Fall of Yugoslavia* (London: Penguin, 1992).

8. A similar charge is contained in the Irish Catholic claim that the Pretestants are 'soupers', i.e. not a legitimate community because they were Catholics who converted to Protestantism to get economic benefits from the English.

9. Norman Cigar, *Genocide in Bosnia. The Policy of 'Ethnic Cleansing'* (College Station, Texas: Texas A&M University Press, 1995), ch. 3.

10. The Martinovic case has become the subject of much Serbian nation-alist poetry. Thus one ran: 'With a broken bottle / On a stake / As though through / a lamb / but alive, / they went through Drordje Martinovic / As if with their first and heavy steps into their future field they treaded ... / When out of the opium and pain / Drordje Martinovic came round / As if from the long past / Turkish times / He woke up on a stake.' (From 'Kosovo, 1389, Kosovo 1989', *Serbian Literary Quarterly*, Serbian Writers Association, 1989, p. 94.) Note the 'Ottoman' themes – opium, kebabs, torture.

11. According to Abdulah Skaljic's *Turkisms in Serbo-Croat*, the *balija* origi-nally referred to a particularly poor and primitive clan or tribe, or to a group of Muslims settled in part of Herzegovina. The *Matica srpska* dictionary gives it as 'a simple and uneducated Muslim peasant'. (I am grateful to my col-league Bernard Johnson for these references.)

12. See the weekly *Information about Yugoslavia*, published by the Yugoslav embassy in London. Characteristic headlines include 'Isatbegovic's Forces Go to Battle on Plum Brandy', 'Muslim Authorities in Sarajevo to Ban Pork', '20,000 Mujaheddin Are Fighting in Bosnia'.

13. *The Guardian*, 2 August 1993.

14. For a critical view of this issue, see Shkelzen Maliqi, 'Athens' Anti-Albanian Campaign', *Balkan War Report*, September 1994, issue no. 28.

15. *Eleftheros Tipos*, 24 May 1993.

16. *Le Monde*, 26 June 1993.

17. This, *inter alia*, confused the difference between Bulgarian Turks, i.e. Bulgarian citizens who were Muslims and had Turkish as their first language, and the Pomaks, the Bulgarian-speaking converts to Islam.

18. Hugh Poulton, *Balkans: Minorities and States in Conflict* (London: Minority Rights Group, 1991), chs 10 and 11.

19. 'Les Turcs de Bulgarie entre l'espoir et la méfiance', *Le Monde*, 21 December 1994.

20. Akbar Ahmed provides a perceptive account of the Indian case, elicit-ing connections with that of Bosnia, '"Ethnic cleansing": a metaphor for our time?', *Ethnic and Racial Studies*, vol. 18, no. 1, January 1995, pp. 12–16.

21. Tapan Basu and others, *Khaki Shorts, Saffron Flags* (Hyderabad: Orient

Longman 1993); Sitaram Yechury, *What is this Hindu Rashtra?* (Madras: Frontline, 1993).

22. 'The Road to Ayodhya', *The Economist*, 6 February 1993.

23. 'Muslims have no right to complain about demolition in Ayodhya, says Nirad. C. Chaudhuri', *The Organiser* (weekly paper of the RSS), 12 September 1993.

24. Under the influence of European fascism, Golwalkar played up the threat of Jews to Hinduism: these sections of his work have been suppressed by the RSS and BJP, who now look to Israel as a potential ally against the Muslim threat. Golwalkar's anti-semitism is explained away as a fashion of the times.

25. See on this Romila Thapa, in Sarvepalli Gopal (ed.), *Anatomy of a Confrontation* (New Delhi: Penguin Books, 1991).

26. The concept of Hindutva was expounded during the 1920s in the influential text by V. D. Savarkar, *Hindutva, who is a Hindu?* This conception of Hindutva was wider than that of the Hindu religion, since it included those who equated their fatherland and a holy land: Hindus, Buddhists and Sikhs were included, Christians, Parsis, Jews and, of course, Muslims were excluded.

27. *Shri Guruji, the Man and His Mission* (Deli: B.N. Bhargava, n.d.), p. 70.

28. *Shri Guruji*, pp. 67–8.

29. Anthony Elenjimmitam, *Philosophy and Action of the RSS for the Hind Swaraj* (Bombay: axmi Publications, 1951), p. 61.

30. Kamal A. Mitra Chenoy, 'Citizen's Inquiry Reports on Ayodhya and Its Aftermath', *South Asia Bulletin*, vol. XIV, no. 2, 1994.

31. M.S. Golwalkar, *Bunch of Thoughts* (Bangalore: Vikrana Prakashan, 1966), ch. 12.

32. *The Organiser*, 12 September 1993.

33. 'Hindu Extremist Fans Bombay Hatred', *International Herald Tribune*, 14–15 August 1993.

34. *Le Monde*, 29 March 1995, quotation retranslated from the French.

35. For more extensive analysis, see *Khaki Shorts*.

36. Norman Daniel, *The Arabs and Mediaeval Europe* (London: Longman, 1975), provides a masterful survey of history, war, theology and literature.

37. Albert Hourani, *Islam in European Thought* (Cambridge: Cambridge University Press, 1991), pp. 28–30.

38. There is no clear etymology for 'Saracen'. Some suggest it refers to the descendants of Biblical Sarah, others that it is a Greek variation on the Arabic *sharqi*, eastern. One other possibility is that it is derived from the word *sirkashi*, Arabic 'Circassian', an ethnic group with a strong military record.

39. 'On War Against the Turk', *Martin Luther: Selected Political Writings*, ed. J. M. Porter (Lanham London: University Press of America, 1988), p. 126.

40. Paul Coles, *The Ottoman Impact on Europe* (London: Thames and Hudson, 1968), pp. 145–8. See also Norman Daniel, *The Arabs and Mediaeval Europe*.

41. *Le Monde*, 9 December 1993.

42. Curiously, one of the borrowings from the Muslim foe, the abusive term 'cretin', is of course but the word for Christian deployed on that side as an

epithet. Another term that has followed a curious semantic journey is the term *kafir*: originally the Arabic word for an unbeliever, it re-entered Dutch and English via South Africa, where it was a term of abuse for the indigenous populations. The result is that in spoken Dutch of today the most common form of abuse of Moroccan immigrants is *stumme kaffr*, stupid kaffir. The French word *giaour* for a North African soldier is derived from the same source.

43. The theme of the Muslims as sea-borne marauders, threatening the Corsican coast, especially in the Sartenes region, is widespread. See Dorothy Carrington, *Granite Island, A Portrait of Corsica* (London: Penguin, 1971). Yet, as she points out (p. 118) 'North African piracy flourished at this period precisely because it was run by Europeans.'

44. 'This word "*Musselmann*", I do not know why, was used by the old ones of the camp to describe the weak, the inept, those doomed to selection.' Primo Levi, *If This Is A Man, The Truce* (London: Sphere Books, 1987), p.94.

45. On this US background, see Laurence Michalak, *Cruel and Unusual. Negative Images of Arabs in American Popular Culture*, American-Arab Anti-Discrimination Committee (ADC), Issue Paper no. 15, third edition, Washington, 1988; Suha Sabbagh, *Sex, Lies and Stereotypes*, ADC Issue Paper no. 23, 1990.

46. The term 'raghead' appears to have originated in the 1920s in reference to turbaned Asian students at the University of California, who would, presumably, have as likely been Hindus or Sikhs as Muslims. *Oxford English Dictionary*, 2nd edn vol. XIII, p. 114.

47. 'Rising Islam May Overwhelm the West', *New Hampshire Sunday News*, 20 August 1989.

48. Thus *The Economist*, 4 April 1992, headed an article on three Islamist movements with the title 'Islam Resumes its march'. See also Charles Krauthammer, 'The New Crescent of Crisis: Global Intifada', *Washington Post*, 16 February 1990. Former French President Valéry Giscard d'Estaing struck a similar note in his interventions in the French press: 'L'immigration, l'invasion', *Le Figaro Magazine*, 21 September 1991.

49. For accounts of anti-Muslimist responses to the Oklahoma bombing, see 'Rush to Judgement Alarms U.S. Arabs', *International Herald Tribune* 25 April 1995; 'Camel Jockeys Killed Your Kids', *Village Voice* 2 May 1995; 'One Man's Jihad', *The Nation* 15 May 1995; 'The Oklahoma City Bombing: the Jihad that Wasn't' by Jim Nanreckas, *Extra!* July/August 1995. Among other incidents an Iraqi refugee living in Oklahoma City, Sahar al-Mawsawi, lost a baby after her home was attacked, a mosque in the city was attacked by a man with a shotgun, and a US citizen of Arab extraction, long resident in Oklahoma, was arrested and aggressively questioned after taking a flight to London.

50. *Bulletin of the Jerusalem Institute for Western Defense*, vol. 6, no. 3, October 1993, quoted in *Information about Yugoslavia*, 10 November 1993.

51. *International Herald Tribune*, 9 November 1993.

52. Christopher Husbands, '"They Must Obey Our Laws and Customs!": political debate about Muslim assimilability in Great Britain, France and The Netherlands', in Alec Hargreaves and Jeremy Leaman (eds.), *Racism, Ethnicity*

Islam and the Myth of Confrontation

and *Politics in Contemporary Europe* (Aldershot: Edward Elgar, 1995).

53. 'France's Not-so-Veiled Message: It Will Not Tolerate Multicultural-ism', *International Herald Tribune* 6 December 1993; Harlem Desire, *Sos Racisme* (Paris: Calmann-Lévy, 1987), pp. 33–4, discusses the relation between racism and hostility to Muslims in France.

54. French terms of abuse for Arabs are many: *bicot*, *melon*, literally 'melon' (with the implication of 'idiot'), *raton*, 'rat', *bougnoul*, 'wog', *crouille* (Foreign Legion slang from the Arabic *ya-akhir*, 'my brother'), again 'wog' but definitely meaning North African.

55. *Le Monde*, 26 April 1995.

56. *International Herald Tribune*, 3 May 1995.

57. *Le Monde*, 4 May 1995.

58. See my *Arabs in Exile, Yemeni Communities in Urban Britain* (London: I.B. Tauris, 1992).

59. 'Strongest among men in enmity to the Believers wilt thou find the Jews and Pagans', sura 5, verse 85, *The Holy Qur'an*, translation and commentary by Abdullah Yusuf Ali (London: The Islamic Foundation, 1975), p. 268.

60. Exodus 17: 14–16; Deuteronomy 25: 17–19.

61. In contrast to the mainstream of Judaism, which stresses pre-ordained fate, the kabbala asserts that human beings can help God and can therefore anticipate redemption by their actions: Gush Emunim and Meir Kahane argued that by expelling Arabs from the land of Israel, and never retreating from an inch of Jewish land, Jews could be seen to be doing God's work. Such work might itself destroy the pious believer who carried it out: here a central figure was Samson, who is held to have said: 'I shall perish with the philistines.' In the aftermath of the Hebron killings, Goldstein was widely hailed as a new 'Samson'. Other titles bestowed on him were 'Kennedy' and 'Martin Luther King' (*The Independent*, 28 February 1994).

62. Israel Shahak, *Jewish History, Jewish Religion. The Weight of Three Thousand Years* (London: Pluto Press, 1994), p. 98.

63. Ibid.

64. Information from Israel Shahak.

65. Ken Brown, 'Iron and a King: The Likud and Oriental Jews', *MERIP Reports*, vol. 13, no. 4, May 1983.

66. The Hebrew poet Haim Nahman Bialik (d. 1934) is reputed to have said: 'I hate Arabs because they remind me of Franks.' This is a saying that was often quoted, against Ashkenazim, by militant Sephardim of the Black Panther movement, but there are many who doubt whether this is an accurate attribution. I am grateful to Israel Shahak and Udi Adiv for elucidation on this point.

67. Louis Marton, 'Destroying the Amalekites', *Israel and Palestine Political Report* (Paris), no. 129, December 1986.

68. *Hared*, literally 'fearful', hence 'religiously observant'.

69. According to Kahane, the Arabs are 'an enemy whose hatred for Jews is an obsession; an enemy whose entire culture and tradition is filled with vicious barbaric cruelty against others and against himself … an enemy whose

origin was already foretold in the Bible'. *The Jewish Press*, 2 March 1990.

70. *The Jewish Press*, 12 January 1990.

71. Robert Friedman, *The False Prophet: Rabbi Meir Kahane – from FBI inform-ant to Knesset member* (New York: Lawrence Hill Books, 1990), p. 260.

72. Ehud Sprinzak, *The Ascendance of Israel's Radical Right*, (Oxford: Oxford University Press, 1991), p. 239. Kahane's ideas were expressed in his regular column in the New York-based *Jewish Press*. See also his interview in Raphael Mergui, *Israel's Ayatollahs: Meir Kahane and the Far Right in Israel* (London: Saqi Books, 1987).

73. As quoted in Israel Shahak, *Report no. 130*, 10 December 1993.

74. Settler support for Goldstein was widely reported at the time of his crime. 'Islam is the poison of humanity ... This is not killing. This is revenge,' one Israeli told reporters ('They Hate Us, and We Hate Them', *International Herald Tribune*, 28 February 1994).

75. *Yerushalaim*, 30 July 1993, translated by Israel Shahak.

76. Baruch Goldstein, in an interview with Israeli radio some weeks before he died, denounced 'the Arab Nazi enemy, who strives to attack any Jew just because he is a Jew in the land of Israel'.

Chapter 7

1. Among other discussions: Bernard Lewis, 'The Question of Orientalism', *New York Review of Books*, 24 June, 1982, and Said's reply, *NYRB*, 12 August 1982; Lata Many and Ruth Frankenberg, 'The Challenge of Orientalism', *Economy and Society*, vol. 14, no. 2; Bryan Turner, 'From Orientalism to Global Sociology', *Sociology*, November 1989; Sadik Jalal al-'Azm, 'Orientalism and Orientalism in Reverse', *Khamsin*, no. 8, 1981; Edward Said, 'Orientalism Revisited', *MERIP Middle East Reports*, vol. 18, no. 1, 1988; Edward Said, 'Orientalism and After', an interview, *Radical Philosophy 63*, spring 1993; Aijaz Ahmad, *In Theory* (London: Verso Books, 1992), ch. 5.

2. For explications of this approach, see C. Wright Mills, *The Sociological Imagination* (Oxford: OUP, 1959); E. H. Carr, *What is History?* (Harmondsworth: Penguin, 1967); E. J. Wilmers, *Systematic Empiricism: Critique of a Pseudoscience* (Hemel Hempstead: Prentice-Hall, 1973).

3. See chapter 1 for one attempt to identify what is, and is not, specific to the Middle East.

4. For discussion of some of these issues see my entry 'Class Analysis' in John Esposito (ed.), *The Oxford Encyclopaedia of the Modern Islamic World* (Oxford: Oxford University Press, 1995).

5. Bill Warren *Imperialism, Pioneer of Capitalism* (London: Verso Books, 1980). Despite some overstatement of his argument, Warren's thesis stands as a powerful corrective to the prevailing literature of anti-imperialism, both in substantive analysis and in its resolutely anti-relativist and anti-whingeing tone. Had Warren lived to see the tide of post-modernism converge with that of underconsumptionist critiques of imperialism, one can only imagine what his

response would have been.

6. This last was the subject of my *Arabia without Sultans* (Harmondsworth: Penguin, 1974).

7. See my 'Letter from Dublin', *MERIP Middle East Reports*, no. 154, September–October 1988.

8. See, among many examples, James Petras, *Politics and Social Structure in Latin America* (Monthly Review: New York and London, 1970), part IV, 'Criticism of Studies of Latin America'; Robert I. Rhodes, *Imperialism and Underdevelopment: a reader* (London: Monthly Review Press, 1970).

9. For earlier critical work on orientalism as such, see the work of Anouar Abdel-Malek, 'Orientalism in Crisis', *Diogenes* 44, winter 1963; Bryan Turner, *Marx and the End of Orientalism* (London: Allen and Unwin, 1978) and the essays contained in Maxime Rodinson, *Marxism and the Muslim World* (French original Paris: Seuil, 1972, English London: Zed Press, 1979). For later discussions, see Maxime Rodinson, *Europe and the Mystique of Islam* (London: University of Washington Press, 1991), and Albert Hourani, *Islam in European Thought* (Cambridge: CUP, 1991).

10. For Lewis, see note 1.

11. His *Culture and Imperialism* (London: Chatto and Windus, 1993) sets writing on the Middle East in a much broader cultural context. For a critical review of his use of Foucault, see Aijaz Ahmad, note 1.

12. See, amongst other places, the series of articles published in *The Review of Middle East Studies* (London): in particular Roger Owen, 'The Middle East in the Eighteenth Century – an "Islamic" Society in Decline: a Critique of Gibb and Bowen's *Islamic Society and the West*', *Review*, no. 1, 1975.

13. His reputation rests on two early works of impressive range and erudition, *The Arabs in History* (1951) and *The Emergence of Modern Turkey* (1961). His subsequent writings have been almost wholly on the writings, attitudes and perceptions of people in the Middle East, always well researched, but failing to analyse the societies or politics in question. Thus his work on race and slavery (*Race and Colour in Islam*, 1971, reissued in amplified form as *Race and Slavery in the Middle East*, 1990) is an account of attitudes and stereotypes. It tells us little about the social and economic institutions of slavery and, as ever, seems innocent of comparison: the only comparisons with the USA are glancing references to attitude, those with Brazil come only in quotes from other writers. His other texts, *The Middle East and the West* (1963), *The Muslim Discovery of Europe* (1982), *Semites and Anti-Semites* (1986), reflect a similar involution, at once methodological and intellectual. One exception is his monograph *The Assassins* (1968).

14. *Covering Islam* (his least illuminating book) is a naive critique of press coverage of the Iranian revolution, collusive (with orientalism) in its very title: *The Question of Palestine* is about attitudes, consciousness, rhetoric, identity, discourse, *not* facts.

15. For a different use of Foucault, one that relates discourse and symbol far more closely to the material structures of power, see Samir al-Khalil, *The Republic of Fear* (London: Hutchinson/Radius, 1989).

16. Said offers three definitions of the term 'orientalism' in the introduction to his book (pp. 2–4). As I shall argue later, there are difficulties with the positing of such a general category, on any of the three definitions: here I am taking a minimal definition relevant to social science work, or rather work that purports to be about Middle Eastern society.

17. One may recommend the wines of Shiraz, the arak of Turkey and Lebanon, the brandies of Baku and much else besides.

18. London: University of Chicago Press, 1988.

19. Why not 'the countries' of Islam? Also note the recurrence in his, and others', writings of the phrase 'where Islam holds sway', suggestive of a vague but pandemic domination and inescapable atmosphere.

20. *Political Language*, p. 3.

21. Bharat was the second son of the Hindu god Ram, and is the conventional Hindi word for India.

22. *New York Review of Books*, 5 December 1991.

23. For a study of political vocabulary that covers some of the same ground as Lewis in an analysis of nineteenth-century Arab writing, see Ami Ayalon, *Language and Change in the Arab Middle East, The Evolution of Modern Arabic Political Discourse* (Oxford: Oxford University Press, 1987). The difference in title between the two is however indicative: Lewis studies the 'language of Islam', Ayalon 'language and change in the Arab Middle East'. Paying little attention to religious determination, Ayalon provides a more subtle and open analysis of changing usages. Yet he too, despite awareness of the general linguistic issues involved, such as that of 'interference' (pp.5–7), ends by presenting the problem as one that is, implicitly, peculiar to the Arabs. His discussion of different meanings of the word *jumhur* ('republic', p. 132) could just as easily be applied to English or any other contemporary political language. Contrast the usages of communist with Western democratic states ('democracy', 'republic', even 'truth'), or the differences between legal or academic terms in, say, the British, French and US systems. Nor is the most rigorously modernized of Middle Eastern languages, Hebrew, immune to such changes and ambiguities.

24. Contrast the methodology implicit in Lewis, *Political Language*, with Raymond Williams, *Keywords* (London: Fontana, 1976). For an interesting discussion of essentialist writing in another field, see Charles Stafford, review of Frank Dikotter, *The Discourse of Race in Modern China*, in *MAN*, vol. 28, no. 3, September 1993.

25. Some among many possible examples: bless, catholic, confess, congregate, create, crucify, damn, diabolical, disciple, ecumenical, faith, inspire, mission, pontificate, sacred, spirit, testify, witness.

26. Two further examples: the root *qll* gives both *qalil*, meaning few, and *istiqlal*, meaning independence: is one to assume from this that independence meant very little to the Arabs and that this explains some subsequent political behaviour? The root *mll* gives us both *mumill*, meaning boring, and *milli* meaning national: what might this entail?

27. *Political Language*, p. 97. For another case see Mohamed Heikal, *The*

Return of the Ayatollah (London: André Deutsch, 1981), p. 88.

28. See, for example, his declarations on the establishment of a Consultative Council in Saudi Arabia, *BBC Summary of World Broadcasts*, part 4, 3 March 1992.

29. According to the German scholar Reinhard Schulze this saying dates from the nineteenth century only: 'How Mediaeval is Islam? Muslim Intellectuals and Modernity', in Jochen Hippler and Andrea Lueg (ed.), *The Next Threat: Western Perception of Islam* (London: Pluto Press, 1995), p. 69, n. 20.

30. For the former, cf. A. J. Wensinck, *Concordance et indices de la tradition musulmane* (Leiden: Brill, 1936–9), vol. 6, p. 51, s.v. *kl'*.

31. *The Social Origins of Dictatorship and Democracy* (London: Allen Lane, 1967), p. 486.

32. The briefest of looks at the ideology of Khomeini will show this to be true: there is nothing in the Koran about *jumhuri-yi islami*, or *sudur-i inqilab* or *istkbar-i jahani* (Islamic republic, export of revolution or world arrogance). The terms he uses of imperialism, *teshne be khun, javan-khor, sheitun-i bozorg* (bloodthirsty, world-devouring, great satan), are terms he has taken from Persian or invented.

33. See Sadik al-Azm, 'Is the "fatwa" a fatwa?', *Middle East Report*, no. 183, vol. 23, no. 4, July–August 1993.

34. Peter Dale, *The Myth of Japanese Uniqueness* (London: Croom Helm, 1986); Dani Botman, 'Some Reflections on Japan, Orientalism and Post-Modernity', unpublished paper.

35. Alexander Dallin, 'The Uses and Abuses of Russian History', in Frederic Fleron and Erik Hoffmann (ed.), *Post-Communist Studies and Political Science* (Oxford: Westview Press, 1993).

36. *Ideology and Utopia: an introduction to the sociology of knowledge* (London: Routledge and Kegan Paul, 1960).

37. Here the almost complete silence of both orientalists and their critics on the question of economics serves to obscure this major dimension of the formation of the contemporary world. Of course, in this they are joined by Islamist thinkers who, while prolix on most other issues, have a blind spot when it comes to the issue of economics. Khomeini was explicit on this, denouncing economics as the subject of donkeys.

38. Said's *Covering Islam*, a critique of US press coverage of the Iranian revolution, misses this point. The hypostases of the *New York Times* pale before those of the mullahs of southern Tehran, or of the likes of Ali Shariati and Jalal Al-i Ahmad.

39. See note 1.

40. For alternative, contingent and social, explanations see the discussion in chapter 1, and in particular Roger Owen, *State, Power and Politics in the Making of the Modern Middle East* (London: Routledge, 1992); Simon Bromley, *Rethinking Middle East Politics: State Formation and Development* (Cambridge: Polity Press, 1994); Halim Barakat, *The Arab World. Society, Culture and State* (London: University of California Press, 1993).

41. *Quran*, sura 49, verse 13.

Index

Abdel-Malek, Anouar, 212
Afghanistan, 64, 71, 81, 89, 91, 118, 119, 147, 182
Afshari, Reza, 133, 140
agriculture, stagnation of, 41
Ahmad, Jalal Al-i, 212
Alawiyya sect, 122
Albanians, 164, 166, 167, 169; in Greece, 169, 170
Algeria, 26, 37, 40, 118, 128, 131, 144, 172, 197
Amalekites, 187, 190, 192
Amariya shelter, bombing of, 100
Amnesty, 135, 137, 177
anti-muslimism, 7, 107, 109, 121, 151, 160–94 see also Europe, India, United Kingdom, United States etc
anti-semitism, 163, 168
apostasy, 134
Arab League, 32
Arab unity, 30–6; irreality of, 33
Arab-Israeli dispute, 11, 12, 16, 18, 31, 79, 182, 202
Arabic, studying of, 202, 206
Arabist, notion of, 207
Arafat, Yasser, 33
arms control, imposed on Iraq, 87, 94
arms sales, 20, 34, 66, 82; to Iraq, 83
army, in Iran, role of, 54–5
Asma bint Marwan, 126
assimilation, 136

Atatürk, Kemal, 121, 157
Austria, 186; racism in, 179
Ayodhya mosque: destruction of, 173; rededication of, 175
al-Azhar university, 142
Aziz, Tariq, 89
al-'Azm, Sadik, 214
al-Azmeh, Aziz, 148

Ba'th party, 21, 40, 84, 92, 95
Bakhtiar, Shahpour, 49
Balfour Declaration, 25
Balkans, 79, 80, 109, 193
Bangladesh, 115, 177, 186
Bani-Sadr, Abol-Hasan, 44, 49, 55
Basra road, shootings on, 101
bazaar sector, 52, 53, 54, 55, 56, 57, 60, 66, 72
Bazargan, Mehdi, 49, 55
Belgium, 186
Benedict, Ruth, 211
Bharatiya Janata Party (BJP), 172, 173, 175
blasphemy, in Islam, 126
Bosnia, 108, 113, 121, 131, 135, 144, 145, 151, 162, 163, 164, 167
Bouarram, Brahim, 185
Brezhnev, Leonid, 66
Bromley, Simon, 156
Buchanan, Pat, 183
Bulgarification of Turks, 171
Bulgaria, 170; exodus of Turks, 171
Bush, George, 79, 90, 98, 99, 101, 102

249

Marxism, 13, 15, 91, 92, 93, 197, 199, 212

massacrology, tendency to, 210

al-Mawdudi, Abul 'Ala, 119

Mayer, Ann, 149

merchants *see* bazaar sector

middle classes, 54, 56, 65, 66

Middle East: and international politics, 11–41; assumed as unique case, 1; boundaries of, 28; conformity of, 27–30; historical formation of, 22–6; perceived poverty of intellectual life in, 213; studying of, 215–17

Middle East peace process, 81, 82

migrants, 111; experiences of, 126; Islamic sentiment among, 108; Islamic, integration of, 130; struggle for soul of, 120–5

migration, 33, 37, 65; into Western Europe, 109; of Jews, 25; of workers, 92; to oil-producer states, 39

Milosevic, Slobodan, 167

minorities, intolerance of, 209

Mitterrand, François, 85

Mladic, Ratko, 168

modernity, 47, 63, 72

modernization, 14, 198, 203

Morocco, 38

Mosaddeq, Mohammad, 48, 54, 58

mosques, 72; as power base, 56; attendance at, 124; building of, 120, 122, 166, 169; closure of, 69, 171; funding of, 52, 123; in Paris, 122

mostakbarin, 62

mostazafin, 62

Mubarak, Hosni, 85

Muhammad, Prophet, 126, 148, 160

Mujahidin groups, 58

mullahs, role of, 46, 60, 66

Muslim League, 173–4

'Muslim Parliament', in UK, 163

Nachmonides, 188

Nagorno-Karabagh, 162

nationalism, 5, 6, 27, 28, 198, 211;

Arab, 13, 17, 18, 23, 81, 84, 91, 202; romantic roots of, 174

New International Order, 79

non-believers, rights of, 134

nuclear weapons, 3, 89, 100, 113, 182

oil: as possible factor of anomaly, 30–6; as weapon, 34; boom of, 33, 39; discovery of, 23; industry in Iran, 51, 65; Iraqi hegemony over supplies, 85; output affected by strikes, 48; price of, 3, 14 (fall in, 82; rises in, 11, 182); protection of supplies, 98, 99, 182, 184; revenues from, 20, 51, 66, 92, 129, 134, 216; social consequences of production of, 39; uniqueness of form of payment, 34

Oklahoma City bombing, 183

Oman, 38

Operation Anfal, 96

Organization of Petroleum Exporting Countries (OPEC), 14

orientalism, 12, 13, 14; as polemical fiction, 204; critique of, 195–217

Ottoman Empire, 22, 24, 59, 108, 109, 113, 165, 166, 171, 178; dismemberment of, 23, 38

Pakistan, 115, 134, 147, 150, 172, 173, 175, 176, 177, 186

Palestine, 18, 23, 24, 25, 26, 28, 30–6, 31, 38, 39, 40, 81, 82, 113, 118, 131, 135, 144, 145, 151, 161, 164, 180, 192, 197, 200; *intifada*, 121; use of issue, 33

Palestine Liberation Organization (PLO), 33, 34

Pan-Arabism, 91, 94

particularism, 14, 136, 137, 141, 146, 151, 211; analytic, 14; historical, 15

Philippines, 161

Poland, 181

political vocabularies, derivation of, 204–5